7/28/06

# ULTIMATE
# BEER

# ULTIMATE
# BEER

## MICHAEL JACKSON

*Photography by*
STEVE GORTON

DK PUBLISHING, INC.
www.dk.com

# A DK PUBLISHING BOOK
www.dk.com

**Senior Editor** SHARON LUCAS

**Senior Art Editor** TIM SCOTT

**Editors** EDWARD BUNTING, ANNA MILNER

**Designer** KEVIN RYAN

**Managing Editor** FRANCIS RITTER

**Managing Art Editor** DEREK COOMBES

**DTP Designer** SONIA CHARBONNIER

**Picture Researcher** JAMIE ROBINSON

**Production Controller** RUTH CHARLTON

**US Editor** CHUCK WILLS

**Research Co-ordinator/Beer Stylist** OWEN D. L. BARSTOW

**Research Team**
LARA BREKENFELD, CASEY CLOGG, BRYAN HARRELL,
ANDREE HOFFMANN, BRITTA VETTER, SILKE WAGLER

First American Edition, 1998

6 8 10 9 7

Published in the United States by DK Publishing Inc.,
375 Hudson Street, New York, New York 10014

Published in Great Britain by Dorling Kindersley Limited.

**Library of Congress Cataloging-in-Publication Data**

Jackson, Michael, 1942-
    Ultimate beer / by Michael Jackson. — 1st American ed.
      p.    cm.
    Includes index.
    ISBN 0-7894-3527-6
    1.  Beer.    I.  Title.
TP577.J295    1998
641.2'3—dc21                  98-16425
                                    CIP

Color reproduction by Colourscan, Singapore
Printed and bound in China by L.Rex Printing Co., Ltd.

# CONTENTS

FOREWORD  7

## WHAT MAKES A GREAT BEER?  8

Where Beer is Grown  10  •  The Grains  12
The Hops  14  •  Additional Flavorings  16
Water and Yeast  18  •  Making Beer  20
Tasting Beer  22

## BEERS FOR THE MOMENT  24

Which Beer, When?  26

### SEASONAL BEERS
Spring  28  •  Summer  32  •  Autumn  36
Christmas  40  •  Celebration Beers  43

### SOCIABLE BEERS
Golden Lagers  44  •  Dortmunder Export  46
Kölschbier  48  •  Altbier  52  •  Belgian Ales  56
English Bitters  58  •  Scottish Ales  62
North American Ales  66
Plain Porters and Dry Stouts  70

### PARTY GREETINGS
Fruit Lambics  74  •  Fruit Beers  76

### THIRST QUENCHERS
Belgian-style Wheat Beers  78
Berlin-style Wheat Beers  82
South German Wheat Beers  84
German-style Hefeweizen  86
German Dark Wheat Beers  90  •  Wheat Ales  92
Flemish "Sweet and Sour" Red Ales  94

### RESTORATIVES
Black Beers  96  •  Dutch "Old Brown" Lagers  98
Mild Ales  100  •  Sweet Stouts  102

### WINTER WARMERS
Bock Beers  104  •  Spiced Beers  108
Old Ales  110  •  Whiskey-malt Beers and Strong
Scottish Ales  114  •  Baltic Porters and Stouts  118

### NIGHTCAP BEERS
Barley Wines  120

### APERITIFS
Extra-dry Pilsner Lagers  124
Dry Abbey Beers  128  •  Strong Golden Ales  130
India Pale Ales  132  •  Extra-hoppy Ales  136

## BEER AND FOOD  138

Beers with Appetizers & Soups  140
Beers with Shellfish  142
Beers with Salads & Starters  144
Beers with Pickles & Pâtés  146
Beers with Sausages  148
Beers with Smoked Foods  150
Beers with Fish  152  •  Beers with Chicken  154
Beers with Pork  156  •  Beers with Lamb  158
Beers with Beef  160  •  Beers with Pizza  162
Beers with Cheese  164
Beers with Fruity Desserts  166
Beers with Creamy Desserts  168
Beers with Chocolate & Coffee  170
Beers for After Dinner  172

## COOKING WITH BEER  174

Beers for Vinaigrettes  176
Beers for Marinades  177  •  Beers for Soups  178
Beers for Stews  179  •  Beers for Braising  180
Beers for Basting  181  •  Beers for Batters & Baking  182
Beers for Desserts  183

SERVING BEER  184
GLOSSARY  185
USEFUL ADDRESSES  186
INDEX  187
ACKNOWLEDGMENTS  192

*So popular is beer, the world's best-selling alcoholic drink, that it
is often taken for granted. Yet scientific analysis shows that a glass of beer
has within it as many aromas and flavors as a fine wine. Not everyone
understands this, but an increasing number of people do.
In an age when more people work at computers than in coal mines, the thirst
for beer is changing. There is a trend toward drinking less but tasting more.
This is shown in the choice of beers now available: from the aromatic, original
golden Pilsner lager of Bohemia, in the Czech Republic, to the tart, hazy wheat
beers of Bavaria and Berlin; the rich, orange or chocolate-colored Trappist brews
of Belgium to the soothing, copper ales of Britain; the dry, black stouts of Dublin
and Cork to the hoppy, amber specialities of Boston and New York – great flavors
from the Sierras and Seattle to Sapporo and Sydney. You might be surprised at
how many of these beers are finding their way into your local supermarket or
speciality beverage store. To track down those that remain elusive,
a beer-hunting vacation might be in order.
Not every beer tastes best by the pint. Many of the beers in this book
have their own goblets and chalices, saucers and flutes. Never before has such
an array been photographed and described. How should these brews taste?
Why do they taste that way? How, and when, might they best be enjoyed?
I have spent years probing the mysteries of malt, the magic of hops.
Now you can see for yourself, and learn, in the pages that follow. Come with
me, inhale the aromas, taste the flavors. Enjoy the world's greatest beers . . .
and some of the most unusual.*

Michael Jackson

# WHAT MAKES A GREAT BEER?

THE TESTS OF A GOOD BEER ARE AROMA, flavor, and finish. Beer is made principally from malted grains, water, hops, and yeast, but there is no point in using those ingredients if the result tastes like fizzy, alcoholic water. As a great beer is enjoyed, its character seems to develop, so that the drinker notices new flavors and finds constant interest. Nor do the flavors suddenly vanish. The drinker looks forward to the beer; enjoys the experience; and is left with a lingering memory of it. A good beer delivers the style it promises on the label. If it says Pilsner, wheat beer, ale, or stout, it truly has the characteristics of that style. A great beer combines aroma, flavor, finish, and fidelity to style with its own distinctive balance and memorability.

# WHERE BEER IS GROWN

JUST AS WINE IS GROWN, so is beer; the first as fruit (usually grapes), the second as grain (most often barley). Both drinks are as old as civilization, and each assumed its present form in central and western Europe. While temperate but warm countries grow grapes and make wine, cooler nations cultivate cereal grains and brew beer. The Czechs, Austrians, Germans, Belgians, Dutch, Danes, British, and Irish shaped modern beer. In the US, the northeast, the midwest, and recently the northwest have been especially influential. The principal flavoring in beer, the hop plant, also grows in cool climates. These are the countries and regions with the great, established brewing traditions.

**BARLEY-GROWING REGIONS**

Just as grapes may be used as a dessert fruit, raisins, or juice, as well as in wine, so barley is the basis for many foods and drinks (*page 12*). Like the wine-maker, the brewer has special requirements. The barley that is used to make beer must have plump, fine-skinned kernels, rich in starch and low in protein.

While grapes are crushed to release their juices, grain is malted to render it soluble. This is a process of soaking, sprouting, and drying. After this, the grain is called malt.

Fine malting barley is cultivated mainly in the northern hemisphere, notably in a band just to the north of latitudes 45 and 55. Famous growing areas include Moravia and Bohemia in the Czech Republic; the Munich Basin of Bavaria, Germany; Denmark; the English regions of Wessex, East Anglia, and the Vale of York; the Scottish Borders and the Moray Firth; the American midwestern states (especially North Dakota) and the northwest; and Saskatchewan and Alberta in Canada.

In the southern hemisphere, similar latitudes cultivate malting barley, although on a lesser scale. Regions include the Australian states of Victoria and South Australia; the southernmost part of New Zealand; Cape Province, South Africa; and a belt across South America, from Uruguay to Peru and Ecuador.

Just as different regions champion their own grapes, so there are debates among brewers as to the merits of "continental" barleys, such as those grown in Bavaria, as against the "maritime" examples of

*A field of beer*
*Not only does barley like temperate, cool, dry climates, it also enjoys well-drained, fertile chalk, loam, or light clay soils. It is vulnerable to wind, and is most easily harvested in flat countryside.*

Denmark or the UK. Continental barleys are said to provide a sweet, nutty flavor, while maritime varieties have a clean, "sea-breeze" character. There are also two races of malting barley, distinguished by the number of rows of grain in each ear. Two-row barleys impart a soft, sweet flavor, favored by lager brewers. Six-row barleys create a firmer, crisper, huskier character, championed by some ale producers. The time of sowing is also a factor. Winter barleys, sown in October or November, tend to be husky. Spring varieties, sown in March, are softer and sweeter.

## HOP-GROWING REGIONS

Just as cool, temperate zones favor barley, so it is with hops, though this plant prefers soil with more clay. The most important hop regions are in the Pacific northwest US, Canada, the South of England, the borders of Belgium and France, Bavaria, Bohemia in the Czech Republic, and Slovenia. In Poland, the Lublin region is growing in importance. The Ukraine grows hops around Zitomir, west of Kiev; China in the Xinjiang region. In the southern hemisphere, Tasmania and Nelson on the South Island of New Zealand are key hop-growing regions.

## THE FIRST BREWERS

Fruit falling from trees and fermenting on the ground introduced humans to wine, but this drink lacks nutrition. When humans ceased to be nomadic hunters and gatherers and began to farm the land, they grew grains. The world's first known recipe, on clay tablets, appears to be a method for making beer. This drink was very nutritious, but it also had the side-effect of making the Mesopotamians feel "exhilarated, wonderful, and blissful." A magical incantation in runic scripts seems to have given us the word *alu*, in the longest-

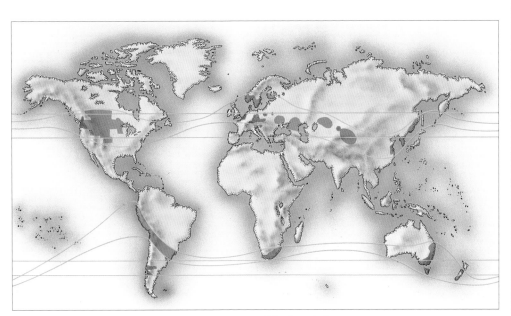

### The first straw
*The golden straw (left) is from Mesopotamia, and is believed to have been used by a high priestess for the consumption of beer. It is in the Museum of the University of Pennsylvania. The Mesopotamian plaque (above) shows beakers of beer taken from an amphora. The gazelle is reminiscent of the goat used today to symbolize Bock beers.*

surviving pagan civilizations in Europe; this is probably the root of the word ale in the English language.

Did the first civilizations live by beer alone, or did they discover the drink while trying to convert grain into edible gruel, porridge, or bread? Beer and bread, both made from grain and water, and fermented with yeast, are companion products. There is a theory that the words bread and brewed have the same origin.

## THE SPREAD OF BEER

Recent work on Mesopotamian pictograms shows that this ancient civilization already distinguished between early forms of barley and wheat. As the cultivation of grain radiated from the earliest sites in the Middle East, the Africans in the hotter south began to brew beer from sorghum and millet; the Asian peoples in the wetter east grew rice, leading to the production of sake in China and Japan (sake, being made from a grain, is really a variant on beer, rather than being rice "wine"); the Slavic people to the north cultivated rye, often on poorer soil, making a version of beer called *kvass*; and the Western Europeans stayed with wheat and barley.

Barley's husk acts as a natural filter in brewing. Barley is less easy to work with in baking – barley breads are hard and crumbly. Conversely, wheat makes good

### The beer belt
*In both the northern and southern hemispheres, the broad belt in which malting barley is cultivated also accommodates the narrower band of hop-growing areas. Cool weather suits both crops.*

bread but is less kind to the brewer. Lacking a full husk, it tends to clog the brewing vessels. As the knowledge of brewing developed, barley gradually became the predominant grain used in beer, while wheat was favored in the bakery. In Germany, especially, beer is often known as liquid bread.

Until recent years, wheat beers were regarded as being old-fashioned, but in the last two decades they have become newly appreciated for their thirst-quenching qualities and fresh flavors.

### Going with the grain
*Stylish symbols survive today, and the image of grain stands high on this tap-handle from the Widmer brewery of Portland, Oregon. Its fruity Hefeweizen beer is a northwestern favorite.*

# THE GRAINS

MANY BEERS ARE MADE entirely from grains that have been malted. Because malt provides natural enzymes needed in fermentation, it always accounts for at least 60 percent of the grain. Even in wheat beers, malted barley usually accounts for at least 40 percent of the grain. The barley imparts a softness and cleanness, and its husks form a natural filter in the brewhouse. Wheat imparts a quenching fruitiness and can contribute to a good head on the beer. Malted or rolled oatmeal, often used in stouts, makes for silky smoothness. Rye, usually malted, adds a spicy tastiness. Cooked rice lightens the beer, as does corn, which can leave an unpleasant "chicken feed" flavor, typically in cheap lagers.

## MALTING

The building in which raw grain is transformed into malt is called a maltings. A number of breweries have their own maltings, but more often the two are separate enterprises.

The process of malting is simple in principle, but control of moisture and temperature is critical if the grain is neither to overgerminate nor die. The soaking of the grains, known as steeping, takes 36–48 hours, with frequent changing of the water. The most traditional method of sprouting is to spread the grains in a layer about 12 cm (5 in) deep on a stone floor for up to a week. During this time, the grains are constantly raked and turned to aereate them and stop them from tangling. Floor malting is very labor-intensive, but some brewers feel it produces an especially clean, dry flavor. Other, more widely used techniques employ ventilated, traylike boxes or rotating drums. The drying of the grains stops the sprouting before it goes too far. It also influences the color and flavor of the malt, and of the finished beer.

## DRYING THE GRAIN

If the grains are dried gently, their appearance will change little and they will make a beer with a naturally golden color and a crackerlike or cookieish malt flavor. There are many other ways of heating the grains, and several combinations of these treatments. For example, if the grains are stewed, their color will turn amber-red, and this will be reflected in the color of the beer, which will have a nutty or toffee flavor. If the grain is toasted, that flavor will emerge in the beer, along with a brown color. Malts roasted in drums (like those used for coffee beans) produce black brews such as stouts, sometimes with flavors reminiscent of espresso.

Some beers are made with only one style of malt, for a simple clarity of flavor. Other beers contain as many as eight or nine malts or grains, providing a layered complexity of aromas, flavors, and textures.

## OTHER SUGARS

Under the German Beer Purity Law, which also applies in Norway, only malted grains are permitted in brewing. This excludes the use of rice, corn, and other sugars. Honey and maple syrup are both old ingredients that have been revived in recent years in the English-speaking world. Traces of their flavors will remain in the beer, but the use of these sugars also changes the natural biochemistry of fermentation; that, too, influences flavor. Lactose, a sugar extracted from milk, is used in some stouts.

Some Belgian beers gain rummy flavors from candy sugar (similar to the crystal sugar sometimes served with coffee). Dark, "luscious" sugars are also used by some British brewers for this purpose. More refined sugars may be used to boost alcohol content, lighten the body of the beer, or reduce costs. Australian lagers sometimes have a cane-sugar flavor and thinness.

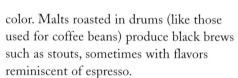

### Hand-made beer
*Malted grains in sacks at a famous regional brewery. In small breweries, "hand-made" beer involves a lot of hoisting and carrying. At bigger breweries, malt is less visible: delivered in bulk into silos, and fed through closed systems.*

# GRAINS AND MALTS, COLORS AND FLAVORS

## THE MALT OF THE CITY

The ways in which grains are malted are sometimes named after the city where a particular process was first used. These malts in turn give their names to styles of beer. In Britain, beer styles such as mild and pale ale also give their names to types of malt. Terms such as amber malt and black malt are also used. Each represents a slightly different process.

## MALTS BY FLAVOR

Some malts are known by the aromas or flavors they impart. Good examples are aromatic malt, which is toasted; honey malt, made by a long, gentle stewing process; and biscuit malt, which is very lightly roasted. Variations in the way the grains are sprouted, the levels of moisture before kilning, and the sequences of drying or drum-roasting make for endless permutations.

## OTHER GRAINS

Originally, brewers used the grains that were most readily available to them. Today, they increasingly choose grains to add distinctiveness to their beers. Rye, traditionally baked into bread, is an example. Rye beers, such as the Slavic *kvass*, are made using bread that has been steeped and fermented. In recent years, though, rye has also begun to feature in variations on wheat beer.

**Munich malt**
*Dark Munich malt has rounded, full flavors with some dryish coffee character. It is an influential ingredient in a dark,* Dunkel-*style lager.*

**Vienna malt**
*The Austrian capital was once known for bronze lagers made with this type of malt. Today, it is typically used in toffeeish* Märzen *or* Oktoberfest *lagers.*

**Pilsner malt**
*The palest malt originates from Pilsen, in Bohemia. It was floor-malted from Moravian barley. Soft, clean, and sweetish, the style is used in golden lagers.*

PILSNER MALT PRODUCED THE WORLD'S FIRST GOLDEN BEER.

**Chocolate malt**
*This style contains no chocolate, but mimics the flavor. Kilned at high temperatures without being burned, it is used in dark beers, such as porters and stouts.*

**Crystal malt**
*Used in reddish-brown ales. Stewing creates a crystal-sugar, nutty character. There are many variations, and the term caramel malt is also used.*

**Smoked malt**
*Once, all malt was dried by wind, sun, or fire. Beechwood fires are still used in Bamberg, Germany. Several brewers also use malt dried over peat fires.*

ALASKAN SMOKED PORTER USES MALT DRIED OVER A FIRE OF ALDER TWIGS.

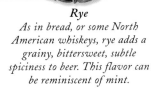

**Rye**
*As in bread, or some North American whiskeys, rye adds a grainy, bittersweet, subtle spiciness to beer. This flavor can be reminiscent of mint.*

**Wheat**
*The refreshing flavors of wheat beers have given them a revival in recent years, especially in Germany and Belgium. The Belgian style is also spiced.*

**Oats**
*The notion of oats as a sustaining, nutritious grain led to their use in stouts, especially after World War II. Oats have been used since Neolithic times.*

MACLAY OAT MALT STOUT IS A PRESENT-DAY EXAMPLE FROM SCOTLAND.

---

ROASTED BARLEY . . . MODEST STRENGTH

*Dark it may be, but the bottled Guinness sold in Ireland and the UK has only 3.4 abw (4.2 abv).*

## COLOR, BODY, AND STRENGTH

Contrary to popular belief, darker beers are not necessarily fuller in body or stronger in alcohol. There is no connection between color, fullness, and potency. Color derives from the malt used. Dark malts do not always create body, and their color has nothing whatever to do with alcohol.

BIG BEER . . . PILSNER MALT

*An innocent-looking golden beer, but Belzebuth has a devilish 12.0 abw (15.0 abv).*

# THE HOPS

THE HOP IS A CLIMBING PLANT, most closely related to hemp, and both plants are members of the botanical order that includes the nettle, mulberry, and elm. Hop shoots were known to the ancients as a salad food similar to bean sprouts, and are still served in this way in growing regions. The part used to aromatize and flavor beer is the resiny cone. Hops may be the plant referred to in relation to "strong drink" in the Jewish Talmud, but firm evidence of their use in beer is much later. The first undisputed reference is from the Benedictine Sister Hildegarde (1098–1179), the abbess of Rupertsberg, in Germany. The hop was to become the dominant flavoring in beer, perhaps because it is also a good preservative.

## PROCESSING THE HOP

Once picked, the hop cone will, like a flower, shrivel within hours unless it is dried and pressed. It is dried in a kiln known as an oast and, in the most traditional method, pressed into tall sacks called pockets. Some brewers feel that this method causes the least abrasion to the resins and essential oils that impart aroma, flavor, and dryness to beer. They also like to see the leaf shape and quality of their chosen variety. Others prefer the modern technique in which the hop is compacted into a tiny, cylindrical pellet and vacuum-packed in foil, like coffee. This method has the benefit of protecting the hop from oxidation. In addition to whole hops in these two forms, hop extract (like a green jam) and hop oils are also used in beer.

## HOP VARIETIES

Those hop varieties with resins high in certain acids are used primarily to give the beer dryness or bitterness, to balance the sweetness of the malt. Varieties high in certain essential oils are employed to impart flavor and, especially, aroma. The latter are known as noble or elegant hops. Just as winemakers usually champion the grapes of their own region, and may even deride other varieties, so brewers can occasionally be dismissive of other countries' hops.

The hop varieties with international reputations for fine aromas and flavors are mainly grown in Europe and North America. The traditional European hops tend toward a herbal delicacy, while those varieties grown in the US, whether originally imported or locally bred, are more scented, piney, and zesty. In recent years, some brewers have experimented by making beers with only one variety of hop. Most beers employ several, and sometimes as many as eight or nine, for balance and complexity. The hops may be added at several stages of the brewing process, sometimes in different blends at each point, variously for aroma, flavor, and bitterness.

**Flowery beer**
*Sunflowers add color to this hop garden in the German Hallertau region. The hop shoots begin to grow in early spring; by late August or September the vine will be up to 20 ft (5 m) tall, and heavy with aromatic cones.*

**Locally farmed**
*The Harvey's brewery, in Sussex, England, takes a pride in using hops from its own county's tiny output, as well as those from across the line in Kent. The name of the farm is chalked on the bin where each pocket is stored.*

# CLASSIC HOP VARIETIES ... AROMAS AND FLAVORS

## CONTINENTAL EUROPE

Poland has its cedary Lublin hops, grown to the west of that town, and Slovenia its Styrians, with a hint of orange zest, but the most famous variety grown in continental Europe is the Saaz, taking its name from the German rendition of Žatec, the famous hop-growing town in the northwest of Bohemia. A wide range of hops are grown in Bavaria and the south of Germany, among which perhaps the most famous is the Hallertau Mittelfrüh.

## BRITAIN

Britain's hop-growing areas, primarily in East Kent, the Weald, and Worcester and Hereford, are relatively small, but have their own range of distinct hop varieties, from the quininelike Challenger to the junipery Progress to the geranial Target. A new variety is the dwarf First Gold, which has a suggestion of tangerines. The most famous English hops, both named after the growers who propagated them, are Golding and Fuggle.

## NORTH AMERICA

The US is one of the world's largest growers of hops, especially in the Pacific Northwest: the Willamette Valley of Oregon, the Yakima Valley of Washington State, and the Snake River Valley of Idaho. Hops are also grown across the Canadian border: in British Columbia around Chilliwack and Kamloops. North America grows European varieties of hops, but also breeds its own, from the piney, flavorsome Chinook to the freshly woody, bitter Nugget.

**Hallertau Mittelfrüh**
*This aroma hop is famously delicate and flowery, perhaps with a suggestion of lemon grass. Hallertau is the region of cultivation, north of Munich, Bavaria.*

**Saaz**
*Sometimes known as the Saazer, or Bohemian Red. This most famous of all aroma hops is cleansing and fresh, with suggestions of camomile or gorse.*

THE SAAZ AROMA, WITH A TOUCH OF STYRIANS, IS EVIDENT IN BELGIAN DUVEL.

**Golding**
*A family of varieties from Canterbury, and dating from 1790. The prized version is the Canterbury, or East Kent, Golding. A lemony, pithy, cedary, earthy aroma hop.*

**Fuggle**
*Noticed in 1861, in Horsmonden, Kent. Propagated in 1875, by Richard Fuggle. A bittering and aroma hop. Soft, with complex, resiny, aniseedy, almost tropical notes.*

THE FUGGLES AROMA AND FLAVOR ARE VERY EVIDENT IN SUFFOLK STRONG ALE.

**Mount Hood**
*Released in 1989, and bred in Oregon from seedlings of the Hallertau-Hersbruck hop. A flowery and herbal aroma hop, with hints of elderberry, apple, sage, oregano, and mint.*

**Cascade**
*Widely used example of the floral, leafy piney, zesty, citrussy American aroma hop. Powerfully aromatic and scenty. Released in 1972. Its parents include the Fuggle.*

ANCHOR LIBERTY ALE IS SOMETHING OF A TRIBUTE TO THE CASCADE HOP.

## HOW THE HOP PROVIDES FLAVOR

Between 250 and 300 natural chemical compounds in beer arise from the essential oils in the hop. Several influential compounds present in the hop are in a group of liquid hydrocarbons called terpenes. One is called pinene; another is limonene, which also occurs in citrus fruits; a third is selinene, which occurs in celery; a fourth is myrcene, which is found in bay leaves. Some of these compounds are also found in lavender, spearmint, and nutmeg. When a panel of specialists in fragrances and flavors was invited to nose 15 varieties of hop at Oregon State University, they arrived at more than 50 comparisons, ranging from anise, basil, and cedar to tobacco, violets, and wet hay. A study at Coors' brewery used 60 herbs as comparisons, dividing aroma hops into spicy, minty, piney, floral, and citric groups.

# ADDITIONAL FLAVORINGS

IN THE DAYS WHEN MAKERS of drinks did not have the technical knowledge to achieve clean aromas and tastes, they used flavorings to cover defects. Long after techniques improved, the flavorings remained as part of the balance of some drinks. This is true of beers (whether the flavoring is the hop, or the other ingredients shown on these pages), vermouths (which are wines with herbs, spices, and fruits), all liqueurs, gins, flavored vodkas, some brandies (with nut or fruit essences), and spiced rums. More conventional wines, brandies, whiskies, rums, and tequilas balance the flavors of their raw materials with tannins and vanilla notes from the casks in which they are aged.

## HERBS, SPICES, AND FRUITS

The Mesopotamians, the earliest known brewers, used "sweet" materials in their beers, but did not record which. Some experts feel this referred simply to the sweetness of malt, but others believe honey, dates, or figs may have been added. This would have been a very early precedent for today's fruit beers.

Pottery shards 4,000 years old, bearing traces of barley and oats, but also honey, heather, and herbs such as meadowsweet (*Spiraea ulmaria*) and royal fern (*Osmunda regalis*) were found on the Scottish island of Rhum. Home brewing of heather ale has never totally vanished from the Scottish islands, especially Orkney.

There are some suggestions that the Romans knew of northern Europeans using heather and bog myrtle (*Myrica gale*). By the 1100s, Sister Hildegarde was mentioning myrtle berries, ash leaves, and hops. By the 1200s, bog myrtle, wild rosemary (*Ledum palustre*), and the daisylike yarrow (*Achillea millefolium*) were typical ingredients in Germany. They were used in a premixed blend of flavors known as grug, or gruit.

In the 1300s, the records of the Archbishop of Cologne mentioned those ingredients but also more exotic items, such as aniseed, caraway, and ginger. To protect the trade in these spices, hops were at times banned, but sometimes the opposite was true. The Bavarian Beer Purity Law in the 1500s, for example, insisted upon hops as the only flavoring in beer.

Coriander is a traditional flavoring in Belgian beers. Another is grains of paradise (*Aframomum melegueta*), a peppery-tasting seed native to West Africa, introduced during colonial times. The use of Curaçao oranges may date from the same era. The Spanish are Europe's principal growers of licorice, which historically was often used in stouts by British and American brewers. The custom survived vestigially on both sides of the Atlantic until the 1970s. A decade later, the revival of interest in speciality beers was bringing back such exotic flavorings.

### PINE TIPS

Pine tips add hoppy, medicinal flavors to the Scottish ale Alba (*page 38*). Birch beer has been made in the US in soft-drink and alcoholic versions. American root beer fits into the former tradition.

*Sweet and dry*
*The small, dryish cherries that grow around Brussels make a perfect foil for the* lambic *beers of the region. The Boston Beer Company (left) makes a sweeter interpretation.*

# REVIVING THE RANGE OF FLAVORS

## HERBS

The term herb is usually applied to a green plant or leaf. Coriander leaf (sometimes known as *cilantro*, or Chinese parsley) features on the label of the peppery, citric-tasting Umbel Ale, from the Nethergate brewery of Clare in Suffolk, England. (An umbel is a flower cluster.) Camomile was used in England in the 1700s, and is employed by several American breweries today. It imparts a flowery, lemongrass flavor to a Belgian-style white beer, Wits' End, made by the Great Lakes Brewing Company of Cleveland, Ohio. Clover is an unusual ingredient, but gives aroma and herbal sweetness to the Winter Vorst ale from the Grolsch brewery in the Netherlands.

## SPICES

This term is usually applied to woody plants, barks, or seeds. Grains of paradise are widely used in Belgium, and were extensively employed in Britain in the 1700s and 1800s. They impart a peppery dryness to Southampton Saison from Long Island. Cinnamon was used in England and Wales as early as the 1300s. It is employed in some porters and widely used in old and winter ales (typically with spices like nutmeg and cloves) in Britain and especially the US. A less common use is in Belgian-style white beers, typically the sherbety Steendonk. The same style of beer almost always uses coriander seeds, along with Curaçao orange zest.

## FRUITS

A drink based on fruit is a wine; a beverage fermented from grain is a beer, even if fruit is added later. In beers of this type, the fruit is primarily a flavoring, even though it contributes sugars that aid fermentation. Technically, a berry is a fruit. Juniper berries are the classic example of such an ingredient in beer, having been used since at least the 1300s. These berries have dry, aromatic flavors, not too much sugar, and good preservative qualities. Damsons and the Belgian type of small cherry are good for color and flavor, with a stone to add almondy dryness. The American fashion for peach "schnapps" encouraged some brewers of *lambic* beers to use this sweet fruit.

## OTHER FLAVORS

Many unlikely sounding ingredients have been used in beer. In the 1700s, roosters, often soaked in Madeira, were used, perhaps to provide nutrition for the yeast, but also as a flavoring. Some domestic brewers continued to add meat well into the 20th century. In 1996, the Boston Beer Company made a Cock Ale in this way. At the same time, some brewers began to use nonnarcotic hemp. By comparison, beers made with chocolate or coffee seem quite conventional. Brewers in the southwest US have in recent years used sagebrush and even chilies, the latter sometimes remaining as a pod in the bottle.

**Coriander leaf**
*In the same family as fennel and European anise, coriander is usually grown in the east Mediterranean.*

**Camomile**
*This daisylike flower is most commonly used in vermouths and teas, and often as a tonic.*

**Clover**
*Its aromas and flavors are also found in whiskeys made on the clovery hillsides of Scotland.*

WINTER VORST ...A SEASONAL BEER FROM GROLSCH.

**Grains of paradise**
*This seed, also known as guinea pepper, is also used to give aromatic dryness and assertiveness to some gins.*

**Cinnamon**
*This tree bark, grown especially in Sri Lanka, has been used in drinks since ancient Egyptian times.*

**Coriander seeds**
*Aromatic, spicy, sweetish, and sometimes orangy, these seeds are also used in gins and vinegars.*

HOEGAARDEN IS THE CLASSIC EXAMPLE OF A BELGIAN WHITE BEER.

**The damson**
*Of Middle Eastern origin. Like the sloe (as used in gin), it is close to the "frontier" between plums and cherries.*

**The peach**
*Originally associated with Persia. Peach "schnapps," like cherry "brandy," is a sweet liqueur, not a spirit.*

**The cherry**
*Best for beer are the "sour," or acidic, varieties, like the kriek of Belgium, the morello, and the maraschino.*

NEW GLARUS USES CHERRIES FROM BRUSSELS, WISCONSIN.

**Coffee**
*The fashions for good espresso and great beer met in the city of Seattle, Washington in the late 1990s.*

**Chili**
*Spice or fruit? It is New Mexico's state vegetable. Chili beers are hot in more than one sense.*

**Chocolate**
*The real thing is sometimes used, but its flavor can be mimicked by "chocolate" malt.*

YOUNG'S OF LONDON MAKE A STOUT FOR CHOCOHOLICS.

# WATER AND YEAST

JUST AS WATER IS THE BIGGEST constituent of wine (in the form of rainfall that becomes juice in the grape), so it is basic to beer. Grain takes far smaller amounts of water from the soil, so the brewer has to help. He runs water through the malted and milled grains in order to make a solution of their fermentable sugars. This solution is then boiled with hops, and sometimes other flavorings, and fermented by the addition of yeast. It could be argued that neither water nor yeast is an ingredient. Water is a medium; yeast is an agent of fermentation. Yet each has its own influence on the character of the finished product.

## "OUR OWN SPRING"

In the days before motorized transport, almost all beer was produced locally, and brewers had to make do with whatever quality of water was available. It was when steam power made it possible to produce beer in far larger volume, and transport it by train to a much wider market, that water became an issue. A brewer planning to expand on an industrial scale would choose a location where there was a guaranteed source of water that was "clean," but also in an inexhaustible, year-round volume of a consistent quality. The best possible source would be a spring or deep well near or inside the premises. The mineral content of the water would be determined by the geological strata from which it rose.

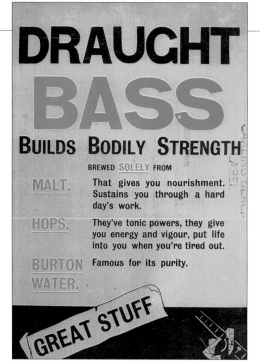

## HOW TASTE IS AFFECTED

The first golden lager was made in Bohemia, at Pilsen, where the water is low in minerals and the beer soft-tasting. The first pale ales were brewed in England, at Burton, where the water is high in calcium sulfate; calcium reduces haze and sulfate enhances hop flavors. Porters and stouts became famous in London, then Dublin, cities with chloride and carbonate water that made for fuller and grainier flavors respectively. In each instance, the water helped shape the beer.

### Pure draft
*The Bass brewery is in Burton in the English Midlands. Malt, hops, and specifically Burton water are the selling points in this 1950s poster.*

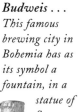

***Budweis . . .***
*This famous brewing city in Bohemia has as its symbol a fountain, in a statue of Samson.*

***. . . and its lager***
*Budvar has a softness enhanced by water from its own wells 984 ft (300 m) deep. The Budweis brewery dates from 1895, though beer has been made in the town since the 1200s.*

***Burton . . .***
*The water tower is salient in this townscape of the Burton breweries.*

***. . . and its ale***
*A calcium sulfate aroma is typical in Marston's famous Burton ales.*

***Dublin . . .***
*Water from the mountains was once held in a cistern at the gates of the city.*

***. . . and its stout***
*Carbonates favor the dark colors and grainy flavors of dry stouts.*

## THE MAGIC MICROORGANISM

Yeast is a microscopic organism belonging to the kingdom of the fungi. It is carried in the air, and can settle anywhere. When it encounters sugar, it converts it into alcohol and acid – a process called fermentation.

Early brewers made solutions of grain, water, and flavorings, then witnessed them turning by apparent magic into beer. They were unaware of the existence of yeast. This method of spontaneous fermentation by wild yeasts that are airborne or resident in the brewery is still used by producers of *lambic* beers in Belgium. Beers made in this way usually taste very acidic and winey.

## CONTROLLED FERMENTATION

When a brew ferments in an open vessel, it warms and develops a foam head that grows and can overflow. By catching the foam, comprising millions of yeast cells, and adding it to the next batch, medieval brewers learned how to achieve a consistent fermentation. This "top-fermentation" technique is still used to make most wheat beers and all true ales, porters, and stouts. It typically produces complex, fruity flavors.

In summer, the atmosphere was so alive with wild yeasts that beermaking became uncontrollable. Brewers would make a final batch of the season in spring, store it in a cool cellar for the summer, and start again in fall. Brewers in Bavaria, who stored their beer in icy caves in the Alps, learned that the cold made the yeast "hide" at the bottom of the brew. Bottom-fermented beer is known as lager (meaning "store" in German), and typically has a clean, rounded taste.

***Recovering the yeast***
*The yeasty foam overflows . . . and is recaptured at the Unertl wheat beer brewery in Bavaria. The equipment is shiningly modern and purpose-built, but the method hardly differs from medieval times.*

## WILD FERMENTATION (LAMBIC)

Spontaneous fermentation has only survived in a handful of tiny breweries around the town of Lembeek, in Belgium, but these make some of the world's most distinctive beers. A brew is made, then left overnight in an open vessel in the attic of the brewery, with open windows or shutters. The wild yeast settles on the beer and begins the fermentation. In the morning, the brew is decanted into wooden casks, in which further yeasts may be resident. The yeasts include a semiwild type called Brettanomyces, which can add "hopsack" aromas.

## TOP-FERMENTATION (WHEAT BEERS)

Two distinct types of top-fermentation give emphatic flavors and aromas to German styles of wheat beer. The *Berliner Weisse* type has a blend of conventional yeast and a lactic culture, imparting a sharp acidity. The south German types use their own family of yeasts, which often impart banana, bubblegum, and clove flavors to the beer. These derive especially from natural compounds called *guaiacols*. Some British and American brewers of wheat beers use more conventional ale or lager yeasts.

## TOP-FERMENTATION (ALES, PORTERS, STOUTS)

Fermentation originally took place at ambient temperatures, as refrigeration had not been invented. These would have been winter temperatures in the traditional brewing nations. With today's sophisticated temperature controls, top-fermentation is normally kept at 59–86° F (15–30° C), followed by a short maturation period at 50–55° F (10–13° C). This type of fermentation can create restrained orangy, strawberryish, or dessert apple aromas and flavors, and sometimes butterscotch, arising from the compound diacetyl.

## BOTTOM FERMENTATION (LAGER)

This technique may have been practiced earlier, but lager-brewers did not begin to understand how it worked until the 1830s. Knowledge improved with Pasteur's studies on yeasts in the 1860s, but a pure culture single cell was not finally identified under a microscope until the 1880s, at the Carlsberg brewery. This work, and the development of refrigeration, were essential to methodical brewing. A lager fermentation classically takes place at 41–48° F (5–9° C), followed by maturation close to 32° F (0° C).

***Geuze Boon***
*This classic from Lembeek itself is a blend of lambic beers. It has a typical rhubarb acidity, imparted by a sequence of wild fermentations for a period of up to three years.*

***Schneider Weisse***
*Among widely available South German wheat beers, Schneider Weisse is a good example of the fruity, bubblegum, clovey style. The yeast and fermentation are carefully monitored to maintain these flavors.*

***St. Ambroise Pale Ale***
*This renowned Canadian ale has an orangy aroma and flavor arising from a famous ale yeast associated with the Ringwood brewery of Hampshire, England. The yeast was earlier used by now-defunct breweries in Yorkshire.*

***Spaten Oktoberfestbier***
*Beers from the pioneering lager brewery of Spaten typically have a creamy, "new-mown hay" aroma that is typical of very traditional bottom-fermenting styles.*

# MAKING BEER

**B**REWING IS AN AGRICULTURAL industry. Whether the brewing takes place in a farmhouse or what appears to be a factory, malted grains are made into an infusion or decoction, boiled with hops, and fermented. For the visitor, these processes are easiest to see and follow in breweries with open vessels. Often, these are local or regional breweries built in Victorian times, where even the newer brewing vessels may be more than 50 years old. Some modern breweries have outdoor fermentation and lagering vessels in clusters known as "tank farms." These can mislead passersby into thinking that a brewery is a chemical works, but even in the most high-tech of breweries there is no such thing as "chemical beer."

### THE MASH

Anyone who has ever made coffee in a filter will find the first stage in the brewhouse familiar. At its simplest, the malted grains are ground in a mill, then put into a vessel with warm water. The grains soak and infuse in the water for an hour or two. Then the false bottom of the vessel is opened so that the infusion can run through a filterlike base. What emerges, like the coffee, is a solution of malt in water; this is known as sweet wort.

As with most stages of beermaking, this process, called mashing, can be varied in many ways to achieve different characteristics in the finished product. These variations are often decided in advance, according to the type of beer being made that day, but they may also be fine-tuned by the brewer on the day if the mash is not developing quite as planned. Despite everyone's best efforts, there might be slight variations in the character of the malt, and the weather may be influencing the water temperature.

### TIMES AND TEMPERATURES

The chief variables throughout beermaking are times and temperatures, and the different regimes of mashing are a good example of that. Lower temperatures release sugars that are fermentable, higher ones liberate unfermentable sugars, making for more body in the beer but less alcohol. Temperatures can be increased, often in several steps, by adding more hot water or by using a vessel with a heated jacket.

A more complex system, often used by traditionalist lager brewers in the Czech Republic and Germany, involves moving proportions of the mash to a second vessel, boiling them, then blending them back. This is known as a decoction: single, double, or triple, depending upon how many times it is performed. Decoction-mashed lagers often have a malt character that is especially aromatic, rich, and soft.

### VISITING A BREWERY

No one should miss the chance to visit a traditional brewery and enjoy, first-hand, the hot, steamy brewhouse with its heady aromas of sweet wort and infusing hops.

*Copper tun*
*Traditionally, the mash was ready when the steam cleared and the brewer could see his reflection in the wort.*

*Lid is raised to release heat and steam.*

**The mash is over**
*Spent grains lie in this drained mash tun at St. Feuillien, a Belgian brewery making malty but spicy, flavorsome, abbey-style beers.*

**Running off**
*Watching the run-off enables the brewer to check clarity and the even spread of filtration. Each tap is connected to a different part of the filter bed.*

**The gift of hops**
*Hops are added to the brew kettle. In this instance, pressed "blossom" or "leaf" hops are being used, as opposed to pellets or the jamlike extract.*

## THE BREW

The simplest brewhouse layout has two principal vessels. One is the mash tub, (this is called the mash tun in Britain), where the infusion of grains is made. The other is the brew kettle, where this infusion is boiled with the hops. The second of these two processes is the actual act of brewing. This usually takes about 90 minutes, though some breweries do it for an hour, and occasional strong beers can demand several hours.

The main function of the boil is to introduce into the sweet wort the aromas and flavors of the hops. It also sterilizes the brew, killing unwanted microorganisms in the wort; to some extent concentrates it, by evaporation; and clarifies it, by coagulating proteins. Most brew kettles are heated by steam coils, but some sit over gas or oil burners. The latter is an older method, called the "direct-flame" system; it creates hot spots in the kettle, making for some caramelization of the malt sugars and perhaps imparting toffeeish flavors to the beer. This system is also sometimes known as "fire-brewing," and some brewers feel that it makes for a more satisfying flavor.

Even in large breweries, the hops are often added by hand. Because the hop is a condiment, it is used in small amounts, like the salt or pepper in a stew. Very small variations in the quantities of hops greatly affect the aroma, flavor, and bitterness of the beer. Hops are added in kilos, pounds, or even ounces; malt in tons.

## THE ART OF HOPPING

Some beers are made with only one addition of hops, but most have more. Brewers, especially in Germany, sometimes refer to these additions as "gifts"; the hops are "given" to the beer as though they were a present. Many master brewers have a love affair with hops, and would like to use more, but are afraid of making their beers too assertive for the consumer. Hops do not contribute alcohol to the beer, but they do make for powerful aromas and flavors.

Varieties of hop intended to impart dryness or bitterness are added early in the boil. Some brewers have a second addition in mid-boil to add flavor. Most have a "gift" around the end of the boil to accentuate aroma. This "late hopping" is done with especially aromatic varieties.

When the brewing is completed, the hop leaves and protein sediment may be removed by centrifugal force. Another method is to run the brewed wort through a strainer, known in the US as a hop jack, in the UK as a hop back. Some brewers add more hops to form a bed in the strainer, causing more aromatic hop oils to be added to the filtering wort. Additional aroma hops may even be placed, sometimes in a muslin sack like a bouquet garni, in the maturation vessel. In Britain, especially, this "dry-hopping" may go into the cask that matures in the pub cellar.

## FERMENTATION AND MATURATION

Advertisements sometimes talk of beer being "fully brewed" or "slow brewed." All beer is fully brewed, and this does not happen slowly. The ads are really referring to fermentation or maturation, usually the latter. Typically, fermentation takes only three or four days, or at most a week, in the case of wheat beers, ales, porters, and stouts, the styles made with "top" yeasts. In most instances, they also mature in a matter of days or weeks. (A notable exception would be beers that have a living yeast in the bottle, where a slower evolution might continue for some years.)

Scarcely more time is given these days to many lager beers, though the very finest, especially in Germany and the Czech Republic, still have the best part of two weeks' fermentation and several months' maturation. The odd very strong lager might approach a year in the making, but that is unusual. The only style of beer that customarily takes more than a year is the old type of Belgian *lambic*.

The oldest techniques of fermentation and maturation use wooden vessels, and some traditionalist brewers still prefer open fermenters to closed ones (despite the risk of contamination by wild yeasts). Top-fermenting beers develop more of their characteristic fruity flavors in such vessels. Even those brewers who use closed vessels sometimes admit that good flavors can be purged, and maturation be uneven, if their vessels are built too tall.

*The meeting of flavors*
*The green of the dry, herbal-tasting hops mixes into the amber of sweet barley wort.*

**Open fermenter**
*The inverted funnel in the middle of this open fermentation vessel is an overflow for the removal of the yeasty head. This is known as "skimming."*

**Lagering vessels**
*Lagering means cold storage, or maturation. The traditional wooden lagering vessels have largely been replaced by stainless steel ones, such as these.*

# TASTING BEER

ALL GOOD BEER TASTES of malted grains and hops, and a truly clean lager of little else. Good ales have both of those elements but also some fruitiness from the use of top-fermenting yeasts. Good porters and stouts have chocolaty or espressolike flavors from the roasted malts used. Good wheat beers are tart and refreshing. But whatever the profile of the beer, if a brew is offered as a lager or ale, porter, stout, or wheat beer, it should live up to the style. If it is a good beer, the flavors will not only be appropriate but also in an interesting balance and combination. This is the meaning of "complexity." A beer with this quality seems to offer further aromas and flavors every time the glass is raised.

## HOW TO APPRECIATE AROMA AND FLAVOR

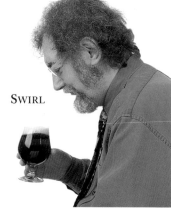  

LOOK

*The pleasures of all food and drink are experienced with the eyes as well as the nose and palate. Clarity is an issue in most, but not all, types of beer. Color certainly is, and the greatest beers often have colors that are distinctive, subtle, complex, and appetizingly attractive.*

SWIRL

*A gentle swirl disturbs the beer enough to help release its aromatic compounds. This level of study might best be pursued at home, as serious swirling might easily be thought pretentious when conducted in a bar or restaurant.*

SNIFF

*Whether the drinker sniffs or not, much of what we think we taste is actually experienced through our potent and evocative sense of smell. In the finest beers, the appetizing aromas are a hugely significant element of the pleasure they impart.*

SIP

*Let the beer lap over the tongue. Sweet flavors (malt for example) may be more obvious at the front of the tongue; salt (as in the water) at the front sides, fruity acidity farther back at the sides; while hop bitterness is best detected at the back.*

## JUDGING BEERS

Enjoyment of great beer does not demand some special tasting talent. All it requires is an open mind, an interest in beer, and a keenness to find aromas and flavors without fear of mockery.

TASTING CONDITIONS: Choose a naturally lit room for better evaluation of color. Music can be a distraction. Avoid cigarette smoke, cooking smells, or perfumes. For judging purposes, the beers should all be sampled in the same type of glass. A large, clear wineglass is ideal, with some curvature to showcase the aroma.

BEER TEMPERATURE: The serving temperatures indicated for each beer in this book are those at which each may be most enjoyable. They are merely suggestions, and do not always accord with the brewers' own guidelines. If, rather than being enjoyed as a drink, the beer is being judged, the aromas and flavors will express themselves most fully at room temperature.

ORDER OF BEERS: Start with the beers expected to be lightest in intensity of flavor, and work upward, especially if they are in several styles.

HOW MANY BEERS?: Even five or six beers can confuse the palate, and 10 or a dozen are more than enough. In order fully to taste the beer, the bitterness must be sensed at the back of the mouth. Beertasters therefore tend to swallow at least some of the fluid, and are less exhaustive in spitting than wine judges. As alcohol is ingested, the faculties become less acute.

SCORESHEETS: In a formal tasting, for a beer or wine club, or class, a scoresheet is a handy *aide-mémoire*. A simple system is to have scores for: fidelity to style (if it is labeled as a Pilsner, wheat beer, or ale, is it a good example?); appearance (head formation, color, and perhaps clarity); aroma (pleasant, appetizing, complex, true to style?); palate (the same criteria); and finish (does it develop late flavor, or simply vanish without saying "goodbye"?).

BETWEEN BEERS: Plain bread, crackers, or matzos will clear the palate. Avoid anything with its own flavors, such as salty pretzels, and butter or cheese, because anything greasy will flatten the beer. A neutral-tasting, still bottled water, generously provided, is the best option.

# A LEXICON OF FLAVORS AND AROMAS

MANY AROMAS AND FLAVORS in beer have more than one origin. Explanations of some typical flavors are given below. Tasters often express flavors in terms of "aroma metaphors" that refer to other drinks and foods.

ACIDITY: An appetizing acidity, sometimes lemony, comes from hops. A fruity acidity derives from the yeast in fermentation, especially in ales and even more so in *Berliner Weisse*, Belgian *lambic* styles, and Flemish brown and red ales.

APPLES: A fresh, delicate, pleasant, sweet apple character arises from the fermentation process in some English ales, famously Marston's. A more astringent, green apple taste can arise from insufficient maturation.

BANANAS: Very appropriate in some South German wheat beers.

BITTERNESS: Sounds negative, but it is positive. "Good" bitterness comes from the hop. It is present to varying degrees in all beers, and especially appropriate in a British bitter. Robust bitterness, as in Anchor Liberty Ale, is appetizing. Astringency is not.

BODY: Not actually a taste, but a sensation of texture or "mouth feel," ranging from thin to firm to syrupy. Thinness may mean a beer has been very fully fermented, perhaps to create a light, quenching character. Firm, textured, or grainy beers may have been mashed at high temperatures to create some unfermentable sugars. Syrupy ones have been made from a high density of malts, possibly with some holding back of fermentation.

BUBBLEGUM: Very appropriate in some South German wheat beers. Arises from compounds called guaiacols created in fermentation.

BURNED: Pleasant burned flavors arise from highly kilned barley or malt in some stouts. Burned plastic, deriving from excessive phenol, is a defect caused by yeast problems.

BUTTERSCOTCH: Very appropriate in certain British ales, especially some from the North of England and Scotland. Unpleasant in lagers. This flavor derives from a compound called diacetyl created in fermentation.

CARAMEL: Most often a malt characteristic, though brewers do sometimes also add caramel itself. A malty caramel character is positive in restrained form in many types of beer. Too much can be overwhelming.

CEDARY: A hop character.

CHOCOLATY: A malt character in some brown ales, porters and stouts. Typically arising from chocolate malt (*page 13*).

CLOVES: Very appropriate in some South German wheat beers. Arises from phenols created in fermentation.

COFFEEISH: A malt character in some dark lagers, brown ales, porters, and stouts.

COOKIELIKE: Typical character of pale malt. Suggests a fresh beer with a good malt character.

EARTHY: Typical character of traditional English hops. Positive characteristic in British ales.

FRESH BREAD: *See* cookielike.

GRAPEFRUIT: Typical character of American hops, especially the Cascade variety.

GRASS, HAY: Can be a hop characteristic. Fresh, new-mown hay is typical in some classic European lagers. It arises from a compound called dimethyl sulfide, caused by fermentation with traditional lager yeasts.

HERBAL: Hop characteristic. Examples of herbal flavors are bay leaves, mint, and spearmint.

HOPPY: Herbal, zesty, earthy, cedary, piney, appetizingly bitter.

LICORICE: A characteristic of some dark malts, in German *Schwarzbier*, English old ales, porters, and stouts. In the English-speaking world, licorice itself is sometimes used as an additive.

MADEIRA: Caused by oxidation. In very strong, bottle-conditioned beers that have been aged many years, this will be in a pleasant balance. In another type of beer, it is likely to be unpleasant.

MALTY: *See* cookielike, fresh bread, nuts, tea, toast, and toffee.

MINTY: Hop characteristic, especially spearmint.

NUTS: Typical malt characteristic in many types of beer, especially Northern English brown ales. Arises from crystal malt (*page 13*).

ORANGY: Typical of several hop varieties. Can also arise from some ale yeasts. Positive if not overwhelming.

PEARS: Yeast characteristic in some ales. If overwhelming, suggests that the beer has lost some balancing hop due to age.

PEPPER: The flavor of alcohol. Suggests a strong beer.

PINEY: Characteristic of some hops, especially American varieties.

PLUMS: Yeast character, found in South German wheat beers.

RAISINY: Typical in beers made with very dark malts and to a high alcohol content, for example, imperial stouts. This flavor develops in fermentation.

RESINY: Typical hop characteristic.

ROSES: Can arise from hops. Also from yeast development during bottle-conditioning, especially in some Belgian beers.

SHERRY: Dry, fino sherry flavors are typical in Belgian *lambic* beers. Sweet sherry can arise in strong, bottle-conditioned beers that have been aged. *See also* Madeira.

SMOKY: Appropriate in "malt whiskey beer," smoked beer, and some dry stouts.

SOUR: Appropriate in *Berliner Weisse, lambic,* or Flemish brown or red specialities, but not in other styles of beer.

STRAWBERRIES: In extremely restrained form, and in balance with malt and hop, an appropriate fermentation characteristic in some British ales.

TEA: A strongish tea, of the type made in England (Indian, especially Darjeeling, with milk) is a good aroma metaphor for malt.

TOAST: Malt characteristic in some dark ales, porters, and stouts.

TOBACCO: Fragrant tobacco smoke can be evoked by the Tettnang hop, grown near Lake Constance in Germany and used in many lagers.

TOFFEE: Malt characteristic, especially in Vienna-style, *Märzen,* and *Oktoberfest* amber lagers. Very appetizing if not overwhelming.

VINEGARY: See acidity.

WINEY: Typical of *lambic* and some other Belgian styles aged in wood.

YEAST: The aroma of fresh yeast, like bread rising, is typical of some ales. Can appear as a "bite" in some from Yorkshire, England.

# BEERS FOR THE MOMENT

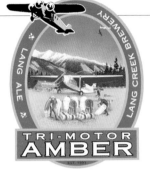

MANY PEOPLE THINK BEER IS MERELY A refresher, but such consumers may not know the world's most quenching, cooling brews . . . and what about the winter warmers, for a cold night? Others believe that the purpose of beer is to intoxicate, but it is very inefficient in this respect: the average strength of beer, worldwide, is about half that of wine, and a tenth that of spirits. Some beers are sociable relaxants, others restoratives after work or exercise. Nothing arouses the appetite like a really hoppy beer. Other brews especially suit certain foods. After dinner, with a cigar? A single-malt Scotch . . . or a very strong, rich, calming beer. With a book at bedtime? As the following pages will demonstrate, there is a beer for each of these moments, and many more.

# WHICH BEER, WHEN?

THE FIRST OBSTACLE to the full enjoyment of beer is the idea that it all tastes the same. The second is the notion that beer is exclusively a thirst-quencher, or an accompaniment to a football game, or may be enjoyed in the pub or at a bar. Just as any wine can be consumed at any time, so can any beer but, like the grape, the grain does have its favored moods and moments. Brewers sometimes fight shy of this idea, fearing that a "perfect moment" for their product would restrict its sale. This seems unlikely. No true beer-lover would be so bound by rules, but there is much to be said for trying a brew in its ideal setting. It is in this spirit that the beers below and on the following pages are presented.

SOME BEERS, from the golden lagers of Munich to the golden ales of Cologne, from the ales of Antwerp to those of America, are soothing and tempting, and ideally suited to sociable drinking. If a beer is to sustain a few hours' conversation, it must be long and easily drinkable, yet not gassy and bloating – and tasty, not tedious. In England, a bitter ale such as Young's Special (*starting the line-up below*) has the qualifications.

A beer that would work better as a greeting drink at a party or barbecue would

**A sociable beer**
*English bitter is usually modest in alcohol, so that it can be consumed in relatively high volume . . . pints to pass an evening.*

**A greeting beer**
*Save the strong stuff for later . . . a small flute of Rosé de Gambrinus provides a perfect, light-hearted start to the proceedings.*

**A thirst-quenching beer**
*Berliner Weisse has a quenching style so acidic that it tends to be sweetened with a herbal or fruit syrup, either green, red, or* au naturel.

be a raspberry or cherry brew, especially a dryish one like Cantillon Rosé de Gambrinus, from Belgium. This elegant, winey brew is the beer world's answer to a pink champagne. It is typically served in a champagne flute: a pretty drink, with a flirtatious flourish.

To cool the brow and quench the thirst on a summer's day, there are better choices than a standard lager. A fruity wheat beer from the south of Germany, or a "sweet and sour" Belgian red ale, might suit. Or a light, fresh, sharp *Berliner Weisse* laced with lemongrassy essence of woodruff. In its

native city, this champagnelike brew is typically served in an oversized saucer.

Summer or winter, to accompany a good movie on television, or a book during a relaxing, restful evening at home, the peppery, warming Old Knucklehead, from Portland, Oregon, is a perfect choice.

But what about dinner? In the pages that follow, styles of beer are nominated, and examples shown, that might accompany soups, salads, fish, poultry, meats, and a variety of other dishes. The spicy, aniseedy,

aromatic La Choulette, a *bière de garde* from northern France, goes wonderfully well with lamb, perhaps served braised with leeks and carrots. There are beers that go well with cheese and with desserts, whether fruity, creamy, or chocolaty. And for a portlike, brandyish, after-dinner digestif, Belgium's opulent, luxurious, relaxing Kasteel Bière du Château is a good example in its chunky goblet.

Only the most dedicated would put beer to all its uses in one day, but each offers its own pleasure . . . not necessarily by the pint.

*A nightcap beer*
Old Knucklehead is typical of the jokingly gnarled names given to barley wines made in the Pacific Northwest of the US.

*A beer to accompany lamb*
La Choulette is a classic example of the spicy bières de garde *made by small breweries in Northern France, near the Channel coast.*

*An after-dinner beer*
Kasteel Bière du Château is a rich, malty, Belgian brew with a stomach-calming potency reminiscent of an after-dinner brandy.

# SEASONAL BEERS FOR SPRING

THE IDEA OF SPECIAL BEERS for spring is strongest in Germany, especially in the state of Bavaria and its capital, Munich. Spring beers there are usually strong lagers, often dark in color. German brewers call a very strong product a *Bockbier*. Some even have "Double" Bocks. In Munich, a *Doppelbock* is regarded as a strong warmer to cure the winter blues as spring arrives. A third variation is the May Bock, sometimes paler and drier.

**Knight rider**
*A jousting tournament is held at Kaltenberg castle, near Munich, over three weekends in July.*

## PAULANER SALVATOR

Germany's most famous spring beer is made by the Paulaner brewery in the city of Munich. This brewery was founded in 1634 by monks in the order of St. Francis of Paula. They brewed an especially malty beer as "liquid bread" to sustain them during Lent. They called it "Salvator," Latin for "The Saviour." The brewery is no longer owned by monks, but its products still include Paulaner Salvator. This extra-strong lager has a head like whipped cream; a rich, deep, amber-brown color; a buttery-malty aroma; and a toffeeish flavor, drying in a long, enticing finish. In honor of this beer, some other Double Bocks have names ending in *-ator*.

**Region of origin**
Munich, Upper Bavaria, Germany

**Style** Double Bock (*Doppelbock*)

**Alcohol content** 6.0 abw (7.5 abv)

**Ideal serving temperature** 48° F (9° C)

**Small but strong**
*A suitably small serving for a very strong, dark lager.*

### A BEER WITH A KICK

A DUKE FROM SAXONY brought strong beer to Bavaria from Einbeck. In the local accent, Einbeck sounded like Einbock. This was shortened to Bock, which also means billy goat, so this animal has become a symbol of the beer style.

## AYINGER CELEBRATOR

Munich's best-known "country" beers are made in the nearby village of Aying, comprising little more than a church, maypole, and brewery (with its own restaurant and inn). Locally grown barley is malted at the brewery. The Ayinger brewery's Double Bock, called Celebrator, has a dark brown to ebony color; soft, rich, coffeeish, malt flavors, and a figgy dryness in the finish.

**Region of origin**
Upper Bavaria, Germany

**Style** Double Bock
(*Doppelbock*)

**Alcohol content**
5.8 abw (7.2 abv)

**Ideal serving temperature**
48° F (9° C)

*Going for the goat*
*The virile symbol appears twice on the label and the glass, and again around the neck of the bottle.*

## KALTENBERG RITTERBOCK

Although Bock beer originated in Einbeck, it was popularized by the royal court brewhouse built by Duke Wilhelm V of Bavaria at the end of the 1500s. One of the Duke's descendants, Prince Luitpold, today brews near Munich at the castle of Kaltenberg. Among his beers is his Ritterbock, available during Lent. It is light-bodied for the style, but with a bitter-chocolate praline character.

**Region of origin** Upper Bavaria, Germany

**Style** Double Bock
(*Doppelbock*)

**Alcohol content**
6.2 abw (7.7 abv)

**Ideal serving temperature**
48° F (9° C)

*Fit for a knight*
*The "Ritter" of "Ritterbock" means rider or knight.*

## BRAND DUBBELBOCK

The oldest brewery in the Netherlands is Brand's, dating from 1341. The Brand family became involved in 1871, and still are – though for 10 years the company has been owned by Heineken. The Brand's brewery has in its range a well-regarded Pilsner-type and three Bock beers. Its Dubbelbock has the creaminess and fruity "warming" maltiness of a Lowland Scotch whiskey.

**Region of origin**
Province of Limburg, the Netherlands

**Style** Double Bock
(*Dubbelbock*)

**Alcohol content**
6.0 abw (7.5 abv)

**Ideal serving temp.**
48° F (9° C)

*Triple Dutch*
*In addition to its Double, Brand's has different Maytime and year-round versions of Bock.*

## VICTORY ST. VICTORIOUS

No fewer than seven German malts are used in this aromatic, creamy, complex Double Bock, which has a finish like a nutty port. It is made by the Victory brewery and pub, established in 1995/96, in Downingtown, Pennsylvania. The brewery's founders met when they were 10 years old. Why Victory? "Being near Philadelphia, we wanted to call our brewery Liberty, but that name was already taken."

**Region of origin** Northeast US

**Style** Double Bock

**Alc. content** 5.9 abw (7.4 abv)

**Ideal serving temperature**
48° F (9° C)

*Victory "V"*
*A whimsical label, but this full-flavored brew is one of the best German-style Bocks in the US.*

## ALFA LENTE BOK

The English word "Lent" probably refers to the lengthening days of spring. In Dutch, "lente" means "spring." This seasonal brew is made by the small, old-established Alfa brewery, north of Maastricht. The brewery is noted for all-malt lagers. This *Bok* has a beautifully retained head and a textured, dryish, fresh, malt character. Strong but light-bodied for the style and very drinkable.

**Region of origin** Province of Limburg, the Netherlands

**Style** Spring Bock (*Lente Bok*)

**Alcohol content** 5.2 abw (6.5 abv)

**Ideal serving temperature** 48° F (9° C)

*A golden Bock*
*Quenching beers for later spring avoid the darker malts.*

## HB MAI-BOCK

The initials stand for Hofbräuhaus: the Royal Court brewhouse. The beer-hall, the world's most famous pub, still functions, on a small square called the Platzl in the center of Munich; the brewery is on the edge of town. The State of Bavaria owns both brewery and beer-hall. The beer claims on its label to be Munich's oldest Bock, though that is not strictly true of this Maytime version. It is a fine beer nonetheless, huge in its malt aromas, nutty flavors, and peppery, warming finish.

**Region of origin** Munich, Upper Bavaria, Germany

**Style** May Bock (*Maibock*)

**Alcohol content** 5.8 abw (7.2 abv)

**Ideal serving temperature** 48° F (9° C)

## HANSA URBOCK

The company name is an old German word for a guild of merchants. "Ur" means "original." This traditional May Bock

is made in the former German Southwest Africa, now known as Namibia. It is surely the most remote example of the style. Hansa Urbock, made according to the German Beer Purity Law, has a bright, tawny color; a sweet toffee aroma and flavor; a smooth, medium body; and a brandyish finish.

**Region of origin** Namibia, Southern Africa

**Style** May Bock

**Alcohol content** 4.8 abw (6.0 abv)

**Ideal serving temperature** 48° F (9° C)

## ROGUE MAIERBOCK ALE

The local Rogue River gives its name to this microbrewery, founded in 1988, in Newport, Oregon, in the beery Pacific Northwest of the US. Rogue is noted for colorful, big-tasting beers. Its brewer's family name is Maier; hence the jokey naming of this product. The beer aims for the smooth yet crisp character of a true May Bock, but is made with an ale yeast. It achieves its objective remarkably well.

**Region of origin** Pacific Northwest US

**Style** May Bock (top-fermenting)

**Alcohol content** 4.8 abw (6.0 abv)

**Ideal serving temperature** 48° F (9° C)

*Rogue brewer*
*Brewer John Maier features on his own label, but just for one beer in a big range of brews.*

# SEASONAL BEERS: SPRING

## ABITA SPRINGS ANDYGATOR

From New Orleans, the bridge-like causeway across Lake Pontchartrain leads to Abita Springs, where one of the American South's earliest micro-breweries was established in 1986. Abita has a Bock at about 4.5 abw (6.0 abv) for Mardi Gras, but at its pub (72011 Holly St.), and occasionally in the bottle, also offers a stronger golden lager with the -ator ending typical of many Double Bocks. Andygator is firm and very smooth, with a clean, whiskeyish, dry maltiness. The brewer who created it is called Andy, and (Alli)'gators abound in swampy Louisiana.

**Region of origin** Southeast US

**Style** Pale Double Bock

**Alc. content** 6.4–6.8 abw (8–8.5 abv)

**Ideal serving temperature** 48° F (9° C)

## ADLER BRÄU DOPPLE BOCK

The name Adler dates from a German-American brewery of the mid-1800s. The brewery was in the home town of Harry Houdini: Appleton, near Oshkosh, Wisconsin. It closed during Prohibition, and was turned into a shopping center. In 1989 a new, small brewery was installed, initially to serve two restaurants in the shopping center. Its oddly spelled Dopple Bock is a tawny brew with a creamy malt aroma, a body that is light for the style, but smooth, with a late development of licoricelike malt flavors.

**Region of origin** Midwest US

**Style** Double Bock

**Alcohol content** 5.2 abw (6.5 abv)

**Ideal serving temp.** 48° F (9° C)

## H.C. BERGER MAIBOCK

Named after Harry Calvin Berger, who was the first pediatrician in Kansas City in pioneering days. Berger, a home brewer, was the grandfather of Sandy Jones, who founded this micro in Fort Collins, Colorado, in 1992. It has since changed ownership and increased its range. Its beers include a deep amber, smooth Maibock that initially seems very light but develops clean, toffeeish, fruity, malt flavors and a late, dry finish.

**Region of origin** Southwest US

**Style** May Bock

**Alcohol content** 4.8 abw (6.0 abv)

**Ideal serving temp.** 48° F (9° C)

## BERLINER BÜRGERBRÄU MAIBOCK

This long-established East Berlin brewery has been given a new life since being acquired by the Bavarian brewing family Häring. It has a golden Maibock as well as a dark Dunkler Bock. The Maibock has a creamy malt aroma; a relatively light body; a faintly buttery malt character; and a crisp, grassy, herbal, hop finish.

**Region of origin** Berlin, Northern Germany

**Style** May Bock (*Maibock*)

**Alcohol content** 6.8 abw (8.5 abv)

**Ideal serving temperature** 48° F (9° C)

## BUDELS MEI BOCK

Very small, long-established (1870) brewery in the village of Budel, North Brabant, the Netherlands. An interesting range of products includes (in the Dutch spelling) a Mei Bock, with a full golden color; hop flavors that are distinctively herbal, almost like wintergreen; and a lingering dryness. Budels also has a brandyish dark Bock.

**Region of origin** Province of North Brabant, the Netherlands

**Style** May Bock (*Mei Bock*)

**Alcohol content** 5.2 abw (6.5 abv)

**Ideal serving temp.** 48° F (9° C)

## DOMINION SPRING BREW

The "Old Dominion" is a nickname for Virginia. Old Dominion Brewing, of Ashburn, Virginia, is one of the most successful microbreweries in the Eastern US. Its beers are readily available at Washington, DC's nearby Dulles Airport. The brewery was established in 1989. Its range has included a Spring Bock that combines a very good malt background with a very assertive hop in the finish.

**Region of origin** Mid-Atlantic US

**Style** Spring Bock

**Alcohol content** 5.8 abw (7.3 abv)

**Ideal serving temp.** 48° F (9° C)

## EINBECKER MAIBOCK

The town of Einbeck, in Lower Saxony, became famous for strong beers when it was the brewing center for the Hanseatic League. This beautifully kept, late-Gothic town still has a (mainly modern) brewery, called Einbecker Brauhaus, making no fewer than three Bock beers, in dark, pale, and Maytime styles. The Maibock is notably spritzy, with a slightly fruity spiciness. It is intended to be more refreshing than the more wintry interpretations.

**Region of origin** Northern Germany

**Style** May Bock (*Maibock*)

**Alcohol content** 5.2 abw (6.5 abv)

**Ideal serving temp.** 48° F (9° C)

## GROLSCH LENTEBOK

This brewery takes its name from its birthplace, originally called Grolle (now Groenlo), in the Netherlands. Its principal product is its lightly hoppy Pilsner-style beer, but it also has a range of specialities. These include an assertive, amber Lentebok, with a lot of hop for the style, both in its grassy aroma and its dry finish.

**Region of origin** Eastern Netherlands

**Style** Spring Bock (*Lentebok*)

**Alcohol content** 5.2 abw (6.5 abv)

**Serving temperature** 48° F (9° C)

## HOLSTEN MAIBOCK

This major North German brewing company takes its name from the Duke of Holstein, who granted brewing rights to Hamburg, its home city. Holsten is most widely known for its dryish, Pilsner-style beer, but it also produces several specialities. One is a Maibock, crimson-tinged dark brown in color, with a licoricelike malt aroma and black treacle flavors, developing to a light, toasty finish.

**Region of origin** Northern Germany

**Style** May Bock (*Maibock*)

**Alcohol content** 5.6 abw (7.0 abv)

**Ideal serving temp.** 48° F (9° C)

# SEASONAL BEERS FOR SUMMER

WARM WEATHER AND BEER go hand in glass, but some brews are much more cooling and refreshing than others. Among the several styles that are particularly quenching, Belgium's traditional *saison* beers were created specifically for the summer season. Most wheat beers are refreshing but some are available only in summer. So are some of the crisp, golden summer ales from brewers of British bitter.

**Lazy Sunday**
*An English summer Sunday means a pint at the pub, with half an eye on the cricket.*

## HOPBACK SUMMER LIGHTNING

After the hops have been boiled in the brew, the leafy cones have to be removed, using a vessel called a hop back. The Hop Back brewery, in Salisbury, England, dates from 1987. Soon after its foundation, it launched Summer Lightning, initially for a beer festival but then as a regular product. At the time, the color was unusually sunny for a British ale. The beer may be light, crisp, and dry, but it is full of subtle flavors: the sweetness of Maris Otter barley malt from Wiltshire, the fragrance of East Kent Golding hops, and the very delicate, bananalike fruitiness of the house yeast.

**Region of origin**  Southern England, UK

**Style**  Summer Ale

**Alcohol content**  4.0 abw (5.0 abv)

**Ideal serving temperature**
Just above 50° F (10° C)

### SINKING THE SAHTI

IN SCANDINAVIA and Finland, midsummer festivities feature farmhouse brews of rye and juniper. Best known of these is the Finnish *sahti*, often served in this two-handled vessel. First a sauna, then a dive into the lake, then a sahti or two . . . and the sun scarcely sinks.

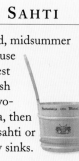

# MARSTON'S SUMMER WHEAT BEER

This brewery is famous for its Pedigree pale ale, but makes a growing number of styles. Its Summer Wheat Beer was launched in 1997. Unlike some wheat beers in the English-speaking world, it uses a Bavarian yeast: hence the pronounced bananalike fruitiness, with dryish vanilla notes and juicy suggestions of bubblegum. Like a Bavarian *Kristall Weizen*, it is filtered. A bright summer refresher.

**Region of origin** Trent Valley, England, UK

**Style** *Kristall Weizen*

**Alcohol content** 3.4 abw (4.2 abv)

**Ideal serving temperature** 48° F (9° C)

# VAUX HOW'S YOUR FATHER SUMMER ALE

The name Vaux sounds Norman-French but is pronounced to rhyme (in British English) with "forks". This Northern English brewery, on the coast at Sunderland, launched How's Your Father in 1997. The phrase derives from ribald holiday humor. This lemon-tinged wheat ale has a sherbety aroma; a firm body; a dryish, crisp palate; and a light finish.

**Region of origin** Northeast England, UK

**Style** Wheat Ale

**Alc. content** 3.7 abw (4.6 abv)

**Ideal serving temperature** 50° F (10° C)

*Wish you were here*
*The label features the fat lady and gawky man from a certain style of British seaside postcards.*

# GOLDEN HILL EXMOOR GOLD

At Wiveliscombe, Somerset, a brewery that had been closed for 20 years was brought back to life in 1980. Six years later, the brewery pioneered golden ales in Britain. This beer is made with only one variety of barley: Pipkin, malted in the next county, at Newton Abbot, Devon. The beer is fresh-tasting, firm, creamy, dryish, with a hint of sweet apples.

**Region of origin** Southwest England, UK

**Style** Golden Ale

**Alcohol content** 4.0 abw (5.0 abv)

**Ideal serving temperature** 50° F (10° C)

*Back-label boast*
*"A Single Malt Beer" is the boast on the back label.*

# McMULLEN HAYTIME SUMMER ALE

The family McMullen, distantly from Ireland, established their brewery in Hertford in 1827, and still run it. The site began as a farm. It was customary on farms to provide a beer to refresh the haymakers, and this product is a revival of such a brew. It has more substance than most summer ales, with the spicy, junipery aroma of the hop variety Progress; a smooth, nutty, crystal-malt background; and appetizing bitterness.

**Region of origin** Eastern England, UK

**Style** Summer Ale

**Alcohol content** 4.0 abw (5.0 abv)

**Ideal serving temperature** 50–55° F (10–13° C)

## SAISON DUPONT

In the French-speaking part of Belgium, the word for "season" sometimes appears on beer labels. The season in question is always summer. As the Belgians like strong beers, even their summer brews are relatively potent. They are firm and dry, with a yeasty, fruity acidity like that of an orange, and usually unfiltered. Saison Dupont is a lively, hoppy classic. It is made at a farmhouse brewery at Tourpes, near Leuze, east of the town of Tournai.

**Region of origin**
Province of Hainaut, Belgium

**Style** *Saison*

**Alcohol content**
5.2 abw (6.5 abv)

**Ideal serving temperature**
50° F (10° C)

## SAISON DE PIPAIX

Spiced with black pepper, anis, and a medicinal lichen, this is a dry, leafy, sourish interpretation of the style. It is brewed by a schoolteacher, Jean-Louis Dits. He revived a steam-powered brewery from the early industrial period, and operates it as a working museum. The brewery is at Pipaix, near Leuze. Another of its beers, La Cochonne, contains chicory root.

**Region of origin** Province of Hainaut, Belgium

**Style** *Saison*

**Alcohol content**
4.8–5.2 abw (6.0–6.5 abv)

**Ideal serving temperature**
50–55° F (10–13° C)

*Hot air*
*The label's "Brasserie à Vapeur" ("Steam Brewery") meant "state of the art" in the early industrial period.*

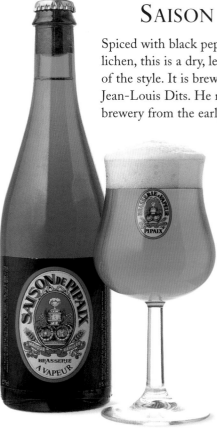

## LEFEBVRE SAISON 1900

The turn of the century was the peak year for the production of *saison* beer at the Lefèbvre brewery, in Quenast, just south of Brussels. The brewery was built in the 1870s to slake the thirst of workers at the nearby stone quarries, where ballast is now dug for the trans-European express railways. Saison 1900 has a firm, hard-toffee maltiness, developing to a spritzy, citric finish.

**Region of origin** Province of Walloon Brabant, Belgium

**Style** *Saison*

**Alcohol content**
4.1 abw (5.2 abv)

**Ideal serving temperature**
50° F (10° C)

*Arty allusion*
*The label typeface alludes to the Art Nouveau style for which Belgium is renowned.*

## SOUTHAMPTON SAISON

New York weekenders heading for Long Island can find some extraordinary Belgian-style beers at the Southampton Publick House (40 Bowden Sq.). This rare American *saison* is aged in wine casks, to which Curaçao orange peels and grains of paradise are added. It emerges with the color of old gold; a big, creamy head; a light but soft body; and a bone-dry palate more reminiscent of a Belgian lambic beer.

**Region of production**
Northeast US

**Style** *Saison*

**Alcohol** 4.4 abw (5.5 abv)

**Ideal serving temperature**
50° F (10° C)

*Publick pints*
*The antique spelling "Publick" is understandable from a brewery that strives to make some very traditional beers.*

# SEASONAL BEERS: SUMMER

## CHOJUGURA BLOND

The name means "Warehouse of Long Life." It refers to a 300-year-old warehouse previously used to store sake, in Itami, Japan. After being damaged in the earthquake of 1994, the warehouse was restored as a tiny sake and beer brewery and restaurant. Its beers include a soft, summery, fragrantly creamy-fruity Blond, with a dry, crisp finish. A Belgian ale yeast is used.

**Region of origin**
Kansai, Honshu, Japan

**Style** Belgian Golden Ale

**Alcohol content** 4.0 abw (5.0 abv)

**Ideal serving temperature**
50° F (10° C)

## COOPERS SPARKLING ALE

Thomas Cooper was a Methodist preacher from Yorkshire, in the north of England, who emigrated to Australia in 1852 and started a brewery in Adelaide. Cooper's is the last of Australia's long-established family breweries. Its Sparkling Ale (which, with its yeast sediment, can in fact be quite cloudy) was originally bronze in color. Since about 1980, it has been golden, and is a quenching classic: fruity, bananalike, and dry, with a long finish.

**Region of origin** South Australia

**Style** Golden Ale

**Alcohol content** 4.7 abw (5.8 abv)

**Ideal serving temperature**
50° F (10° C)

## DE DOLLE BROUWERS ARABIER

When their local brewery closed down, an architect and his family revived it, initially working

weekends only. They call themselves De Dolle Brouwers ("The Mad Brewers"). The 1840s brewery is at Esen, near Diksmuide, not far from Ostend, Belgium. Its robust seasonal products include summer's Arabier, a golden ale that is packed with flavors: honeydew fruitiness, gingery, peppery dryness, and intense hop.

**Region of origin**
Province of West Flanders, Belgium

**Style** Strong Summer Ale

**Alcohol content** 6.4 abw (8.0 abv)

**Ideal serving temperature**
50° F (10° C)

## FULLER'S SUMMER ALE

The London ale-brewer Fuller's, known for amber bitters, added this golden brew to its range in 1996. Fuller's Summer Ale has a flowery aroma; pours with a dense, white, head; has a soft, creamy, clean palate; and a lemony, crisp finish. It contains 15 percent wheat malt, and is hopped with the famous Saaz variety, more commonly used in Pilsner-style lagers.

**Region of origin**
London, England, UK

**Style** Summer Ale

**Alcohol content** 3.2 abw (3.9 abv)

**Ideal serving temperature**
50–55° F (10–13° C)

## MARTENS SEZOENS

The Flemish rendition of *saison* is the brand name of a superb summer beer from the Martens brewery in the Belgian province of Limburg. This strong golden ale has a flowery hop aroma; a light

but very firm body; a restrained fruitiness; and a delicately appetizing dryness. A sedimented version is softer, fruitier, and spicier. Martens, at Bocholt, near the German border, is also famous for its museum of brewing equipment.

**Region of origin**
Province of Limburg, Belgium

**Style** Strong Golden Ale

**Alcohol content** 4.8 abw (6.0 abv)

**Ideal serving temperature**
48° F (9° C)

## NEW BELGIUM PORCH SWING ALE

Belgian beers have inspired several American brewers. An enthusiast started the New Belgium brewery in the basement of his home in Fort Collins, Colorado, in 1992. The brewery expanded quickly to become of America's most successful micros. Its Porch Swing Ale has a full golden color, and a clean orangey dryness that is both refreshing and satisfying. It is reminiscent of the "Single" brewed at Westmalle, Belgium for the monks' own consumption.

**Region of origin** Southwest US

**Style** Abbey Single

**Alcohol content** 4.2 abw (5.2 abv)

**Ideal serving temperature**
45–50° F (7–10° C)

## PETE'S SUMMER BREW

Home-brewer Pete Slosberg, who has a degree in space mechanics, created the Wicked Ale range in California. The beers have been made at several breweries. The best-known is along the lines of brown ale, but there are also seasonal specialities. Pete's Wicked Summer Brew is very pale, with a hint of lemon. Many American breweries have summer specials.

**Region of origin** California, US

**Style** Summer Ale

**Alcohol Content** 3.9 abw (4.9 abv)

**Ideal serving temperature**
50° F (10° C)

## SAISON SILLY

To English-speakers, it sounds Silly, but it is the name of a village near Enghien, south of Brussels, Belgium. A farm-style brewery there produces, among several other beers, a good example of the summer *saison* style. This beer has a fruitiness reminiscent of nectarines, tartly refreshing, with some winey notes. The beer is made by a traditional process of ageing and blending.

**Region of production**
Province of Hainaut, Belgium

**Style** *Saison*

**Alcohol content** 4.0 abw (5.0 abv)

**Ideal serving temperature**
50° F (10° C)

## USHERS SUMMER MADNESS

This British brewery, once owned by Watney's (then a national giant), is now proudly independent. It makes a wide range of interesting ales, including several seasonals. Ushers Summer Madness is a wheat ale, very lightly flavored with honey and ginger. There is a good, flowery, leafy, hop balance and the beer has a crisp, dry finish. The brewery, established in 1824, is in the Wiltshire town of Trowbridge, originally a Belgian settlement.

**Region of origin**
Southern England, UK

**Style** Summer Ale

**Alcohol content** 3.2 abw (4.0 abv)

**Ideal serving temperature**
50–55° F (10–13° C)

# SEASONAL BEERS FOR AUTUMN

LAGER WAS "INVENTED" in Bavaria in the days before artificial refrigeration, when the brewing season ended in March or April and did not begin again until September or October. To provide for summer, quantities of beer were stored in nearby Alpine caves, and the cold maturation made for a smoother style of beer. When summer ended, the last of the March (*Märzen*) beer was consumed at autumn celebrations. This is why the words for March and October sometimes appear on the same label.

**A style for celebration**
*The malt-accented, medium-strong lagers produced for the season are ceremonially served at the* Oktoberfest.

## STEINER MÄRZEN

Stein is a hamlet where a rocky cliff on the Traun River once formed the frontier between Bavaria and Austria. Caves in the cliff face are still used for the lagering of beer, and contain the lagering vessels of the Schlossbrauerei ("Castle Brewery") Stein. Its Märzen (March) beer, brewed to be consumed in September, is a good example of the style. It has the reddish bronze color that was traditional in *Märzen-Oktoberfest* lagers; a richly malty aroma (also with some spicy hop balance); and juicy, almost chewy, barley-sugar flavors.

**Region of origin**
Upper Bavaria, Germany

**Style** *Märzen/Oktoberfest*

**Alcohol content** 4.4 abw (5.5 abv)

**Ideal serving temperature** 48° F (9° C)

### THE OKTOBERFEST

MANY PLACES IN GERMANY have annual festivals centered on beer tents on the village green or town fairground. Some take place after the harvest, or mark summer's end. Munich's *Oktoberfest*, the most famous such celebration, has more formal origins. The first marked the wedding of Crown Prince Ludwig and Queen Theresia, in 1810. The 16-day festival actually starts in late September.

## SPATEN OKTOBERFESTBIER

Lager-brewing had its beginnings as a modern technique at the Spaten brewery in Munich, around the end of the 1830s. The brewery dates from 1397. The custom of making reddish-bronze, malt-accented lagers specifically for *Oktoberfest* also began with Spaten, but in recent years the brewery has produced only a golden version. This beer has a creamy aroma and a clean, firm, smooth, light malt accent. It is traditionally the first beer to be tapped at the *Oktoberfest*.

**Region of origin**
Munich, Upper Bavaria, Germany

**Style**
*Märzen/Oktoberfest*

**Alcohol content**
4.7 abw (5.9 abv)

**Ideal serving temp.**
9° C (48° F)

## HB OKTOBERFESTBIER

HB – the Hofbräuhaus – takes a special interest in a festival that began with the wedding of the Crown Prince. Its label illustrates the horses and drays that take part in the procession to "Queen Theresia's Meadows." Its Oktoberfestbier forms a head of Alpine proportions, and has a creamy, malty spiciness reminiscent of licorice or aniseed.

**Region of origin**
Munich, Upper Bavaria, Germany

**Style** *Märzen/Oktoberfest*

**Alcohol content**
4.6 abw (5.7 abv)

**Ideal serving temperature**
48° F (9° C)

*Beautiful bloom*
*One result of all-malt beers is a solid foam, prized as a "beautiful bloom."*

## AYINGER OKTOBER FEST-MÄRZEN

None of the breweries outside the city limits is permitted to have its beer at the Munich *Oktoberfest*, but many make the seasonal style. Ayinger, in the countryside nearby, has a good example. The beer has a gold-to-bronze color, very fresh hop and malt aromas, nutty flavors, and a lightly firm body. The Ayinger brewery organizes many smaller festivals in the countryside around Munich.

**Region of origin**
Upper Bavaria, Germany

**Style** *Märzen/Oktoberfest*

**Alcohol content**
4.6 abw (5.8 abv)

**Ideal serving temperature**
48° F (9° C)

*Special claim*
*Ayinger's label refers to its beers as "specialities." The brewery makes about a dozen styles.*

## DINKEL ACKER VOLKSFEST BIER

Around the same time as the Munich *Oktoberfest*, the other great southern German capital, Stuttgart, has its own "People's Festival" (*Volksfest*). The city's breweries make special beers for the occasion. The Carl Dinkelacker brewery makes a lively example with a big, malty start and a good hop balance. The city's Schwaben Bräu has a similar *Märzenbier*, with a delicate hop aroma and sweetish malt character.

**Region of origin**
Baden-Württemberg, Germany

**Style** *Märzen/Festbier*

**Alcohol content**
4.4 abw (5.5 abv)

**Ideal serving temperature**
48°F (9°C)

## FRAOCH HEATHER ALE

The purple heather that warms the mountains of Scotland was a flavoring in the local beers long before hops were used. In the early 1990s, brewers Bruce and Scott Williams restored the tradition with their Fraoch ("heather" in Gaelic) ale. The beer has a sunny, amber color; a flowery bouquet; a slightly oily body; and a spicy, applelike, faintly winey finish. The heather is picked in July, and the new season's beer is available in August/September.

**Region of origin**
Central Scotland, UK

**Style** Heather Ale

**Alcohol content**
4.0 abw (5.0 abv)

**Ideal serving temperature**
55° F (13° C)

*Ceramic chalice*
*The vessel favored by the brewers of Fraoch conceals the color of the beer.*

## GROZET GOOSEBERRY & WHEAT ALE

The name is Scottish for gooseberry. Literary references to a beer of this name spurred the brewing brothers Williams to recreate the style. Their gooseberry beer is flavored with bog myrtle and meadowsweet. The beer is perfumy and spritzy, with a tangy suggestion of gooseberry skins. The beer is available in September.

**Region of origin**
Central Scotland, UK

**Style** Gooseberry Ale

**Alcohol content**
4.0 abw (5.0 abv)

**Ideal serving temperature**
55° F (13° C)

*Hide and sink*
*Leather drinking vessels such as this one were once common.*

## ALBA SCOTS PINE ALE

Another unusual Scottish brew from the Williams brothers is an ale with no hops at all – just pine sprigs and spruce shoots. This is available earlier in the year, but might best be saved until the cooler weather. It is aromatic, oily, peppery, and medicinal. The brothers produce these beers at the Maclay's, in Alloa, but plan their own brewery in a watermill at Strathaven, south of Glasgow.

**Region of production**
Central Scotland, UK

**Style**
Pine/Spruce Beer

**Alcohol content**
6.0 abw (7.5 abv)

**Ideal serving temperature**
55° F (13° C)

## TRAQUAIR JACOBITE ALE

Traquair House is a castle on the Scottish side of the border with England, owned by a branch of the Scottish royal family Stuart. Bonnie Prince Charlie is said to have visited the house during campaign in the autumn of 1745. Jacobite Ale, produced in the house's own brewery, was launched in 1995. It is a purple-to-black ale, rich, with a sweetish, spicy, soft, rooty flavor.

**Region of origin**
Scottish Borders, UK

**Style**
Spiced Scottish Ale

**Alcohol content**
6.4 abw (8.0 abv)

**Ideal serving temperature**
55° F (13° C)

*Loyalty to royalty*
*Jacobite, after King James II, means a supporter of the royal Stuart succession.*

## USHERS AUTUMN FRENZY

One of the first English brewers to launch an autumn beer was Ushers, which has a speciality for each of the four seasons. When the leaves begin to fall, look out for the autumnal hue of this gently sustaining, dryish brew. Both the color and the smooth, nutty, spicy palate owe something to the use of rye, a grain once found only in some Baltic and Russian speciality brews.

**Region of origin**
Southern England, UK

**Style** Rye Ale

**Alcohol content**
3.2 abw (4.0 abv)

**Ideal serving temp.**
50–55° F
(10–13° C)

## BRECKENRIDGE AUTUMN ALE

The Rocky Mountain ski resort and former gold-mining town of Breckenridge, Colorado, gained its first brewpub in 1990, probably America's highest, at 9,600 ft (2,926 m). Branches have since opened in Denver and other cities. Breckenridge produces a wide range of beers. Its bottled Autumn Ale has a chestnut colour; a firm, toffeeish, textured body; and hints of sugar and cocoa. A delicious beer.

**Region of origin**
Southwest US

**Style** Brown Ale/Old Ale

**Alcohol content**
5.4 abw (6.8 abv)

**Ideal serving temperature**
50–55° F (10–13° C)

## HALE'S HARVEST ALE

Inspired by a brief spell in 1981, working as an "apprentice" at near-namesake Gale's brewery, in Hampshire, England, young American Mike Hale fired his own kettles in Washington State in 1983. He now has an English-accented microbrewery in Spokane and a brewpub in the Seattle suburb of Fremont. His Harvest Ale has the aroma of fruit gums; a juicy palate; and a clean apple note in a dry, perfumy finish.

**Region of origin**
Pacific Northwest US

**Style** Strong Ale

**Alcohol content**
3.6 abw (4.5 abv)

**Ideal serving temperature**
50–55° F (10–13° C)

***Hale and hearty***
*"Rich, robust and distinctive . . . as brisk and refreshing as a fall morning," says Hale's publicity material.*

## LEINENKUGEL'S AUTUMN GOLD

The name means "Linen Bobbin." The German Leinenkugel family established their brewery in Chippewa Falls, Wisconsin, in 1867. The family still run the brewery today, though it is now owned by the national giant Miller. There is now a second Leinenkugel brewery in Milwaukee. The Autumn Gold, slightly fuller in color than its name suggests, has spicy, malt-loaf aromas and flavors, and a dryish hop balance.

**Region of origin**
Midwest US

**Style** Vienna Lager

**Alcohol content**
3.9 abw (4.8 abv)

**Ideal serving temperature**
48° F (9° C)

# SEASONAL BEERS FOR CHRISTMAS

THE COLDER COUNTRIES, especially in the far north, have a long tradition of comforting themselves with strong beers during the darkest, shortest days of winter. Elsewhere, the new season's barley and hops make for seasonal specials that are released in November. This assumes that the barley has two months' dormancy, to permit the biological changes that will ease germination in malting, and that the beer has also had a reasonable period of maturation. In North America, some brewers make pumpkin ales for Halloween and for Thanksgiving, the beginning of a winter holiday season that stretches through to New Year.

**Tankard time**
*Ale-and-hearty images are part of the folklore of British Christmas past.*

## SAMICHLAUS BIER

The name is "Santa Claus" in the Swiss-German dialect of Zürich. This immensely rich, darkish lager is brewed there each year on St. Nicholas' Day, December 6. The beer matures for the best part of 12 months, gaining strength in the lagering tank, and is released on the same date of the following year, with a vintage date. Samichlaus was first made in 1980, in both dark and pale versions. Because the beer is so dense, there was still plenty of color in the pale. Eventually, the brewery decided to make only the dark. Of the world's super-strong lagers, Samichlaus is the most complex and satisfying. It has a reddish chestnut color; a brandyish aroma; a firm, oily body; creamy and cherryish flavors; and a warming, spicy, peppery finish. It is made by the Hürlimann brewery, now owned by Feldschlösschen.

**Big beer, tiny serving**
*With Swiss caution, a stein the size of an espresso cup was issued by the brewery.*

| | |
|---|---|
| **Region of origin** | Northern Switzerland |
| **Style** | Double Bock |
| **Alcohol content** | 11.0 abw (14.0 abv) |
| **Ideal serving temperature** | 48° F (9° C) |

### SANTA'S OFFICE

SANTA CLAUS, Saint Nicholas, Father Christmas . . . neither his name nor his nationality are certain but a strong claimant works from an office at Rovaniemi, in Finnish Lapland. He answers letters from children all over the world. This Santa has been known to drink the amber seasonal *Jouluolout* (Christmas beer) from the nearby brewery Lapin Kulta (Lapp Gold).

## GORDON XMAS

Scotland may celebrate Christmas less than it does New Year's, but it definitely counts as a cold northern country. Rich and warming Scottish ales were introduced to Belgium by British regiments in two world wars. Scottish Courage brews this beer in Edinburgh for the Belgian market. It is a ruby-to-black ale, pouring with a mountainous head. It has a clean, sweet maltiness, but finishes with a toasty dryness. Much the same brew is made for France under the name Douglas.

**Region of origin**
Southern Scotland, UK

**Style** Strong Scottish Ale

**Alcohol content**
7.0 abw (8.8 abv)

**Ideal serving temperature**
55° F (13° C)

## ABBEY AFFLIGEM NÖEL CHRISTMAS ALE

The Benedictine abbey of Affligem, west of Brussels, was founded in 1074. It ceased to make its own beers during World War I, but some fine products are created on its behalf by a local brewery. Its Christmas brew is garnet in color, and hugely complex, with notes of prunes, spiciness, and sappy dryness.

**Region of origin**
Province of Flemish Brabant, Belgium

**Style** Strong Spiced Ale

**Alcohol content**
7.2 abw (9.0 abv)

**Ideal serving temperature**
55° F (13° C)

*Nöel or Noël?*
*This label has the umlaut (dots) in the wrong place on the French word,* Noël.

## BUSH DE NOËL

The Dubuisson family brewery, of Pipaix, Belgium, translated its name into the English "Bush" after the premises were liberated by a British battalion in World War I. In the US, to avoid confusion with the St. Louis brewer, Busch, the beer is known as Scaldis (after the Schelde River). The Christmas beer has an attractive, full amber color; a delicately leafy, hop aroma; and a beautiful balance of sweet malt and fruitiness.

**Region of origin**
Province of Hainaut, Belgium

**Style**
Strong Ale/Barley Wine

**Alcohol content**
9.6 abw (12.0 abv)

**Ideal serving temperature**
50–55° F (10–13° C)

## KOFF JOULUOLUT

The Sinebrychoff brewery in Finland was founded in 1819 by a Russian. In 1987 this brewery (its name is often abbreviated to Koff these days) introduced a lager in the amber-red, malt-accented Vienna style, as a Christmas beer. The word *Joulu* has the same origin as "Yule." The Finnish word for beer is *olut*. The word itself shares a root with the English "ale." This example is on the pale side for the style, with a firm, clean, nutty maltiness.

**Region of origin** Finland

**Style** Vienna Lager

**Alcohol content**
3.7 abw (4.6 abv)

**Ideal serving temperature**
48° F (9° C)

## VAUX ST. NICHOLAS'S CHRISTMAS ALE

Vaux is one of many English brewers that produce Christmas beers. These are often darker, stronger versions of a bitter. Although described as a bitter, St. Nicholas is more of a dark ale. It has a rich chestnut color; a light body for the style; a fruity palate reminiscent of sweet pears; and a dry, toasty finish.

**Region of origin**
Northeast England, UK

**Style** Bitter/Dark Ale

**Alcohol content**
4.0 abw (5.0 abv)

**Ideal serving temperature**
55° F (13° C)

## MOCTEZUMA NOCHE BUENA

The name means "Good Night," referring to Christmas Eve. This is the time when Mexicans have their Christmas dinner. Noche Buena, a strong, dark lager, is one of the tastiest beers from Mexico. It has a deep, amber-brown color, and is very smooth, with both malty sweetness and hoppy dryness in its long finish. Noche Buena is made by Moctezuma, which also produces the popular Vienna-style Dos Equis.

**Region of origin**
Province of Vera Cruz, Mexico

**Style** Munich Dark Lager/Bock

**Alc. content** 4.8 abw (6.0 abv)

**Ideal serving temperature**
48° F (9° C)

*Scarlet leaves*
*The label shows a poinsettia.*
*Because it turns red in midwinter,*
*it is a symbol of Christmas.*

## ANCHOR "OUR SPECIAL HOLIDAY ALE"

San Francisco's Anchor Brewery is famous for its dry, sparkling Steam Beer, but the company has several other specialities. Its Special Holiday Ale is released after Thanksgiving and is available until New Year. It is almost always spiced, but the ingredients change from one year to the next. In various "vintages," tasters think they have detected allspice, cinnamon, cloves, coriander, juniper, licorice, nutmeg, and zest of lemon.

**Region of origin**
California, US

**Style** Spiced Ale

**Alcohol content**
4.4–4.8 abw (5.5–6.0 abv)

**Ideal serving temperature**
55° F (13° C)

## SIERRA NEVADA CELEBRATION ALE

Perhaps the most famous new-generation brewery in the US is near the Sierra Nevada mountains, at Chico, California. The brewery is known for beers full of character and complexity. Its winter holiday Celebration Ale is typically aromatic and lively in flavor, with hints of oily dark chocolate and lots of lemony hop bitterness. The variety of hops varies each year, and experimental growths are sometimes used. The beer is broadly in the style of an India Pale Ale.

**Region of origin**
California, US

**Style** Ale/IPA

**Alc. content** 4.8 abw (6.0 abv). May vary

**Ideal serving temperature**
50–55° F (10–13° C)

# CELEBRATION BEERS

Beer lovers do not need excuses, but it is always pleasant to celebrate an anniversary. The appropriate beer for the day adds a splash of color, and the chance to explore new flavors. If you do not have the good fortune to be in the appropriate nation at the time, or cannot find its best beers nearby, try at least to find something from that country. It may even accompany a national dish for dinner.

## JANUARY

New Year is still a legitimate moment for a Gordon's Xmas and, at a stretch, that beer could be served to honor the poet Robert "Rabbie" Burns on the 25th. Russian Orthodox Christmas, on the 7th, might be an excuse for a Baltika Porter. Australia Day, on the 26th, calls for a Burragorang Bock.

BALTIKA PORTER

## FEBRUARY

Sri Lankan Independence Day, on the 4th, demands a Lion Stout. On the 6th, New Zealand celebrates one of its most important national days, to mark the Waitangi treaty between colonists and Maoris: raise a Mike's Mild or Emerson's 1812. The Independence Day of Estonia, on the 24th, could be celebrated with a Saku Hele.

## MARCH

Wales marks St. David's Day on the 1st: it's Brain's you'll want. Ireland's celebration of St. Patrick's on the 17th tends to prompt Guinness, though several beers may be required. Namibian Independence Day, a more esoteric anniversary, on the 21st, suggests a Hansa Urbock.

HANSA URBOCK

## APRIL

England marks St. George's Day, once the end of the brewing season, on the 23rd: a case for London Pride. The 25th is Liberation Day in both Italy and Portugal, calling for a Moretti La Rossa or a Sagres Dark respectively. It is also Anzac Day in Australia and New Zealand, to be celebrated with a Toohey's Old or Coopers Sparkling Ale.

## MAY

The 1st is a public holiday almost everywhere: settle for any May Bock you can find. The 5th is Liberation Day in the Netherlands, with plenty of Dutch beers on offer: try Het Elfde Gebod. The same date, in the guise of Cinco de Mayo, is perhaps Mexico's best-known national day: any Nochebuena left? The 17th is Norwegian Independence Day: celebrate with an Aass Bock.

## JUNE

Denmark celebrates Constitution Day on the 1st: an opportunity for a Ceres. Traditionalist Finns like to drink home-brewed, rye-and-juniper *sahti* at Midsummer's Eve. In the absence of such delights, seek out a Koff Porter. If your inclinations are more Swedish, try a Carnegie Porter.

## JULY

Salute Canada Day with a Molson Signature or Granite Peculier on the 1st. American Independence on the 4th calls for an Anchor Liberty Ale or a Sam Adams Triple Bock. The Flemish have their national day on the 11th: the moment for a De Koninck. France's Bastille Day, on the 14th, suggests a Sans Culottes.

ANCHOR LIBERTY ALE

## AUGUST

In England, the 1st is Yorkshire Day, demanding a Black Sheep or a Samuel Smith's. Swiss Confederation Day, on the 1st, calls for an Ueli Reverenz Spezial. Jamaica begins the month with Emancipation Day, then celebrates Independence on the 6th: either day will do for a Dragon Stout.

## SEPTEMBER

The first Monday of the month is Labor Day in the United States: perhaps a Climax ESB? South

African Heritage Day on the 24th suggests a Mitchell's Raven Stout. The French-speaking part of Belgium celebrates its National Day on the 27th: a case for Cuvée de l'Ermitage.

## OCTOBER

Germany's Day of Unity is the 3rd, calling for a Berliner Bürgerbräu. Japan's National Sports Day, on the 10th, sounds like a good moment for a restorative Csarda Sweet Stout. Austria's National Day is on the 26th: celebrate with an Eggenberg Urbock or something from Baron Bachofen von Echt. The Czechs mark Independence on the 28th: time for Pilsner Urquell or Budweiser Budvar.

CSARDA SWEET STOUT

## NOVEMBER

Polish Independence Day is on the 11th, suggesting an Okocim Porter. The United States celebrates Thanksgiving on the fourth Thursday of this month, perhaps calling for a Sierra Nevada Celebration. On the 30th, the Scots honor St. Andrew: take the Flying Scotsman, from the Caledonian Brewery, or try for a sighting of Nessie.

## DECEMBER

Switzerland's super-strong lager Samichlaus launches on the 6th, beginning the Christmas beer season. It has been another great year for John Barleycorn.

# SOCIABLE BEERS: GOLDEN LAGERS

IN THE ORIGINAL HOME OF LAGER, that term is rarely used. A German drinker fancying an everyday lager would order a *Helles*, from the German word for "bright." The term sounds odd to the English speaker, but the word *Helles* has the same origins as "howl" or "yell." A "bright" sound; a "clear" colour. Not so much "yell" as yellow. A *Helles* is a golden lager with a sweetish, malt accent but a delicate balance of spicy hop. *Helles* lagers, originally made in Munich, are less bitter than the famous golden style of Pilsen, and not as firm-bodied as the Dortmund Export type.

*Friday picnic, after work*
In a Munich beer garden, the food must include salted radishes . . . and the beer is probably a Helles.

## OTARU HELLES

German brewer Johannes Braun created this outstanding *Helles*, albeit an especially far-flung example of the style. He has worked in many countries, but developed this beer at a brewpub in Otaru, a college town and major port on Hokkaido, the northern island of Japan. The pub is decorated with scenes of German village life and photographs of Braun's family. In the center is a copper-clad brewhouse built in Bamberg, Bavaria. Otaru Helles pours with a huge, rocky head, and has a bright gold color. It has the flowery aroma and flavor of German Tettnang hops, with a cookielike maltiness in the middle. The brewpub also produces an orangey-brown dark lager with a firm, smooth, Vienna-malt character, and seasonal specialities such as a smoked beer.

*Deep "growler"*
Unfiltered beer is filled into one-liter "growlers," but the yeast sediment drops during storage to reveal a bright brew.

OTARU BIER **Helles** ●ヘレス

小樽ビール

モルトを3種類ブレンドしたものを、下面発酵させ、約40日間熟成しました。
モルトの風味とホップの香ばしい
まろやかなくちあたりの黄金色ビールです。

厳選麦芽100%

(非熱処理)生(アルコール分約5.0%) BREWED AND BOTTLED BY OTARU BREWERY

| | |
|---|---|
| **Region of origin** | Hokkaido, Japan |
| **Style** | *Helles* Lager |
| **Alcohol content** | 4.0 abw (5.0 abv) |
| **Ideal serving temperature** | 48° F (9° C) |

## UNIONS BRÄU HELL

One of the smallest and most interesting breweries in Munich is Unions, on Einstein Strasse. Once it was larger, formed by the union of four breweries. That incarnation ended in the 1920s, in a merger with Löwenbräu. The Unions premises reopened in 1991, as a brewpub. Its principal product is its *Helles*: sweet, malty, smooth, and slightly oily; and served from pitch-lined oak barrels. Organically grown barley and hops are used.

**Region of origin**
Munich, Upper Bavaria, Germany

**Style** *Helles* Lager

**Alcohol content**
3.8 abw (4.7 abv)

**Ideal serving temperature** 48° F (9° C)

## FISCHERSTUBE UELI REVERENZ

One of the first new-generation brewpubs in Europe was established at the Fischer café, in Basel, Switzerland, in 1975. The owner is a doctor of medicine, who playfully calls his brewery Jester *(Ueli)*. Among the beers is a *Helles* rather seriously called Reverenz. It is light and malty in its aroma and palate, with some cookielike flavors in the middle and a touch of hoppy tartness in a dryish finish.

**Region of origin** Basel, Northwest Switzerland

**Style** *Helles* Lager

**Alcohol content**
4.3 abw (5.4 abv)

**Ideal serving temperature**
48° F (9° C)

## SAKU HELE

A German landowner established a brewery on his estate at Saku, near Tallinn, the capital of Estonia, in 1820. The Saku brewery, now owned by a Baltic group, is especially known for its cedary, coffeeish, strong Christmas porter. Its year-round *Hele* (Estonian spelling) pours with a dense, bubbly head and has a very pale color; a light but firm body; and a very hoppy, appetizing finish. Fairly dry for the style.

**Region of origin**
Estonia

**Style** *Helles* Lager

**Alcohol content**
3.9 abw (4.9 abv)

**Ideal serving temperature**
48° F (9° C)

## HÜBSCH SUDWERK HELLES

Sudwerk is one of the best German-style breweries in the US (Sudwerk is from the German for a brewhouse). Hübsch is a family name of one of the founders. A brewpub and microbrewery in Davis, in northern California, Sudwerk makes a wide range of German styles, including this firm, smooth *Helles*, with a textured, malty start and a clean, crisp smack of hops.

**Region of origin**
California, US

**Style** *Helles* Lager

**Alcohol content**
3.9 abw (4.9 abv)

**Ideal serving temperature**
48° F (9° C)

*Drinking in the study*
*The Sudwerk beers are made in Davis, home of California's wine university. The subject of beermaking is also studied at the college.*

# SOCIABLE BEERS: DORTMUNDER EXPORT

Dortmund became Germany's biggest brewing city in the days when its beers soothed the souls of coalminers and steelworkers in the Ruhr valley. Its style of golden lager, known as Dortmunder Export, is distinctively firm-bodied (from the local water), dryish, and very slightly stronger than the golden lagers of the Munich or Pilsner types. Some Exports are also slightly fuller in color.

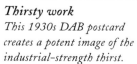

**Thirsty work**
*This 1930s DAB postcard creates a potent image of the industrial-strength thirst.*

**Original style**
*Once, Dortmund's own style was sold far and wide. Hence "Export." Today, the city makes more Pilsner.*

## DORTMUNDER UNION EXPORT

Dortmunder Union Brauerei (DUB) is the best-known of the city's brewing companies. Its Export has a firm, mouth-filling body; a restrained, malty sweetness; and a lightly dry, rounded finish. DUB acquired Dortmunder Ritter, which also has an Export in its range. The two Exports are similar, but the Ritter seems smoother and more assertive. DUB's traditional local rival is Dortmunder Actien-Brauerei (DAB), which has a light-tasting Export and a similar brew under the name of Dortmunder Hansa. DAB has in recent years acquired Dortmunder Kronen, with a clean, soft Export.

**Region of origin**
Dortmund, North Rhine-Westphalia, Germany

**Style** Dortmunder Export

**Alcohol content** 4.5 abw (5.3 abv)

**Ideal serving temperature** 48° F (9° C)

### DORTMUND DRAYMAN

This ten-foot bronze was given to Dortmund by DAB in 1979 to symbolize the city's major industry. It stands in the *Neuer Markt* (New Market). To mark ten years of their being twin cities, the same figure was presented to Leeds, England. The bronze there is in Dortmund Square in the city center. The sculptor was Artur Schulze-Engels.

## GREAT LAKES DORTMUNDER GOLD

The most traditional examples of the Dortmunder Export style, in their fuller color and body, are today found in the US. This one is perhaps even too generous in color and maltiness, though its grainy dryness and touch of new-mown hay are exemplary. The Great Lakes micro and pub is at 2516 Market St., Cleveland, Ohio. The pub still has original bullet holes from Prohibition days.

**Region of origin**
Midwest US

**Style** Dortmunder Export

**Alcohol content**
4.5 abw (5.6 abv)

**Ideal serving temperature**
48° F (9° C)

*Inspirational study*
*Great Lakes' co-founder Patrick Conway, a Jungian academic, was inspired by German beers when he studied in Europe.*

## ST. GALLER KLOSTERBRÄU SCHÜTZENGARTEN NATURTRÜB

The oldest brewery plans in Europe, dating from the ninth century, are from the abbey of St. Gallen, founded in Switzerland by an Irish monk. The town still has a brewery, Schützengarten, albeit a mere 220 years old. Its "naturally turbid" (unfiltered) speciality has the appropriate strength and color to be deemed an Export. It has an excellent balance of malty sweetness and flowery, herbal, peppery hop.

**Region of origin**
Switzerland

**Style** Unfiltered Lager/Export

**Alcohol content**
4.1 abw (5.2 abv)

**Ideal serving temperature**
48° F (9° C)

## GULPENER DORT

The village of Gulpen is south of Maastricht, in the Netherlands, but close to Belgium and Germany. The Gulpener brewery's products include this Dort, a shorter but darker and stronger echo of the German style. It has a marshmallowy maltiness, balanced by a leafy hop finish. Nearby, Leeuw has a slightly drier Dortmunder; Alfa a creamy Super Dortmunder, even stronger; and De Ridder the well-balanced Maltezer.

**Region of origin**
Province of Limburg, the Netherlands

**Style** Dutch Strong Dortmunder Export

**Alcohol content**
5.2 abw (6.5 abv)

**Ideal serving temperature**
48° F (9° C)

## CERES DANSK DORTMUNDER

The mythological Roman goddess of farming and cereal grains, Ceres, gives her name to this brewery in the Danish city of Aarhus. This

brewery has a strong "Danish Dortmunder." The beer has a buttery maltiness and some fruitiness. Ceres' other products include a beer flavored with rum and lemon essence, named after the navigator Bering (who died of scurvy); and a peppery, phonetic Stowt.

**Region of origin**
Denmark

**Style** Danish Strong Dortmunder Export

**Alcohol content**
6.2 abw (7.7 abv)

**Ideal serving temperature**
48° F (9° C)

# SOCIABLE BEERS: KÖLSCHBIER

AT A GLANCE, THEY LOOK LIKE Pilsner-style lagers, but the beers of the Cologne area are less assertively bitter and have an ale-like fruitiness, albeit very light. This style of beer, gaining its special character from a top-fermenting yeast, is very delicate, soft, and digestible. More than a dozen breweries in a defined region around Cologne make about 20 examples, almost always serving the beer in its own cylindrical glass. Cologne, a city of neighborhoods, has a strong culture of taverns, and several make their own *Kölschbier*. For all their similarity of style, each has its own subtle personality.

**Cologne cartridges**
*Cologne's uniformed waiters are, by custom, addressed as Jakob, or 'Köbes. Also shown is one of the perforated trays into which glasses are loaded like cartridges into a six-shooter.*

## FRÜH KÖLSCH

Opposite the cathedral, on a street called Am Hof (after the Archbishop's court), the turn-of-the-century tavern of P. J. Früh is the best-known destination for visitors wishing to sample *Kölschbier*. The beer was made on the premises until the 1980s, but is now brewed on a separate site, and is bottled for general sale. P. J. Früh is a classic Cologne pub, with the typical standing area jokingly known as the *Schwemme*. When it is crowded, the Schwemme may seem like a swimming pool, but the reference is actually to a place where horses are watered. Deeper into the pub are scrubbed wooden tables where the beer is enjoyed with snacks of cheese, blood sausage, and pork *Mettwurst*. The beer has a faint strawberry fruitiness of aroma; a creamy malt background; and an elegant balancing dryness of hop.

**Region of origin**
Cologne, North Rhine-Westphalia, Germany

**Style** *Kölschbier*

**Alcohol content** 3.8 abw (4.8 abv)

**Ideal serving temperature** 48° F (9° C)

### KINGS OF THE CITY

THE TAVERNS' OFTEN-BRISK waiters have become symbols of Cologne, as shown in this rendition by Franz Mather, a local writer who has done much to publicize the city's beer. The illustration is from his book, *Waiter, another Kölsch!* This particular waiter seems also to be bringing the classic meal, "Three Kings": knuckles of three different meats.

## DOM KÖLSCH

The name means cathedral, and that is the trademark of this medium-sized brewery. Dom is on the corner of Tacitus and Goltstein Streets, just south of the center of Cologne. Its Tacitus tavern there was dubbed "the best kitchen in town" by the influential French critics Gault and Millau. Local dishes are offered. The beer is fresh, clean, and well balanced, with a smooth maltiness and lemony, hop dryness. Dom, founded in 1894, is now part of the same group as Stern, of Essen.

**Region of origin** Cologne, North Rhine-Westphalia, Germany

**Style** *Kölschbier*

**Alcohol content** 3.8 abw (4.8 abv)

**Ideal serving temperature** 48° F (9° C)

*Slow maturation*
*Cologne's cathedral was not completed until the 1800s. It is a symbol of the entire city, as well as this beer.*

## GARDE KÖLSCH

The first golden beer in the region, a heavier parent to today's *Kölsch*, is said to have been brewed by Garde in 1898. Today's Garde Kölsch is very soft and fresh, with a light, clean, sweet-apple fruitiness and a dry finish. It is a very good example of the style, and one of the fuller in flavor. The beer is bottled, but can also be found on draft in Cologne at the Bei d'r Tant in Cäcilienstrasse. Garde Kölsch is popular on the town's north side. The brewery is north of the city, at Dormagen, in the direction of Düsseldorf.

**Region of origin** Dormagen, North Rhine-Westphalia, Germany

**Style** *Kölschbier*

**Alcohol content** 3.8 abw (4.8 abv)

**Ideal serving temperature** 48° F (9° C)

*Guarding the style*
*Garde, named after the German Imperial Guard, stands at the perimeter of the defined* Kölsch-*producing region.*

## GILDEN KÖLSCH

Very flowery in aroma – an attribute of a good *Kölsch*. The palate is light, sherbety, and slightly winey. This beer is made by the Bergische Löwen brewery, in Mülheim, across the river from the city center of Cologne. This brewery is owned by the national group Brau und Brunnen. The brewery also produces Sion Kölsch, which seems maltier, with a pear-brandy fruitiness and a late hop dryness. Sion has a tavern in the city center, in a street called Unter Taschenmacher.

**Region of origin** Cologne, North Rhine-Westphalia, Germany

**Style** *Kölschbier*

**Alcohol content** 3.8 abw (4.8 abv)

**Ideal serving temperature** 48° F (9° C)

*Gilding the glass*
*Gilden takes its name from a trade guild. Today's Association of Brewers in Cologne protects the* Kölsch *style and its region of production.*

## KÜPPERS KÖLSCH

One of the few *Kölsch* beers to be found on occasion in export markets. Gustav Küpper brewed in the city in the 1800s, but the *Kölsch* and the present brewery date from the 1960s. It is a large brewery, on the banks of the Rhine. With a relatively "new" *Kölsch* to promote, Küppers emphasized heritage by establishing at the brewery an excellent museum of beer advertising. The brewery also has a restaurant serving local dishes. The beer is flowery, perfumy, and sweetish.

**Region of origin** Cologne, North Rhine-Westphalia, Germany

**Style** *Kölschbier*

**Alcohol content** 3.8 abw (4.8 abv)

**Ideal serving temperature** 48° F (9° C)

*Coopering the barrel*
*Like the English word "cooper," Küpper probably means "barrel-maker," but in an old dialect of the Rhine. The modern German word, Küfer, is more often understood as "cellarman." A barrel-maker is a* Fassbinder *("vat-binder").*

## MÜHLEN KÖLSCH

The *Malzmühle* (Malt Mill) is a long-established, unpretentious brewpub making a distinctly malty, almost marshmallowlike *Kölschbier*. Mühlen Kölsch pours with a dense head, has a very fresh aroma, and a balancing spicy dryness. The brewpub is in the center of Cologne, on the square called the Haymarket (*Heumarkt*). An interesting contrast is offered at the opposite end of the square by Päffgen, a smarter bar-restaurant offering a hop-accented *Kölsch*. Päffgen has a brewpub in Friesen Strasse.

**Region of origin**  Cologne, North Rhine-Westphalia, Germany

**Style**  *Kölschbier*

**Alcohol content**  3.8 abw (4.8 abv)

**Ideal serving temperature**  48° F (9° C)

### Brewing in the wind
*Was the Malt Mill wind-powered? Unlikely, as the brewery dates from only 1858. Perhaps there were windmills by the banks of the Rhine.*

## REISSDORF KÖLSCH

Heinrich Reissdorf, who came from an old agricultural family, established this brewery in 1894. After World War II, it pioneered the style of *Kölsch* as universally brewed in Cologne today. The company is still privately owned, and said to be very conservative. It is in the St. Severin district, in the south part of Cologne's inner city. Its beer has a minty, hop aroma; sweet, vanillalike, malt flavors; and a crisp, dry, cedary finish. A delicious *Kölsch*, which briefly inspired a very fruity beer called St. Severin's Kölsch in California.

**Region of origin**  Cologne, North Rhine-Westphalia, Germany

**Style**  *Kölschbier*

**Alc. content**  3.8 abw (4.8 abv)

**Ideal serving temperature**  48° F (9° C)

## RICHMODIS KÖLSCH

A spritzy, lemony, dryish *Kölsch*, with a crisp finish, from a Cologne brewery. The original brewery, built in 1888, was destroyed by Allied bombs in 1944. Richmodis is in Gremberghaven, south of the river. The beer is widely available in Cologne taverns and restaurants. A good outlet is *Zum Neuen Treffpunkt* (The New Meeting Point), 25 Nussbaumer Strasse. The brewery is owned by Königsbacher, of Coblenz.

**Region of origin**  Cologne, North Rhine-Westphalia, Germany

**Style**  *Kölschbier*

**Alcohol content**  3.8 abw (4.8 abv)

**Ideal serving temperature**  48° F (9° C)

### Mother country
*In Roman times, Cologne was a colonial capital, hence the name. This beer's label remembers "Colonia est Mater." Coeln and Cöln are old spellings, Köln today's German form.*

## SESTER KÖLSCH

A very fragrant, firm-bodied *Kölsch*, smooth and slightly oily, with an orangey fruitiness. The long-time slogan, *Trink Sester mein Bester*, means "Drink Sester, my friend". The firm of Sester was founded in 1896, but in recent years the beer has been made by the Bergische Löwen brewery. Sester's symbol is a team of dray horses, called Max and Moritz after two characters in a series of stories by German poet, painter, caricaturist, and satirist Wilhelm Busch (1832–1908). The stories inspired the American comic strip, "The Katzenjammer Kids."

**Region of origin**  Cologne, North Rhine-Westphalia, Germany

**Style**  *Kölschbier*

**Alcohol content**  3.8 abw (4.8 abv)

**Ideal serving temperature**  48° F (9° C)

## HELLERS WIESS

In premises that formerly housed a distillery making a bitter liqueur, this new-generation brewpub, dating from the 1980s, is something of a maverick in Cologne's brewing industry. Hubert Heller makes one brew called Ur-Wiess, this term implying a "meadow" beer as served at festivals. In this case, that means an unfiltered beer. This perfumy, fruity brew, with a good hop bitterness, is also served in filtered form as *Kölsch*, in which version the malt emerges more clearly and the hop is slightly subdued. By definition, *Kölschbier* is filtered.

**Region of origin** Cologne, North Rhine-Westphalia, Germany

**Style** *Kölschbier*

**Alcohol content** 3.6 abw (4.5 abv)

**Ideal serving temperature** 48° F (9° C)

## SÜNNER KÖLSCH

After five generations, Sünner is the oldest family concern still making its own beer in Cologne. Christian Sünner founded the brewery in 1830 and it has been on the same site since 1859. It is across the river from the city center, in the high street of the Kalk neighborhood. There is a beer garden at the brewery. Sünner Kölsch has a fresh, creamy aroma; a peachy fruitiness; and a dry, spicy, almost salty, hop tang in its crisp finish. The brewery also makes a rye whiskey.

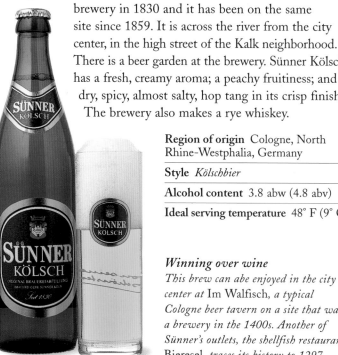

**Region of origin** Cologne, North Rhine-Westphalia, Germany

**Style** *Kölschbier*

**Alcohol content** 3.8 abw (4.8 abv)

**Ideal serving temperature** 48° F (9° C)

### Winning over wine
*This brew can abe enjoyed in the city center at* Im Walfisch, *a typical Cologne beer tavern on a site that was a brewery in the 1400s. Another of Sünner's outlets, the shellfish restaurant* Bieresel, *traces its history to 1297.*

## BUDELS PAREL KÖLSCH

Not made in the region, or even in Germany, and a little stronger than the original, but broadly in the style of a *Kölsch*. This beer is made across the Dutch frontier, beyond even the border province of Limburg, in the Brabant town of Budel. The enterprising Budels brewery launched it in 1985 as a novel speciality. *Parel* is Dutch for "pearl." The beer has a very good, resiny, hop aroma; a firm, smooth body; a dry palate; a faint hint of raspberry and vanilla fruitiness; and a dry, appetizing finish.

**Region of origin** Province of North Brabant, the Netherlands

**Style** *Kölsch*-type

**Alcohol content** 4.8 abw (6.0 abv)

**Ideal serving temperature** 47–48° F (8–9° C)

## FIREHOUSE KÖLSCH LAGER

Germany's restrictions on the term *Kölsch* have not yet reached the US, where many breweries try to emulate the style. This example is oddly subtitled a "Kölsch Lager." It is produced in a brewery and pub in a former fire station in Cleveland, Ohio. It has a lightly hoppy aroma; delicate flavors; a firm, slightly oily, creamy body; and a dry, faintly tart finish.

**Region of origin** Midwest US

**Style** *Kölsch*-type

**Alcohol content** 3.8 abw (4.7 abv)

**Ideal serving temperature** 48° F (9° C)

### Hot beer
*The horses on this label are pulling a fire engine. Several new-generation American breweries are located in former fire station buildings.*

# SOCIABLE BEERS: ALTBIER

THERE ARE STRONG SIMILARITIES between the ales of England and Belgium and the *Altbier* made in Düsseldorf and other northwestern German cities – not only in typical colour, but also in method of production. These copper-colored German beers are really ales, in that they are made with top-fermenting yeasts. *Alt* is German for "old," and these are beers still loyal to the "old" style that was common before lager brewing spread from southeastern cities such as Munich and Pilsen. Today, Düsseldorf is one of Germany's most cosmopolitan cities, and its lively bars take a pride in their *Altbier*, a style widely emulated in the US and Japan. Perhaps the Japanese acquired the taste in Düsseldorf, home to the European headquarters of many Japanese companies.

*Over a barrel*
Altbier *blends the generations at Düsseldorf's* Zum Uerige.

*A tasty drop . . .*
*. . . is the meaning of* "dat leckere Dröppke." *Some labels display the word* "Obergärige," *which means* "top-fermenting."

## UERIGE ALT

Fashion icons, rock stars, punks, men in suits, old ladies with big hats . . . everyone in Düsseldorf drinks at Zum Uerige by the river in the *Altstadt* (Old Town). The inn has its own sausage butchery, and its specialities are head-cheese and a cheese marinated in beer. The beer at this rambling old brewpub, the classic example of *Alt*, is also bottled for general sale. It has a fresh hop aroma; a firm, smooth, almost slippery, clean maltiness; and a robust punch of bitterness. The name "Uerige" refers to a cranky past proprietor. A slightly stronger, "secret" version, given extra aroma with an additional hop treatment, is brewed once or twice a year under the name *Sticke Bier*, a Düsseldorf tradition. Uerige Alt inspired the excellent Ur Alt of the Widmer Brewery in Portland, Oregon.

**Region of origin**
Düsseldorf, North Rhine-Westphalia, Germany

**Style** *Altbier*

**Alcohol content** 3.6 abw (4.5 abv)

**Ideal serving temperature** 48° F (9° C)

### BARD OF BEER

THE HOUSE OF the German lyric poet Heinrich Heine (1797–1856) is near the *Altbier* brewpub *Zum Schlüssel*. He noted that "Germans have a thousand words for beer." On travels in Bavaria, he criticized the "best beer" there, preferring "English Porter."

## IM FÜCHSCHEN ALT

The name means "The Fox Cub." This is another rightly renowned brewery and pub in the Old Town of Düsseldorf. Its *Alt*, also a favourite among lovers of the style, is a well-balanced but hoppy interpretation. It has a creamy malt character; a restrained, pearlike fruitiness; and a hoppy acidity in the dry finish. The brewery, a classic of its type, stands like a miniature industrial building behind the tavern. Inside, customers share scrubbed tables, and the beer accompanies a hearty menu. The house speciality is *Eisbein:* boiled knuckle of pork.

**Region of origin**
Düsseldorf, North Rhine-Westphalia, Germany

**Style** *Altbier*

**Alc. content** 3.6 abw (4.5 abv)

**Ideal serving temperature**
48° F (9° C)

## SCHUMACHER ALT

A family-owned brewery and pub in the modern center of the city. The Schumacher family were beer-makers even before they owned their first brewery, in 1838, and the present premises date from the 1870s. This is a quieter, more cafélike brewpub, with a beer garden. Its beer is one of the paler examples in color; sweetish, malt-accented, and softly, nuttily fruity; but with a good balance. Typical dishes served include *Sauerbraten*, the marinated beef dish of the Rhineland.

**Region of origin** Düsseldorf, North Rhine-Westphalia, Germany

**Style** *Altbier*

**Alcohol content** 3.7 abw (4.6 abv)

**Ideal serving temperature** 9° C (48° F)

*Symbols of brewing*
*The malt shovel and mashing fork on the label are symbols of the brewer's art. The mini-barrel is used like a ladle. The big vessel is a mash tun.*

## FRANKENHEIM ALT

This light, dry, peppery, spicy *Altbier* is from a major privately owned brewery in Düsseldorf. The brewery dates from the 1870s, and is still in the Frankenheim family. Another family-owned brewery, Diebels of Issum, produces the biggest-selling *Altbier* nationally: a smooth, firm, malty example. Other privately owned breweries include Rhenania (making a sweetish, slightly thick-tasting *Altbier*) and Gatzweiler (very fruity).

**Region of origin**
Düsseldorf, North Rhine-Westphalia, Germany

**Style** *Altbier*

**Alc. content** 3.8 abw (4.8 abv)

**Ideal serving temperature**
48° F (9° C)

*Private pride*
"Privatbrauerei" *means that the brewery is privately owned – so the brewers can take pride in making great beer, rather than just making money for shareholders.*

## SCHLÖSSER ALT

The name derives from the word for "lock." The Schlösser family founded the enterprise as a brewpub in the Old Town in 1873. Between the two world wars, a series of mergers and expansions began. Schlösser is now the biggest *Altbier* brewery within Düsseldorf, and is part of the national Brau und Brunnen group. Its beer is on the light side in both body and taste. It has a syrupy start, with flavors like brown sugar, becoming nuttier, firmer, and drier in the finish.

**Region of origin**
Düsseldorf, North Rhine-Westphalia, Germany

**Style** *Altbier*

**Alcohol content** 3.8 abw (4.8 abv)

**Ideal serving temperature**
48° F (9° C)

*The true tradition*
*Schlösser's short, cylindrical glass is the most traditional shape used for* Altbier. *Some brewers have moved to taller, slimmer vessels more reminiscent of* Kölschbier.

# BOLTEN UR-ALT

A truly "old" brewery, tracing its history to 1266, in Korschenbroich, west of Düsseldorf. Since the 1600s, the brewery, inn, and farm have been owned by the Bolten family. The early beers of the region used peat-smoked malt, were spiced, and were fermented with wild yeast. The term *Altbier* was introduced in the 1890s. The beers had a low carbonation until the post-World War II period. Bolten Alt has deep, complex, dry, malty flavors. The version called Ur-Alt is unfiltered, more textured, and juicier.

**Region of origin**
Korschenbroich,
North Rhine-
Westphalia, Germany

**Style** *Altbier*

**Alcohol content**
3.8 abw (4.7 abv)

**Ideal serving
temperature**
48° F (9° C)

# PINKUS MÜLLER ALT

This golden, wheat-tinged interpretation – very dry, crisp, and quenching but with some buttery maltiness – is a quite different style of "old" beer. It evolved in the the university city of Münster, capital of North Rhine-Westphalia. This version is made only at a famous brewery and pub called Pinkus Müller.

This establishment began in 1816 as a bakery and brewery in the Old Town, and has expanded over the years through nine houses. In summer, the beer is offered laced with soft fruits.

**Region of origin**
Münster, North Rhine-
Westphalia, Germany

**Style** Münster *Altbier*

**Alc. content** 4.0 abw (5.0 abv)

**Ideal serving temperature**
48° F (9° C)

# NUSSDORFER ST. THOMAS BRÄU

Thomas, the patron saint of the village of Nussdorf on the edge of Vienna, Austria, gives his name to this *Altbier*, produced there by Baron Bachofen von Echt. A Nussdorfer brewery established in 1819, and run by the Baron's family for five generations, closed in the 1950s, but he revived the tradition in 1984. His *Altbier* has robust malt flavors – sweet, creamy, nutty, and juicy – with a good hop balance.

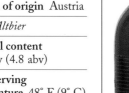

**Region of origin** Austria

**Style** *Altbier*

**Alcohol content**
3.8 abw (4.8 abv)

**Ideal serving
temperature** 48° F (9° C)

***Pure by law***
*The top line of the label
makes clear that this
Austrian beer is brewed
according to the German
Purity Law.*

# WARTECK ALT

A director of the Warteck brewery developed a love of *Altbier* from his wife, who came from the Lower Rhine. From such chance origins, this brewery in Basel, Switzerland, gained its own *Altbier* in the late 1970s. The beer has a malty aroma; a lightly toffeeish start, developing to cinnamon spiciness and perfumy fruitiness; and a balancing touch of hoppy dryness. Warteck was acquired by a local rival, and the beer is now produced in the cathedral-like brewhouse of Feldschlösschen.

**Region of origin**
Northwest Switzerland

**Style** *Altbier*

**Alcohol content**
3.8 abw (4.7 abv)

**Ideal serving temperature**
48° F (9° C)

## BUDELS ALT

Few European breweries are as eclectic in their beer styles as Budels of North Brabant in the Netherlands. Its range includes not only a *Kölsch* type but also this *Altbier*, albeit at an alcohol content that is higher than typical. This interpretation has a pale color for the style; fresh spicy hop and fudgy malt in the aroma; lively flavor development, with hints of ginger; and a firm, very dry finish.

**Region of origin**
Province of North Brabant, the Netherlands

**Style** *Altbier*

**Alc. content** 4.8 abw (6.0 abv)

**Ideal serving temperature**
48° F (9° C)

*Toasting Alt*
*On this label, the historical crowned head of Brabant, Jan Primus, is shown as Gambrinus, mythical King of Beer and alleged inventor of the toast.*

## ALASKAN AMBER

A beer that seems to have been very like an *Alt* was produced by a German immigrant brewer in Alaska around the start of the 20th century. This was discovered by Geoff and Marcy Larson when they established their microbrewery in the state capital, Juneau, in 1986. They decided to brew an *Alt*, which they called Alaskan Amber.

This has become their principal product. It is a very complex beer, with a malty aroma; a slightly oily, clean, malty palate; and a spicy dryness in the finish.

**Region of origin**
Alaska

**Style** *Altbier*

**Alcohol content**
4.2 abw (5.2 abv)

**Ideal serving temperature**
48° F (9° C)

## SOUTHAMPTON SECRET

Modeled on a *Sticke (see p. 52)* and made with imported German ingredients: no fewer than five malts (pale, Vienna, Munich, black, and wheat) and three varieties of hops (Northern Brewer, Hallertau Tradition, and Spalt) and an *Altbier* yeast. Very fresh in aroma and palate, with a sweetish, slightly chocolatey, smoothly malty start but a good balance of late dryness. It is from the Southampton Publick House, on Long Island, New York.

**Region of origin**
Northeast US

**Style** *Altbier*

**Alcohol content**
4.2 abw (5.2 abv)

**Ideal serving temperature**
48 F° (9° C)

*First resort*
*The summer houses and sandy beaches of Southampton seem a far cry from the coziness of Old Town taverns by the Rhine in Düsseldorf.*

## SCHMALTZ'S ALT

The jocular-sounding alliteration derives from a local nickname in the largely German-American town of New Ulm, Minnesota. In this instance, it applied to the late father of the brewery's principal. The August Schell brewery, founded in 1860, is one of the few long-established regional breweries left in the US. It is also the prettiest, set in woodland with its own deer park. Schmaltz's Alt is a very dark, roasty, vanilla-tinged, dry interpretation of the style.

**Region of origin** Midwest US

**Style** *Altbier*

**Alcohol content** 4.7 abw (5.9 abv)

**Ideal serving temperature**
48° F (9° C)

*Frontier spirit*
*In the early pioneering days, perhaps because of finely tuned diplomatic skills, the Schell family, who still own the brewery today, survived a Native American uprising.*

# SOCIABLE BEERS: BELGIAN ALES

THE WORD "ALE" IS USED IN BELGIUM to describe bronze or amber-red brews for everyday drinking. While English ale is often more fruity or bitter, and German *Altbier* notably rounded and smooth, the Belgian members of this family can have an appetizing spiciness, usually deriving from the character of the local top-fermenting yeasts. These softly teasing brews perfectly suit the pace of café life in a country where neither food nor drink is consumed in a hurry.

***Symbolic sculpture***
*A Brabant draft horse, shown here sculptured in bronze, is the symbol of Palm ale and appears on both bottle and glass.*

***Vulgar fractions***
*In Antwerp bars and cafés, this goblet is called a* bolleke *(little ball), which has a vulgar ring to English speakers. Meanwhile the word for the ladies' glass, a* flûte *(*fluitje *in Flemish), has phallic connotations locally.*

## DE KONINCK

The name of this beer means "king," but it was the surname of a man who owned a beer garden in Antwerp, capital of Flanders and second city of Belgium. The beer garden has long gone, but its brewery survives. Its principal product is known simply as De Koninck. This is the much-loved local beer of Antwerp. It is not described on the tap handle or label as an ale, but it certainly is one. As a bottled brew, De Koninck is good, but its fresh, yeasty, dusty, cinnamon-like spiciness is at its best when the beer is served on tap. It has a dense head that leaves lacework with every swallow. It is subtle, dryish, but beautifully balanced, toasty, soothing, and drinkable. A stronger (6.4 abw/8.0 abv), spicier, brandyish version is called Cuvée De Koninck.

**Region of origin** Province of Antwerp, Belgium

**Style** Belgian Ale

**Alcohol content** 4.0 abw (5.0 abv)

**Ideal serving temperature** The brewery suggests 45° F (7° C), but the flavors are more evident at a less severe temperature, around 54° F (12° C)

### DE KONINCK YEAST

OPPOSITE THE DE KONINCK brewery is the Pilgrim café, where the brewery's surplus yeast is traditionally offered to customers by the shot-glass as a tonic. Some chase it down with a glass of De Koninck, while others add it to their beer. In recent years, the practice has spread to other De Koninck cafés in the city.

## PALM SPECIALE

This ale was introduced in the 1920s. It became Belgium's best-selling ale and the brewery is now known as Palm. The beer is made in Steenhuffel, northwest of Brussels. Palm Speciale has a malty accent, with a rounded, orange, yeasty finish. The brewery also produces a stronger (6 abw/7.5 abv), drier, hoppier ale called Aerts 1900.

**Region of origin**
Province of Flemish Brabant, Belgium

**Style** Belgian Ale

**Alcohol content**
4.0 abw (5.0 abv)

**Ideal serving temperature**
54° F (12° C)

*Uncommon style*
*The term "Speciale" is sometimes used on labels in Belgium to indicate an ale, rather than the more common lager style.*

## OP-ALE

In Flemish, *op* means "up", as in "drink up" – an apt abbreviation for Opwijk, the town where this ale is made. Op-Ale has a refreshing, sweet-apple fruitiness; a light, clean, dry, crisply malty palate; and a citric spritziness in the finish. It is made by the De Smedt brewery, which also produces beers for the abbey of Affligem.

**Region of origin** Province of Flemish Brabant, Belgium

**Style** Belgian Ale

**Alc. content** 4.0 abw (5.0 abv)

**Ideal serving temperature**
The brewery suggests 45° F (7° C), but the flavors are more evident at around 50° F (10° C)

*Pride of the province*
*Not only the local breweries, but also the province adopts the Brabant horse as a symbol.*

## GINDER ALE

Not "ginger": the man who created this beer was called Van Ginderachter. It is a lively, appetizing beer with apple-brandy flavors deriving from a distinct yeast. Ginder Ale is made by the same company as Stella Artois, in the brewing city of Leuven. The same company, Interbrew, also makes the smooth, anise-tinged Horse Ale and the sherbety, faintly smoky Vieux Temps.

**Region of origin**
Province of Flemish Brabant, Belgium

**Style** Belgian Ale

**Alcohol content**
4.1 abw (5.1 abv)

**Ideal serving temperature**
50° F (10° C)

## PETRUS SPECIALE

The name Petrus sounds like a famous Bordeaux wine but is intended simply to signify St. Peter, known as "holder of the keys to Heaven." The Petrus range is made by the De Brabandere brewery, of Bavikhove, West Flanders. Its Speciale is an assertive ale, with an earthy aroma; a textured malt background; coriander in the palate (this spice is added); and a rooty, hoppy finish.

**Region of origin** Province of West Flanders, Belgium

**Style** Belgian Ale

**Alc. content** 4.4 abw (5.5 abv)

**Ideal serving temperature**
50° F (10° C)

*Hop happy*
*Hops feature on many beer labels. In this case, the illustration is justified. Petrus Speciale is one of the hoppier Belgian ales.*

# SOCIABLE BEERS: ENGLISH BITTER

ALL BREWS BALANCE the sweetness of the malt with the bitterness ("dryness" might be a better term) of the hop. The English term for an ale that is well hopped is a "bitter." Some are only very slightly bitter, others have a real smack of hops. The best examples gain a teasing complexity of flavor as they mature in the cellar of the pub.

**Pulling power**
*In Britain, a high proportion of beer is consumed on draft.*

*Bottled strength*
*The bottled version of London Pride is slightly stronger than the draft. Pints in the pub are often of modest strength.*

## FULLER'S LONDON PRIDE

In some parts of the world, Fuller's ales are gaining a cult following. Within Britain, much of the beer is sold very locally, in the suburbs around the brewery. Fuller's has three examples of bitter. The low-strength Chiswick Bitter (named after the brewery's neighborhood), is refreshingly flowery in its hop character. This is a typically English approach: a beer that is full of flavor but light in body and alcohol, so that several pints can be consumed in an evening. In the middle comes London Pride, with beautifully combined flavors of light, smoothly nutty malt; crisply bitter hop; and faintly honeyish yeast. This is a more satisfying, soothing bitter. Drinkers wanting a little more punch, and perhaps only one pint, opt for the bigger Extra Special Bitter, with its robust hits of malt and hop.

**Region of origin**  London, England, UK

**Style**  Bitter Ale

**Alcohol content**  In bottle: 3.8 abw (4.7 abv)
On draft: 3.2 abw (4.1 abv)

**Ideal serving temperature**  50–55° F (10–13° C)

### HAND-RAISED ALE

GENUINE HAND-PUMPS are more than a decoration in a British pub. They pull beer from the cellar without the use of nitrogen or carbon dioxide pressure. The gentle carbonation in the beer is caused by a secondary fermentation in the cask at cellar temperature. During this "conditioning," the yeast in the cask precipitates.

# ADNAMS SUFFOLK STRONG ALE

The barley-growing and malting region of East Anglia is home to this family brewery. Adnams is in the county of Suffolk, in the seaside town of Southwold. The company owns the Swan pub, where there may have been a brewery in 1345.

Adnams Suffolk Strong Ale, extravagantly named, is firm-bodied and dry – with a pronounced aroma and flavor of the hop variety Fuggles. A draft counterpart is called Adnams Extra.

**Region of origin**
Eastern England, UK

**Style** Bitter Ale

**Alcohol content**
3.6 abw (4.5 abv)

**Ideal serving temperature**
50–55° F (10–13° C)

# BATEMANS XXXB

British beer lovers have cherished this brewery ever since George Bateman won a family battle to ensure its independence. Its XXXB recalls the days before mass literacy, when the strength of a beer was indicated by numerals or symbols branded onto the wooden cask. This robust but smooth, sweetish, fruity, full-flavored beer has a touch of "aniseedy" spiciness. The brewery is in farmland near Skegness, Lincolnshire.

**Region of origin**
Eastern England, UK

**Style** Bitter Ale

**Alcohol content**
3.9 abw (4.8 abv )

**Ideal serving temperature**
50–55° F (10–13° C)

*Stylish logo*
*The trademark is a stylized depiction of the windmill under which the brewery stands, in flat countryside near the coast.*

# CAINS FORMIDABLE ALE

The formidable Robert Cain, from Cork, Ireland, founded this Victorian brewery across the water in Liverpool. He also built some of the city's famously elaborate pubs, several of which are still in operation. After several changes of ownership, the brewery restored the name Cains around 1990. Formidable Ale, pale in color, seems crisp at first, but builds to a surge of gingery bitterness.

**Region of origin**
Northwest England, UK

**Style** Bitter Ale

**Alcohol content**
4.0 abw (5.0 abv)

**Ideal serving temperature**
50–55° F (10–13° C)

# BRAKSPEAR SPECIAL

The name rhymes with Shakespeare. This long-established brewery is on the Thames River at the regatta town of Henley. Brakspear Special is beautifully balanced; light, smooth, and drinkable; with a late, lingering bitterness. The "double" fermentation mentioned on the label refers to a traditional system of two vessels. The first encourages the development of complex flavors. The dropping of the brew into the second vessel refines those flavors.

**Region of origin**
Central England, UK

**Style** Bitter Ale

**Alcohol content**
3.4 abw (4.3 abv)

**Ideal serving temperature**
50–55° F (10–13° C)

## JENNINGS COCKER HOOP

Far northern brewery, in Cockermouth near the English Lakes. Apart from being a pun on the location, the name is a reference to drinking. The beer's back label suggests that the cock (tap) and hoop were both parts of the barrel. Cocker Hoop rolls smoothly over the tongue, at first nutty, then lightly orangey and perfumy, and finally hoppy and grassy. A summery, sociable ale with lots of character. Despite its far-flung location, the brewery's products are widely available.

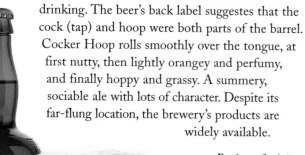

**Region of origin**
Northwest England, UK

**Style** Bitter Ale

**Alcohol content**
3.8 abw (4.8 abv)

**Ideal serving temperature**
50–55° F (10–13° C)

## TIMOTHY TAYLOR'S LANDLORD

A renowned brewery on the edge of the moors in Yorkshire's Brontë country, Timothy Taylor's is located in the small wool town of Keighley. Its Landlord Strong Pale Ale was allegedly designed to cleanse the throats of Yorkshire coalminers. It is a very drinkable beer, with a heathery hop aroma (Styrian Goldings are used); a firm, grainy palate; some juicy maltiness; and a touch of refreshing acidity in the finish. The brewery recommends only a gentle chilling.

**Region of origin**
Northern England, UK

**Style** Pale Ale/Bitter

**Alcohol content**
3.3 abw (4.1 abv)

**Ideal serving temperature**
52–58° F (11–14° C)

## SHEPHERD NEAME SPITFIRE

Hop Country brewery in the heart of East Kent. Its home town of Faversham is believed to have had an abbey brewery in the 1100s. Shepherd Neame itself dates from 1698, and is, as a business, Britain's oldest brewing company. Its Spitfire is a sedimented, bottle-conditioned ale. The brew has a fresh hop aroma; a light, firm body; a lively, dry palate; and a lingering bitterness.

**Region of origin**
Southeast England, UK

**Style** Bitter Ale

**Alcohol content**
3.8 abw (4.7 abv)

**Ideal serving temperature**
50–55° F (10–13° C)

***Fighting spirit***
*Spitfire is named after the fighter aircraft that flew from bases in Kent during World War II. The beer was launched some 50 years later.*

## YOUNG'S SPECIAL

Known for its dray horses, ram mascot, and geese – all in an inner-city brewery in London. Young's stands on Britain's oldest brewing site; beer has been made there continuously since 1581. The present company dates from 1831. While some of Young's beers have lost a little of their typical dryness in recent years, the Special has become flintier, with long, firm flavors.

**Region of origin**
London, England, UK

**Style** Bitter Ale

**Alcohol content**
3.4 abw (4.3 abv)

**Ideal serving temperature**
50–55° F (10–13° C)

***Historic trademark***
*The "Ram Brewery" trademark may date from a pub on the site.*

# ENGLISH BITTER

## CHILTERN JOHN HAMPDEN'S ALE

Just north of the Chiltern Hills in Aylesbury, historic county town of Buckinghamshire. The brewery, established in 1980, revived Aylesbury's beer-making tradition after a gap of 40-odd years. The farm-based Chiltern brewery also sells beer-flavored condiments and cheeses, and even hop-based toiletries. John Hampden's Ale is straw-colored, with the aroma of lemons and ginger and a very dry, crackerlike maltiness.

**Region of origin**
Southeast England, UK

**Style** Bitter Ale

**Alcohol content** 3.8 abw (4.8 abv)

**Ideal serving temperature**
50–55° F (10–13° C)

## EVERARDS' TIGER

This brew was once produced in Britain's beer capital, Burton upon Trent, but is today made elsewhere in the Midlands, at the Everard family's modern brewery near Leicester. Everards' Tiger is named after a local regiment that spent a great deal of time in India. The beer, as in a classic Burton ale, has a hint of sulfur on the nose. Its palate is rounded, nutty, and oily, with some orangey flavors and a dry finish.

**Region of origin**
Central England, UK

**Style** Bitter Ale

**Alcohol content** 3.6 abw (4.5 abv)

**Ideal serving temperature**
50–55° F (10–13° C)

## MORDUE'S WORKIE TICKET

Judged "Champion Beer of Britain" two years after this new-generation brewery was established. Founders Matthew and Gary Fawson were inspired to their profession when they discovered that their house near Newcastle had been a brewery called Mordue in the 1800s. "Workie Ticket" is a Geordie (Newcastle) expression for a troublemaker. This full-colored beer has a robust maltiness, balanced by a surge of nutty dryness in the finish.

**Region of origin**
Northeast England, UK

**Style** Bitter Ale

**Alcohol content** 3.6 abw (4.5 abv)

**Ideal serving temperature**
50–55° F (10–13° C)

## MORLAND "OLD SPECKLED HEN"

Georgian landscape painter George Morland was a member of the family. The brewing company dates from 1711. It bought its present premises, at Abingdon, Oxfordshire, in 1863. The town has a history of malting and brewing, but MG cars were also a local industry. The Old Speckled Hen was a locally famous MG. The beer is malt-accented, but with a distinctly yeasty dryness and appetizingly lively, long finish.

**Region of origin**
Southern England, UK

**Style** Bitter Ale

**Alcohol content** 4.2 abw (5.2 abv)

**Ideal serving temperature**
50–55° F (10–13° C)

## RINGWOOD OLD THUMPER

New-generation beer makers all over the world took their initial advice from veteran brewer Peter Austin. He started his own first brewery here in the New Forest, at Ringwood, Hampshire. His Old Thumper is a bronze ale, with a sherbety aroma; clean, syrupy flavors; a smooth body; and a gentle hop balance. A good interpretation of Old Thumper is made in the US by the Shipyard brewery of Portland, Maine.

**Region of origin**
Southern England, UK

**Style** Strong Ale/Bitter

**Alcohol content** 4.5 abw (5.6 abv)

**Ideal serving temperature**
50–55° F (10–13° C)

## WADWORTH 6X

An open copper kettle is still used and wooden casks are supplied to local pubs by the tradition-minded Wadworth brewery in the market town of Devizes, Wiltshire. The classic tower brewery was built in 1885, though earlier premises from at least the 1830s still stand. Wadworth's 6X is modest in alcohol but big in flavor and texture: an oaky aroma, with hints of cognac; a toasted-nut maltiness; and a sappy, slightly tart dryness in the finish.

**Region of origin**
Southern England, UK

**Style** Bitter Ale

**Alcohol content** 3.4 abw (4.3 abv)

**Ideal serving temperature**
50–55° F (10–13° C)

## CHARLES WELLS BOMBARDIER

Sizable regional brewery, long-established, and still family-run, in Bedford. Its best-known beer evokes the memory of boxer Bombardier Billy Wells, British heavyweight champion from 1911 to 1919. This satisfying, smooth, malt-accented beer has a slightly sulfury, rooty aroma; fruity, cherry-pie flavors; and a cookielike dryness in the finish. A firmer, drier, stronger ale is neatly named Wells Fargo.

**Region of origin**
Eastern England, UK

**Style** Bitter Ale

**Alcohol content** 3.4 abw (4.3 abv)

**Ideal serving temperature**
50–55° F (10–13° C)

## WOODFORDE'S NORFOLK WHERRY

New-generation farmhouse brewery near Norwich. Some of the buildings are thatched with reeds from the nearby system of waterways known as the Norfolk Broads. A wherry is a type of shallow boat typically used in the area. The beer named after the boat is hoppy, with a leafy, sharp, fresh-lime aroma and flavor; a crisp, cookielike, malt background; and a dry, candied-peel finish.

**Region of origin**
Eastern England, UK

**Style** Bitter Ale

**Alcohol content** 3.1 abw (3.8 abv)

**Ideal serving temperature**
50–55° F (10–13° C)

# SOCIABLE BEERS: SCOTTISH ALES

SCOTLAND CULTIVATES BARLEY for malting, but its climate is too cool for hops. Scottish ales emphasize the malt, typically having a soothing maltiness and roundness. In the days before refrigeration, Scotland's weather made for relatively low temperatures of fermentation and maturation, and this helped to round the beers. The examples shown here are substantial, without being too strong for sociable drinking.

**Cross-border café**
*Scotland's capital, Edinburgh, has ornate pubs such as the Café Royal.*

*Towering trademark*
*The trademark on the glass depicts the kiln in which grain is dried at the end of malting. Some whiskey distilleries use a similar symbol.*

## CALEDONIAN FLYING SCOTSMAN

The small Caledonian brewery in Edinburgh produces Scotland's maltiest beers. The brewery dates from 1869, and still boils its kettles by direct flame (as opposed to the more usual steam). This "fire-brewing" creates hot spots and a caramelization that can heighten malty flavors. Since 1987, the brewery has been run by a malt expert who formerly worked in the whiskey industry. The brewery stands near the Edinburgh-London railway, and the Flying Scotsman beer is named after a famous train on that route. The ruby-colored brew also contains a tiny amount of rye. It is is profoundly malty in its aroma and flavors, but very well rounded, with hints of raisiny spiciness and toasty dryness. There is a yet greater maltiness, but not as much balancing dryness, in the marginally less strong Merman and the more potent Edinburgh Strong Ale.

**Region of origin**  Southern Scotland, UK

**Style**  Scottish Ale

**Alcohol content**  3.9 abw (5.1 abv)

**Ideal serving temperature**  50–55° F (10–13° C)

### SHILLING FOR ALE

SCOTTISH ALES ARE OFTEN LABELED 60/-, 70/-, 80/-, or 90/-. The symbol represents the shilling, a former unit of British currency. In the past, these ratings represented tax bands. Today they indicate ascending strength, but in general terms. There is no specific link between the shillings and the alcohol.

# MACLAY EIGHTY SHILLING EXPORT ALE

Classic Victorian brewery in the old beer-making town of Alloa. The Alloa breweries used hard water from the Ochil Hills and local coal. Maclay Eighty Shilling has a dense head; a perfumy malt aroma; a hint of chocolatey sweetness; and a creamy dryness in the finish. The slightly stronger, paler, drier Maclay Scotch Ale has more of a fresh-bread maltiness.

**Region of origin**
Central Scotland, UK

**Style** Scottish Ale

**Alcohol content**
3.2 abw (4.0 abv)

**Ideal serving temperature**
50–55° F (10–13° C)

# BROUGHTON BLACK DOUGLAS

This new-generation brewery is in the Borders, at Broughton, birthplace of novelist John Buchan. The first beer was called Greenmantle after one of Buchan's stories. It has a rather English taste, emphasizing the hop. This newer ale is named after an ally of the Scottish patriot Robert the Bruce, and clearly has north-of-the-border qualities of color and maltiness. Its aroma suggests malted milk, the palate is lightly sugary, and the finish has the bitterness of black chocolate.

**Region of origin**
Scottish Borders, UK

**Style** Scottish Ale

**Alcohol content**
4.1 abw (5.2 abv)

**Ideal serving temperature**
50–55° F (10–13° C)

# BELHAVEN 80/- EXPORT ALE

A Benedictine monastery on a nearby island gave rise to this brewery at Belhaven, near Dunbar, between the border and Edinburgh. The brewery traces its commercial origins to 1719. Its 80/- (labeled with the shilling symbol rather than the full spelling) has a tawny color; a smooth, firm, toasty palate; and a good flavor development, with a faint, jammy, pineapple note from the house yeast.

**Region of origin**
Scottish Borders, UK

**Style** Scottish Ale

**Alcohol content**
3.1 abw (3.9 abv)

**Ideal serving temperature**
50–55° F (10–13° C)

# MCEWAN'S 80/-

Scotland's biggest beer maker, which merged with Younger's, then acquired Newcastle Breweries and later Courage. The resultant company, Scottish Courage, is the biggest brewer in Britain. In Edinburgh, McEwan's products include this 80/-, very slightly lighter in body than its competitors, on the dry side, with a touch of burnt toast. The label emphasizes the use of roasted barley, suggesting that this is a "classic" ingredient.

**Region of origin**
Southern Scotland, UK

**Style** Scottish Ale

**Alcohol content**
3.6 abw (4.5 abv)

**Ideal serving temperature**
50–55° F (10–13° C)

## BERT GRANT'S SCOTTISH ALE

Dundee-born beer maker Bert Grant was a brewpub pioneer in the hop town of Yakima, Washington, in 1982. He is still associated with the Grant's brewery, though it is now owned by a local winery. His Scottish Ale is inspired by his origins as much as the classic style, though it does have a lot of malt in both aroma and palate, as well as the hop character appropriate to the region.

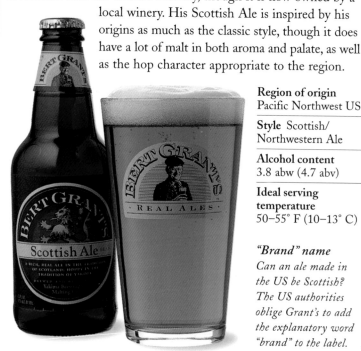

**Region of origin**
Pacific Northwest US

**Style** Scottish/
Northwestern Ale

**Alcohol content**
3.8 abw (4.7 abv)

**Ideal serving
temperature**
50–55° F (10–13° C)

*"Brand" name*
*Can an ale made in
the US be Scottish?
The US authorities
oblige Grant's to add
the explanatory word
"brand" to the label.*

## ODELL'S 90 SHILLING

Doug Odell is an American of Welsh extraction who visited Scotland on vacation, enjoyed the beers, went home to Colorado, gave up his landscaping business, and in 1989 established a microbrewery in Fort Collins. One of his first beers was his 90 Shilling. It is appropriately malty in both its fresh aroma and satisfying balance of light, smooth syrupiness and nuttiness, finishing with a restrained, enticing dryness.

**Region of origin**
Southwest US

**Style** Scottish Ale

**Alcohol content**
4.5 abw (5.6 abv)

**Ideal serving
temperature**
50–55° F (10–13° C)

## PORTLAND BREWING MACTARNAHAN'S GOLD MEDAL

Portland, Oregon, has 20-odd breweries, more than any other city in the world. The boom began in the mid-1980s, and Portland Brewing dates from that time. In 1992, the brewery won a gold medal at the Great American Beer Festival for its MacTarnahan's. The product is named after a friend of the brewery. It has a touch of butterscotch maltiness in the aroma, rounding out to a fruity, hoppy dryness.

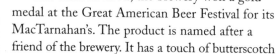

**Region of origin**
Pacific Northwest US

**Style**
Scottish/Northwestern Ale

**Alcohol content**
3.4 abw (4.2 abv)

**Ideal serving temperature**
55° F (13° C)

*Read the small print*
*The small print on the label
describes MacTarnahan's as
a Scottish-style amber ale.*

## FLATLANDER'S EIGHTY SHILLING ALE

People from the midwestern US states sometimes self-mockingly call themselves flatlanders. This brewery is on the premises of a spacious restaurant in the Illinois town of Lincolnshire. Despite the town's English name, the brewery's most noteworthy product is a very authentic Scottish ale: typically full in color and textured in body, with a dryish, very faintly peaty maltiness. Scottish malt is used.

**Region of origin**
Midwest US

**Style** Scottish Ale

**Alcohol content**
3.0 abw (3.7 abv)

**Ideal serving temperature**
50–55° F (10–13° C)

# SCOTTISH ALES

## BOULDER CREEK HIGHLANDS AMBER

In the Redwood Hills, in the old logging town of Boulder Creek, north of Santa Cruz, California. This rather remote brewpub specializes in British styles. Its Highlands Amber is made with pale and brown malts and roasted barley, all from Scotland. The beer has a dense, bubbly head, leaving good lace; a tawny color; and a delicious interplay of fruity, chocolatey maltiness and crisp, dry toastiness. It is a fine example of a really quaffable Scottish ale.

**Region of origin** West US

**Style** Scottish Ale

**Alcohol content** 3.7 abw (4.6 abv)

**Ideal serving temperature**
50–55° F (10–13° C)

## FLYING DOG SCOTTISH ALE

The owner of a ranch called the Flying Dog is a partner in this cellar brewpub in the fashionable ski resort of Aspen, Colorado – hence its unusual name. Flying Dog's beers are also produced for bottling in the associated Broadway brewery, in Denver. The Scottish ale, sub-titled Road Dog, is notably smooth, with flavors suggesting cocoa, raisins, and rum, and a balancing dryness of lively, yogurty acidity.

**Region of origin** Southwest US

**Style** Scottish Ale

**Alcohol content** 4.6 abw (5.8 abv)

**Ideal serving temperature**
50–55° F (10–13° C)

## HARVIESTOUN MONTROSE ALE

A 200-year-old stone cowshed was the original home of this brewery near the Firth of Forth in Central Scotland. Harviestoun's brews have ranged from a crisp wheat ale to an unfiltered lager. Its more traditional ales have a Scottish maltiness that leans to the dry, nutty side, sometimes with touches of vanilla, and are quite fruity. The brew named after the town of Montrose is a full-flavored 80/-, with a suggestion of blackcurrant.

**Region of origin** Central Scotland, UK

**Style** Scottish Ale

**Alcohol content** 3.4 abw (4.2 abv)

**Ideal serving temperature**
50–55° F (10–13° C)

## MOLSON DAVE'S SCOTCH ALE

This Canadian national giant was founded in Quebec in 1786 by John Molson, from Lincolnshire, England. It is the oldest brewing company in North America, though it is now partly owned by Foster's of Australia. Molson is better known for golden ales and lagers, but its specialities include a deep amber Scotch Ale: firm, malty, dry, and faintly peaty. This tasty brew is part of a range created for supermarket principal Dave Nichol.

**Region of origin**
Province of Ontario, Canada

**Style** Scottish Ale

**Alcohol content** 4.5 abw (5.6 abv)

**Ideal serving temperature**
50–55° F (10–13° C)

## MOULIN ALE OF ATHOLL

The Moulin Hotel is in the Perthshire town of Pitlochry (known for its theater festival), near the Duke of Atholl's castle.

The hotel had a brewery when it opened in 1695, and the idea was revived for its 300th anniversary. Among its several beers is the bottle-conditioned Ale of Atholl: tawny and toffeeish, with some fruit in the finish.

**Region of origin** Central Scotland, UK

**Style** Scottish Ale

**Alcohol content** 3.6 abw (4.5 abv)

**Ideal serving temperature**
50–55° F (10–13° C)

## ORKNEY DARK ISLAND

Off the northern tip of the Scottish mainland are the Orkney Islands, where the winters are long and dark. On the main island, known simply as Orkney, is this new-generation brewery in an 1870s school building. The brewery was established in 1988 by a former pub owner and his schoolteacher wife. Its products have become widely known. Among them, Dark Island is a mahogany ale: peaty, chocolatey, creamy, and juicy.

**Region of origin** Orkney Islands, Northern Scotland, UK

**Style** Scottish Ale

**Alcohol content** 3.7 abw (4.6 abv)

**Ideal serving temperature**
50–55° F (10–13° C)

## SHERLOCK'S HOME PIPER'S PRIDE

This punning pub in a suburb of Minneapolis, Minnesota produces a classic Scottish ale, using malted oats and, in addition to hops, an earlier bittering ingredient called quassia (an extract from a tree that grows in Central and South America). The brewer is a Scot who on occasion plays the bagpipes. The ale is tawny and malt-accented, with a touch of butterscotch and a spicy-herbal balancing dryness.

**Region of origin** Midwest US

**Style** Scottish Ale

**Alcohol content** 3.7 abw (4.6 abv)

**Ideal serving temperature**
50–55° F (10–13° C)

## TOMINTOUL WILD CAT

The last syllable rhymes with owl. Tomintoul is a village at 1,164 ft (355 m) in the Grampian mountains of northern Scotland. It is known for snow-blocked roads and a malt whiskey made near the Livet River. The brewery is in a 1700s grain mill, once driven by water. Its Wild Cat ale has a full amber color; a whiskeyish aroma; a light, firm, cookielike maltiness; and a dryish finish.

**Region of origin**
Highlands, Northern Scotland, UK

**Style** Scottish Ale

**Alcohol content** 4.0 abw (5.1 abv)

**Ideal serving temperature**
50–55° F (10–13° C)

# SOCIABLE BEERS: NORTH AMERICAN ALES

THE NEW GENERATION of microbreweries in the US and Canada makes more ales than other beers. Many of their brews taste fresh and are delightfully drinkable. These new ales usually combine the appetizingly fruity, piney aromas of American hops with a light maltiness and a dry finish. For sociable drinking, try a lightish cream ale, a drier pale ale, or a rounder ESB (extra special bitter).

**Badge drinking**
*Designer labels belong to beers when they are worn at the annual Great American Beer Festival, in Denver, Colorado.*

## OLIVER ESB

A family called Oliver from Kent, England, by way of Canada, brews this ESB in Baltimore, Maryland. The Olivers' brewery and Wharf Rat pub opened in 1993. The ESB is served on hand-pumps at the pub, and in half-gallon "growlers" to go. It has an attractive, reddish-amber color and fine bead; pours with a pillowy head, leaving a good lace; has a peppery hop-and-malt aroma; a nutty palate; a quenchingly tart finish; and a late, typically appetizing dryness.

**Region of origin** Northeast US

**Style**
American Ale/Extra Special Bitter

**Alcohol content** 4.5 abw (5.6 abv)

**Ideal serving temperature**
50–55° F (10–13° C)

### JOHNS' BRONZE

BALLANTINE'S WAS ONE of a handful of ales widely known in the US before the days of the microbrewery movement. This golden, hoppy brew is such a legend that artist Jasper Johns cast it in bronze.

## CLIMAX ESB

"The name represents the point of greatest excitement," according to one of the principals of this outstanding ale brewery. Climax, one of the first new-generation breweries in the state, was established in Roselle Park, New Jersey, in 1996. Its products range from a dryish, perfumy cream ale to an India pale ale with a rooty, almost artichokelike bitterness. Between these two extremes is a fruitier, maltier, clean, soft ESB full of appetizing flavors.

**Region of origin**
Northeast US

**Style** American Ale/
Extra Special Bitter

**Alcohol content**
4.4 abw (5.5 abv)

**Ideal serving
temperature**
50–55° F (10–13° C)

## REDHOOK ESB

A name that suggests fishing, for a brewing company based in the maritime towns of Seattle, Washington, and Portsmouth, New Hampshire. Established in 1982, this was one of the first new-generation ale breweries. It introduced a winter ale in 1987 and later dubbed it ESB, pioneering that term in the US. The beer is pale for the style, and it is hop-accented in its big bouquet and appetizing dryness; but with a firm malt balance.

**Region of origin**
Pacific Northwest US

**Style**
American Ale/ESB

**Alcohol content**
4.3 abw (5.4 abv)

**Ideal serving
temperature**
50–55° F (10–13° C)

***Traditional brew***
*The small print on the label emphasizes the use of a traditional, top-fermenting ale yeast.*

## OASIS CAPSTONE ESB

Every good watering hole is an oasis, but this microbrewery and pub pushes the point with its Egyptian-style interior. The brewpub is in the college town of Boulder, Colorado. Its bottled Capstone ESB has a full reddish-amber color and fine bead; a dense head, creamy aroma, and malt accent; and satisfying flavor development. It is silky smooth, with toast and marmalade notes, and a cedary finish.

**Region of origin**
Southwest US

**Style** American Ale/
Extra Special Bitter

**Alcohol content**
4.5 abw (5.6 abv)

**Ideal serving
temperature**
50–55° F (10–13° C)

***Watchful eye***
*The thirst-making Egyptian sun god peers out from the label.*

## BRIDGEPORT ESB

The bridges of Portland, Oregon, unite a city framed by the Columbia and Willamette Rivers, both flowing from hop-growing regions. BridgePort, founded in 1984 as Columbia River Brewing, is the oldest micropub in this great city of small beers. Its ESB is perfumy and fruity, rounded off by an appetizingly dry, hoppy acidity.

**Region of origin**
Pacific Northwest US

**Style**
American Ale/ESB

**Alcohol content**
4.6 abw (5.8 abv)

**Ideal serving
temperature**
50–55° F (10–13° C)

# MOLSON SIGNATURE CREAM ALE

The Canadian giant Molson introduced its Signature range in 1993 as a rival to the tasty products being made by new-generation micros. Its Signature Cream Ale became a local speciality in British Columbia. Cream ales are traditionally pale, light in body and palate, and fruity. This ale has a perfumy aroma; a light, soft body; and flavors reminiscent of lemon jelly, drying in a "fruit gums" finish.

**Region of origin** Province of British Columbia, Canada

**Style** Cream Ale

**Alc. content** 4.1 abw (5.1 abv)

**Ideal serving temperature** 50° F (10° C)

*Form and character*
*The tall, slender, waisted glass is perhaps intended to convey a light-but-tasty character.*

# WALNUT BIG HORN BITTER

America's lively home-brewing scene traces much of its growth and sophistication to an association in Boulder, a college town in the mountains of Colorado. The town's first brewpub was established on Walnut Street in 1990 and now bottles its beers. The Western-sounding Big Horn is, true to its designation, a very English-tasting bitter. It is refreshingly drinkable, with a lightly textured maltiness; restrained, clean fruitiness; rounded with a really appetizing hop-bitterness in the finish.

**Region of origin** Southwest US

**Style** English Bitter

**Alcohol content** 4.2 abw (5.2 abv)

**Ideal serving temperature** 50–55° F (10–13° C)

# HALE'S SPECIAL BITTER

Apart from some well-regarded seasonal brews, Mike Hale makes a solid range of regulars at his microbreweries in Seattle and Spokane, Washington. Hale's Special Bitter has a big, rocky head and is dark reddish-amber. It is full of flavor: malty and rounded, with fruity notes reminiscent of glacé cherries and candied peel. It has a spritzy, dry finish. Its initials, HSB, are shared with a similar beer made by Hale's inspiration, Gale's, in Horndean, near Portsmouth, England.

**Region of origin**
Pacific Northwest US

**Style** English Bitter

**Alcohol content**
3.8 abw (4.7 abv)

**Ideal serving temperature**
50–55° F (10–13° C)

*Hale's and Gale's*
*The tankard forms an "H" for Hales, though it could equally stand for Horndean.*

# DESCHUTES BACHELOR BITTER

The Deschutes river, in Oregon, shoots over rapids and curves sharply at the town of Bend, near the ski resort of Mount Bachelor. A pub and microbrewery at Bend produce a wide range of flavorsome beers with alliterative names, and distribute them bottle-conditioned. Bachelor Bitter is big-tasting and is notably firm and assertive, with a fresh dryness of American hop flavors and clean, orangy fruitiness. The beer is also quite bitter, particularly in its lingering finish.

**Region of origin**
Pacific Northwest US

**Style** American Ale/Bitter

**Alcohol content**
4.2 abw (5.2 abv)

**Ideal serving temperature**
50–55° F (10–13° C)

# NORTH AMERICAN ALES

## ELYSIAN THE WISE ESB

The Greek word for blissful might, for the beer lover, describe the city of Seattle, Washington. The city has a good dozen small breweries and invented the notion of an "ale house." Elysian is a pub and brewery that makes extremely assertive ales with names alluding to mythical qualities. Its ESB, named The Wise, has a deep amber color; a leafy aroma; and a thick, malty palate, sweet at first, developing to an intense orange-zest bitterness.

**Region of origin** Pacific Northwest US

**Style** American Ale/ESB

**Alcohol content** 4.6 abw (5.7 abv)

**Ideal serving temperature** 50–55° F (10–13° C)

## GOOSE ISLAND HONKER'S ALE

The "island" is a neck of land near Chicago's Halsted Street nightlife area. In a competitive city where many breweries have been short-lived, Goose Island is the success of the new generation. It is both a pub and brewery, producing a wide and changing range of beers, some available in the bottle. Its principal regular brew is Honker's Ale: orangy-colored with an appetizing aroma of the hop variety Styrian Goldings; a firm, crisp body; and lively, dry, lightly fruity flavors.

**Region of origin** Midwest US

**Style** American Ale

**Alcohol content** 3.0 abw (3.8 abv)

**Ideal serving temperature** 50–55° F (10–13° C)

## GRITTY MCDUFF'S BEST BITTER

The founder of this brewery had a friend called Sandy, who was nicknamed Gritty. McDuff somehow followed. Gritty McDuff's began as a British-style pub and brewery in an old harbor warehouse in Portland, Maine. Now the beer is also bottled. The dry-tasting Best Bitter has a bright amber-tan color; a light, spritzy body; some spicy, fruity notes; and a good balance of malt and hop.

**Region of origin** Northeast US

**Style** English Bitter

**Alcohol content** 4.0 abw (5.0 abv)

**Ideal serving temperature** 50–55° F (10–13° C)

## LANG CREEK TRIMOTOR AMBER

The remote Lang Creek brewery is in a former aircraft hangar in Marion, near Kalispell, in western Montana. The brewery's founder, a hobby pilot and aviation enthusiast, honors the pioneering, three-engined 1930s passenger plane with this beer. Trimotor Amber is a deep amber ale, broadly in the style of an ESB. It is smooth, tasty, malty, and nutty, with late flavors of chocolate and leafy hop.

**Region of origin** Pacific Northwest US

**Style** American Ale/ESB

**Alcohol content** 4.2 abw (5.3 abv)

**Ideal serving temperature** 50–55° F (10–13° C)

## OTTO BROTHERS' TETON ALE

Brothers Charlie and Ernie Otto and their partner Don Frank run their brewery in a pine cabin at Wilson, in Jackson Hole, between the Teton and Gros Ventre ranges of the Rockies, in Wyoming. Here, in the Snake River Valley, the super-rich visit their weekend ranches and enjoy Teton Ale: a deep, reddish-amber brew; malty, light but textured, with suggestions of caramel, well-done toast, and applelike tannin in the finish.

**Region of origin** Pacific Northwest US

**Style** English Bitter

**Alcohol content** 3.8 abw (4.8 abv)

**Ideal serving temperature** 50–55° F (10–13° C)

## OXFORD CLASS ALE

A British diplomat's son founded this brewery in a suburb of Baltimore in 1988. It was originally called British Brewing but that name proved too colonial-sounding. It is now Oxford Brewing, and American-owned. Oxford Class Ale is in the style of an English Bitter. It has a bright, full, amber color and is light-bodied but firm, with a hoppy aroma, malty-grainy palate, and dry finish. A cask-conditioned version is available locally as Oxford's Real Ale. There has also been a maltier Special Old Bitter.

**Region of origin** Northeast US

**Style** English Bitter

**Alcohol content** 4.0 abw (5.0 abv)

**Ideal serving temperature** 50–55° F (10–13° C)

## RIVERSIDE PULLMAN PALE ALE

The river is the often-dry Santa Ana, east of Los Angeles. The town of Riverside is in orange-growing country and its pub and brewery are in the former Fruit Exchange. In more leisurely days, Riverside was an inland resort, hence names like Pullman. This Pale Ale is intended to be English in style. It has a sunny, mid-amber color; a lemony hop aroma; a firm, rounded, lightly malty body; and a very dry finish.

**Region of origin** California, US

**Style** English Pale Ale/Bitter

**Alcohol content** 4.5 abw (5.6 abv)

**Ideal serving temperature** 50–55° F (10–13° C)

## WATERLOO BREWING ED'S BEST BITTER

The famous battle was honored in the names of several American towns. This particular Waterloo, in Texas, was soon renamed Austin, after a family that settled there. It is now the state capital, home to the vast main campus of the state university, and known for its many small breweries. The Waterloo pub and brewery, a meeting place for beer enthusiasts, has touches of a 1950s cafe. Its Ed's Best Bitter is a superb, subtle brew with a minty hop aroma; soft, sweet maltiness; and a fresh, grassy finish.

**Region of origin** Southwest US

**Style** English Bitter

**Alcohol content** 3.5 abw (4.4 abv)

**Ideal serving temperature** 50–55° F (10–13° C)

# SOCIABLE BEERS: PLAIN PORTERS AND DRY STOUTS

THERE IS NO EXPERIENCE more sociable than lingering in an Irish pub over a pint of the country's famous black brew: soft, creamy, and dry as Irish humor. When the Irish writer Flann O'Brien said: "A pint of plain is your only man," he was referring to a porter of modest strength. After a few decades' absence, "plain porter" has returned to Ireland to stand alongside its stouts. Despite the term "stout," these beers are not especially full in body, or alcohol.

*Literary liquid*
*The black stuff seems to lubricate the wit in every Irishman, especially in the pubs of Dublin.*

## BURTON BRIDGE PORTER

Britain's brewing capital, the Midlands town of Burton, has, on Bridge Street, one of its livelier new-generation microbreweries with its own pub. Small enterprises like the Burton Bridge Brewery, established in 1982, reintroduced porter decades after the country's bigger brewers had dropped the style. The Burton Bridge range includes a fine porter at an easily drinkable strength. Burton Bridge Porter has a ruby-to-black color and a pillowy head. There are hints of crystal sugar in the aroma; smoky, fruity notes; and a sappy dryness in the finish.

| | |
|---|---|
| **Region of origin** | Trent Valley, England, UK |
| **Style** | Plain Porter |
| **Alcohol content** | 3.6 abw (4.5 abv) |
| **Ideal serving temperature** | 55° F (13° C) |

BURTON PORTER

A BOTTLE CONDITIONED BEER

ALC 4.5%       AC 500ml

BREWED AND BOTTLED AT

BURTON BRIDGE BREWERY

BURTON-ON-TRENT UK

BEST BY ▶ 22 FEB 1998

500ml

### THE STUFF OF DREAMS

PORTER WAS ORIGINALLY a London brew, and was hugely popular in England in the mid- and late-1700s. A porter brewery was "not a parcel of boilers and vats but the potentiality of growing rich beyond the dreams of avarice," commented the contemporary lexicographer, essayist, and critic, Dr. Samuel Johnson (*left*). He nursed a jealous passion for Hester Thrale, wife of a gentleman brewer. Johnson's extravagant phrase was intended to help the Thrales sell their porter brewery, in Southwark, London.

## CARNEGIE STARK PORTER

A Scotsman called Carnegie first brewed this beer in the 1830s, in Gothenburg, Sweden (the two countries historically have strong trading links). Doctors traditionally prescribed the porter, enriched with an egg yolk, for nursing mothers. There are two strengths, the lower of which makes more of a "session" beer. The stronger version leans towards being an imperial stout. Carnegie Stark Porter is creamy and licorice-tasting with a long, dry finish. A top-fermenting yeast is used.

**Region of origin** Sweden

**Style** Baltic Porter

**Alc. cont.** 2.8 abw (3.5 abv) and 4.4 abw (5.5 abv)

**Ideal serving temperature** 50–55° F (10–13° C)

*Vintage porter*
*Carnegie is year-dated. Each "vintage" seems slightly different, though the flavors meld with age.*

## SHEPHERD NEAME ORIGINAL PORTER

This brewery, in the county of Kent, is not far from London, the traditional home of porter. Shepherd Neame reintroduced porter in the early 1990s. Its soothing and very tasty example has hoppy and oaky, sherryish notes in its aroma; a hint of dry, rooty licorice (an ingredient); and a good malt background reminiscent of barley-sugar sweets.

**Region of origin** Southeast England, UK

**Style** Porter/Stout

**Alcohol content** 4.1 abw (5.2 abv)

**Ideal serving temperature** 50–55° F (10–13° C)

## HARVEYS 1859 PORTER

A traditional brewery in the old river port of Lewes, East Sussex. The business dates from the 1700s, and the timbered brewery from the following century. Reintroduced in 1993, this porter is based on an 1859 recipe and uses traditional brown malt. The beer has hopsack and cedar in the aroma; medicinal, bitter chocolate notes in the palate; and a powerful, roasty dryness in the finish.

**Region of origin** Southeast England, UK

**Style** Porter/Stout

**Alcohol content** 3.8 abw (4.8 abv)

**Ideal serving temperature** 50–55° F (10–13° C)

*Best bottlings*
*Harveys Porter occasionally appears in bottle-conditioned form. This is less stable but can develop great complexity.*

## OKHOTSK MILD STOUT

Close to the Okhotsk Sea, at the small town of Kitami near the east coast of Hokkaido, Japan, a pub and brewery make some delicious beers – flavorsome interpretations of classic styles. This mildly dry, very drinkable stout has a purply-black color; pours with a dense, rocky head; has an earthy hop aroma; roasted chestnuts in the palate; a creamy body; and a yogurty tartness in the finish.

**Region of origin** Hokkaido, Japan

**Style** Dry Stout

**Alcohol content** 4.0 abw (5.0 abv)

**Ideal serving temperature** 50–55° F (10–13° C)

*Mild-mannered*
*The word mild usually implies a sweetish ale. This brew is certainly mild in flavor, but a stout in style.*

# BERT GRANT'S PERFECT PORTER

Bert Grant is one of the personalities of the American brewing industry. He is an expert on hops, was a pioneer of both brewpubs and microbreweries in the US, and once used advertising seeming to take credit for human happiness. His brand name Perfect Porter is hardly modest, but the alcohol content is; despite this, the beer is astonishingly well rounded in both body and flavor, with subtle suggestions of cocoa powder, toasted nuts, and a touch of peat.

**Region of origin**
Northwest US

**Style** Plain Porter

**Alcohol content**
3.2 abw (4.0 abv)

**Ideal serving temperature**
50–55° F (10–13° C)

*Looking glass*
*Bert Grant sees himself every time he raises a glass of his own beer.*

# CATAMOUNT PORTER

The name celebrates the mountain lion, state animal of Vermont. The Catamount microbrewery began in White River Junction, Vermont, in 1987. It now has a second brewery a few miles downriver in Windsor. Catamount Porter is among the best American examples of the style. It has a fragrant, clean fruitiness of aroma; a remarkably smooth, creamy body; and a chocolaty, fruity dryness, with perhaps a hint of blackcurrant.

**Region of origin**
Northeast US

**Style** Porter/Stout

**Alcohol content**
4.2 abw (5.3 abv)

**Ideal serving temperature**
50–55° F (10–13° C)

# FISH TALE MUD SHARK PORTER

Coastal name for a brewery founded in Olympia, capital city of Washington State, in 1993. Founder Crayne Horton also offers that his star sign is Pisces and that he once kept fish. The brewery's beers are big and robust. Mud Shark Porter has a peppery aroma, with hints of pears in cream and rich, dark chocolate that are carried through in the palate. The finish is toasty, roasty, and dry.

**Region of origin**
Northwest US

**Style** Porter/Stout

**Alcohol content**
4.4 abw (5.5 abv)

**Ideal serving temperature**
50–55° F (10–13° C)

*The beer that got away*
*The small print above the illustration on the label brings the fisherman's boast to the beer-drinker.*

# BLACKSTONE ST. CHARLES PORTER

New-generation brewery and restaurant established in the mid 1990s in Nashville, Tennessee. The beers were created by star brewer Dave Miller. "Saint" Charles is the son of one of the owners. The porter that takes his name has a firm body and offers the sensation of biting into a praline filled with cream. The richness rounds into bitter chocolate. The beer is smooth, sociable, and dry enough in the finish to demand another round.

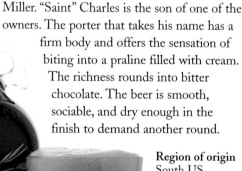

**Region of origin**
South US

**Style** Porter

**Alcohol content**
4.0 abw (5.0 abv)

**Ideal serving temperature**
50–55° F
(10–13° C)

# PLAIN PORTERS AND DRY STOUTS

## EMERSON'S LONDON PORTER

Some outstanding beers are made by the Emerson's new-generation brewery, established in 1993 in Dunedin, New Zealand. The company's London Porter is black with purply highlights, forming a dense head with good lace. It has a perfumy aroma reminiscent of a dessert with pistachio nuts and cream. The flavors start coffeeish and become rummy, with a big, rounded, dry finish. Both soothing and satisfying.

**Region of origin**
South Island, New Zealand

**Style** Porter/Stout

**Alcohol content** 3.9 abw (4.9 abv)

**Ideal serving temperature**
50–55° F (10–13° C)

## GREAT DIVIDE SAINT BRIGID'S PORTER

The continental divide is not far from Denver, Colorado, home of this brewery, but the company was conceived in the union of Brian and Tara Dunn. They married on a Saturday and started their first brew on the Sunday. Their porter is named after the 6th-century Irish saint who allegedly could turn her bathwater into beer. Saint Brigid's Porter has an earthy, sappy, rooty aroma; is light but very smooth; and has well-combined flavors of licorice and toffee. It finishes lightly creamy but dryish.

**Region of origin** Southwest US

**Style** Porter/Stout

**Alcohol content** 4.5 abw (5.6 abv)

**Ideal serving temperature**
50–55° F (10–13° C)

## HOEPFNER PORTER

The only porters made in Germany within living memory seem to have been from the now-defunct Dressler brewery of Bremen and the very active Hoepfner of Karlsruhe. After a gap of nearly two decades, Hoepfner revived its porter in 1998. The beer has a mahogany-to-black color; a smooth, toffeeish palate; and a powerful burned character in a rounded finish. The tower of Hoepfner's 1898 brewery is replicated in a lidded stein 17 in (43 cm) tall.

**Region of origin**
Baden-Württemberg, Germany

**Style** Porter/Stout

**Alcohol content** 4.6 abw (5.8 abv)

**Ideal serving temperature**
50–55° F (10–13° C)

## KALAMAZOO BREWING BELL'S PORTER

The Michigan town of Kalamazoo has a local reputation for its eccentrics. There is a café called The Eccentric at this colorful brewery, founded in 1985 by former baker and jazz disc jockey Larry Bell. The brewery makes something of a speciality of porters and stouts. Bell's Porter is full of whiskeyish, grainy flavors, with a long finish.

**Region of origin** Midwest US

**Style** Plain Porter

**Alcohol content** 4.6 abw (5.7 abv)

**Ideal serving temperature**
50–55° F (10–13° C)

## KING AND BARNES OLD PORTER

Bottle-conditioned beers have in recent years become the speciality of this family brewery, in Horsham, just across the Surrey-Sussex border, south of London. The brewery's Old Porter pours with a huge, rocky head; has a ruby-tinged, black color; a fresh, creamy aroma; a light but smooth palate; and a distinctly dry finish. When young it is cocoaish, but it develops more peppery, spicy, bitter notes with bottle age.

**Region of origin**
Southeast England, UK

**Style** Porter/Stout

**Alcohol content** 4.4 abw (5.5 abv)

**Ideal serving temperature**
50–55° F (10–13° C)

## MITCHELL'S RAVEN STOUT

Lex Mitchell, who previously worked for South African Breweries, founded Africa's first microbrewery in 1984 in Knysna, Western Cape. He has since opened Mitchell's pubs in Johannesburg and Cape Town. His smooth, firm, malty beers are unfiltered and unpasteurized. Raven Stout has a slatey black color; a creamy aroma; a rummy middle; and a hopsack, burlaplike dryness in the finish.

**Region of origin**
Western Cape, South Africa

**Style** Strong Dry Stout

**Alcohol content** 4.8 abw (6.0abv)

**Ideal serving temperature**
50–55° F (10–13° C)

## NUSSDORF SIR HENRY'S DRY STOUT

Nussdorf is on the edge of the Vienna Woods. The name means "nut village," referring not to its inhabitants but to the local walnuts. In the wine cellars of his château at Nussdorf, Baron Henrik Bachofen von Echt makes Sir Henry's Stout. With its chocolaty flavors, this stout could be over-

rich, but there is an appealing dryness in the fruity finish.

**Region of origin** Vienna, Austria

**Style** Dry Stout

**Alcohol content** 4.5 abw (5.6 abv)

**Ideal serving temperature**
50–55° F (10–13° C)

## PORTERHOUSE PLAIN PORTER

Porter as a beer style was once especially associated with Dublin. In 1996 it was restored in a brewpub called The Porterhouse, by lawyer Oliver Hughes and his publican cousin Liam LaHart. The Porterhouse is at the corner of Parliament Street and Temple Bar. Its Plain Porter has a slatey color and is light but textured in body, with a fruity dryness. The brewery also makes two outstanding stouts.

**Region of origin** Dublin, Ireland

**Style** Plain Porter

**Alcohol content** 3.4 abw (4.3 abv)

**Ideal serving temperature**
50–55° F (10–13° C)

## YELLOW ROSE VIGILANTE PORTER

The state's symbol lends a name to the Yellow Rose microbrewery in San Antonio, Texas. The brewery was established in 1994. The local sheriff seems to have awarded a star to Vigilante Porter. The beer pours with a dense head; has a light but smooth body; with dark chocolate and bitter orange flavors; and a dry, spritzy finish.

**Region of origin** Southwest US

**Style** Plain Porter

**Alcohol content** 3.5 abw (4.4 abv)

**Ideal serving temp.** 50° F (10° C)

# PARTY GREETINGS: FRUIT LAMBICS

A GLASS OF CHAMPAGNE or mimosa, a chilled chardonnay, sangria, punch, or cocktail? The welcoming drink at the barbecue, cookout, or party should look stylish and perhaps sparkling and be both refreshing and appetizing, but not too filling. Ideally, it should also be novel. The drier style of Belgian fruit beer does the job perfectly . . . especially the spritzy, tart type based on a *lambic* – a style of wheat beer fermented and matured with wild yeasts in the area around the town of Lembeek, near Brussels. Fruits are added to the maturing beer, creating both a distinct flavor and the sparkle and life of a further fermentation.

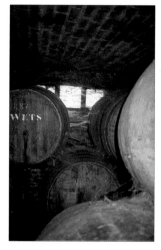

***Wild website***
*Cobwebs can house wild yeasts, in this case a blessing as these are valued ingredients in* lambic-*making.*

## FRAMBOISE BOON

The French *framboise* (raspberry) is preferred on this label to the Flemish *frambozen*. The brewer, though, is Flemish, and he makes his *lambic* beers in Lembeek itself. A brewery dating from the 1600s was due to close in 1977 when young revivalist Frank Boon acquired the business. He now produces a range of *lambic* beers at a brewery on the banks of the Zenne, the river whose valley helps define the region. The wild yeasts of the valley impart a perfumy, flowery, chardonnaylike dryness, and oak-aging offers a touch of vanilla, to balance the raspberry-jam sweetness of this fresh, delicate brew. Although the beer is lightly sweetened, a lemony acidity emerges to dry the finish. For every 1¾ pints (1 liter) of beer, 7 oz (200 g) of rasperries are used, and a small proportion of cherries. If this *lambic* is not sufficiently dry, look out for Boon's Mariage Parfait range, which contains a higher proportion of long-matured *lambics*, typically 18 months to two years old.

***Party dress***
*Champagne bottles dressed with foil offer an elegant presentation for many Belgian beers, especially* lambics. *Belgian brewers like their beers to please the eye as well as the nose and palate.*

**Region of origin**
Province of Flemish Brabant, Belgium

**Style** *Framboise/Frambozen-lambic*

**Alcohol content** 5.0 abw (6.2 abv)

**Ideal serving temperature** Store at 50–55° F (10–13° C). Lightly refrigerate for two or three hours before serving. Serve at 47° F (8° C)

## KRIEK MORT SUBITE

The small, dark, dry-tasting cherry typically used in Belgian fruit beers is called a *kriek* in Flemish. *Mort Subite*, meaning "sudden death," is a version of a dice game that was played in a famous café in Brussels. Mort Subite became the name of the café and its house beer, made in the Zenne Valley. Mort Subite contracts orchards to grow specific cherries for its beer. It is a beautifully balanced beer, with a creamy, almondy, cherry-pit note, and a lightly tart finish. Look out, also, for the drier Mort Subite Fond Gueuze, an unfiltered blend of young and old *lambics*.

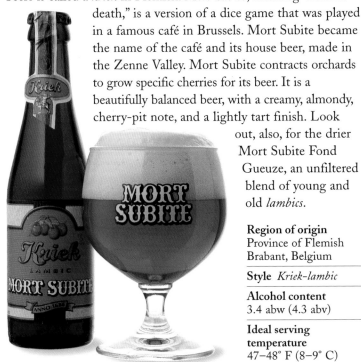

**Region of origin**
Province of Flemish Brabant, Belgium

**Style** *Kriek-lambic*

**Alcohol content**
3.4 abw (4.3 abv)

**Ideal serving temperature**
47–48° F (8–9° C)

## BELLE-VUE KRIEK

The Zenne Valley inspired the landscapes of Brueghel, but the Belle-Vue *lambic* brewery, in Molenbeek, is on the urban edge of Brussels. Its *kriek* has an oaky, irony note, as well as some currantlike fruitiness. A richer, sweeter, cherry character is usually found in Belle-Vue's Kriek Primeur, which is a different blend each year. A batch of Kriek Primeur is launched each April, using the cherries from the previous year's harvest.

**Region of origin**
Province of Flemish Brabant, Belgium

**Style** *Kriek-lambic*

**Alcohol content**
4.2 abw (5.2 abv)

**Ideal serving temperature**
47–48° F (8–9° C)

***Stellar view?***
*Belle-Vue is owned by the Belgian national group Interbrew, producer of Stella Artois.*

## TIMMERMANS KRIEK

The Timmermans brewery dates from 1888, though there may have been a brewery on the site, in Itterbeek, since 1650. The founding family still has a share in the company, though control is in the hands of John Martin's, better known for Pale Ale. Among the widely available examples of *kriek*, Timmermans' has a more obvious *lambic* character than its competitors – a delicate, fino sherry acidity – before the cherry flavors emerge. An unfiltered *gueuze* called Caveau is yet drier.

**Region of origin**
Province of Flemish Brabant, Belgium

**Style** *Kriek-lambic*

**Alcohol content**
4.0 abw (5.0 abv)

**Ideal serving temperature**
47–48° F (8–9° C)

## GUEUZE VIGNERONNE CANTILLON

The Cantillon brewery is near Brussels South station, where the Anderlecht district is a gateway to the Zenne Valley. Cantillon's very traditional *gueuze* has an addition of muscat grapes during maturation. It is very light on the tongue, and very dry indeed. A hint of grape skins in the aroma, and a touch of tannin in the finish, round the lemony flavors that are typical of the Cantillon beers. If this is just too dry, try the brewery's *framboise*, Rosé de Gambrinus.

**Region of origin** Province of Flemish Brabant, Belgium

**Style** Fruit *lambic*

**Alc. content** 4.0 abw (5.0 abv)

**Ideal serving temperature**
47–48° F (8–9° C)

# PARTY GREETINGS: FRUIT BEERS

NOT ALL FRUIT BEERS ARE BASED on the winey, *lambic*-style brews. There is a wide variety of non-*lambic* fruit beers, and several of these are dry enough to serve as a welcoming brew. They vary from Belgian cherry beers based on brown ales to French *bières de garde* with raspberries, English ales with damsons, and American ales with grapes. Many American breweries make raspberry wheat beers. Among the more unusual fruit brews is Rogue-N-Berry. This is made with the marion berry, a hybrid of raspberry, blackberry, and loganberry. The Rogue Brewery, in Newport, Oregon, devised this beer to satirize the controversial Washington mayor, Marion Berry.

Even goed... maar... véél gezonder !

Specialiteit der Brouwerij Verhaeghe Vichte

**ECHTE KRIEK en VERA**

***The real thing***
*The Echte ("Real") Kriek of the Verhaege family's brewery in Vichte, West Flanders, uses morello cherries. Its brandyish Kriek and its hoppy Vera Pils are a better tonic than a visit from the district nurse, according to this 1950s poster.*

## LIEFMANS KRIEKBIER

This cherry beer is based on a classic brown ale in the local sweet-and-sour style of Oudenaarde, in East Flanders, Belgium. Liefmans' brewery was founded in 1625, but its kettles were retired in 1991. The brown ale is now brewed in nearby Dentergem, but fermented and matured in Oudenaarde. This stage of production, using a semiwild yeast, is essential to the acidic character of the beer. The classic Liefmans' brown ale is called Goudenband (Gold Riband). In the fruit variation, the beer lies with a blend of Danish cherries and the smaller, drier, Belgian *kriek* variety for at least six months. About 30 lb (13 kg) of cherries is used for every 100 litres (180 pints) of the fruit – roughly 2 oz per pint (60 g per half litre). The beer has an excellent fruit aroma, brandyish flavors, and a balancing, tannic dryness.

***Wrapped with pride***
*At any one time, four people are engaged in wrapping the beers, each handling between 3,000 and 5,000 bottles a day. The tissue announces a triumph in a British tasting.*

**Region of origin**
Province of East Flanders, Belgium

**Style** Oudenaarde Brown Ale, with fruit

**Alcohol content** 5.2 abw (6.5 abv)

**Ideal serving temperature** 50° F (10° C)

KRIEKBIER

Liefmans
OUDENAARDE - BELGIUM

Liefmans KRIK

has been... ...tegory for
...est Beer in the...
EUROPEAN BOTT... BEERS
...drinkers at 18th Annual...arborough
...mpaign for Real Ale
Beer Festival
August 1995

Signed

Chairman

## LA CHOULETTE FRAMBOISE

The name refers to a northern French game that was an antecedent of lacrosse. La Choulette is a farmhouse brewery, founded in 1885, at Hordain, south of Valenciennes. The basic La Choulette is a strong, amber brew in the local style known as *bière de garde*. It is the basis for the *framboise*, which is made with natural raspberry extract. This ruby-colored brew has an almost blackberryish aroma and a hint of cherry brandy in a smooth, cleanly nutty, dryish palate.

**Region of origin**
Northern France

**Style** *Bière de Garde*, with fruit

**Alcohol content** 5.6 abw (7.0 abv)

**Ideal serving temperature**
50° F (10° C)

*Towering brew*
*This beer is brewed in Ostrevant, a small region centered on Valenciennes. The landmark tower of Ostrevant is a 12th-century fortification.*

## STRAWBERRY BANK DAMSON BEER

The fruit, also known as the "Damascus plum," possibly introduced by the Crusaders, has been grown for centuries in the Lyth Valley near Kendal in the Lake District of England. First used to make a dye, then for jam and homemade gin, this fruit is now used in beer. With a view to utilizing the damson crop, the beer was created at a nearby pub, the Masons' Arms, Cartmel Fell, Windermere. The beer has a winey bouquet, an intense fruitiness, and a dryish finish.

**Region of origin**
Northwest England, UK

**Style**
English Ale, with fruit

**Alcohol content**
5.6 abw (7.0 abv)

**Ideal serving temperature**
50° F (10° C)

## NEW BELGIUM OLD CHERRY ALE

This pioneering Belgian-style brewery in Fort Collins, Colorado, makes an elegant fruit beer from locally grown Montmorency "sour" pie cherries. The beer has a pale, orange-pink color; a very lightly fruity, dryish aroma; a slightly oily, barley-sugar, malt background; and a very lightly acidic, balancing dryness in the finish. The brew is based on a lightly hopped amber ale. The cherries are intended to add the tart edge.

**Region of origin**
Southwest US

**Style** American/Belgian Ale, with fruit

**Alcohol content**
4.0 abw (5.0 abv)

**Ideal serving temperature**
50° F (10° C)

*From Paris to Fort Collins*
*Montmorency cherries are named after their place of origin, near Paris, France. They are known for their bright color and sour taste.*

## PECONIC COUNTY RESERVE ALE

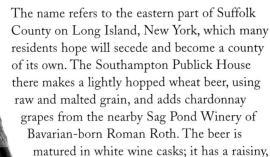

The name refers to the eastern part of Suffolk County on Long Island, New York, which many residents hope will secede and become a county of its own. The Southampton Publick House there makes a lightly hopped wheat beer, using raw and malted grain, and adds chardonnay grapes from the nearby Sag Pond Winery of Bavarian-born Roman Roth. The beer is matured in white wine casks; it has a raisiny, brandyish aroma; a crisp attack; a fresh-apple and maple palate; and a big, woody, dry finish.

**Region of origin**
Northeast US

**Style** Wheat Beer, with fruit

**Alcohol content**
5.0 abw (6.2 abv)

**Ideal serving temperature**
50° F (10° C)

# THIRST QUENCHERS: BELGIAN-STYLE WHEAT BEERS

BEERS MADE WITH A SUBSTANTIAL PROPORTION of wheat in addition to the usual barley malt are especially refreshing and quenching. Wheat can give a tartness reminiscent of plum or apple. In the Belgian style of wheat beer, there is usually also a fruitiness from the use of Curaçao orange peels, as well as citric, minty, peppery flavors from coriander seeds, and other spices. These ingredients are used in addition to the normal hops.

*Pierre Celis*
*Wheat beer revivalist*
*. . . see also page 80.*

## HOEGAARDEN SPECIALE

The country town of Hoegaarden, east of Brussels, in the heart of wheat-growing country, once had more than 30 breweries making the local wheat beer. The last closed in the 1950s, when traditional brews were being driven out by lagers, but in the 1960s enthusiast Pierre Celis revived the style. In the 1980s, his brewery was acquired by Interbrew. The regular Hoegaarden is perfumy and spicy in aroma, with a fruity palate and a honeyish background. A newer Hoegaarden Speciale, for winter, is slightly firmer and nuttier. Hoegaarden Grand Cru has the same spices, but is stronger in alcohol, and has no wheat. Hoegaarden recently revived a spiced amber ale, DAS.

**Region of origin**
Province of Flemish Brabant, Belgium

**Style**  Belgian Wheat Beer

**Alcohol content**  4.0 abw (5.0 abv)

**Ideal serving temperature**  48–50° F (9–10° C)

*Why "white"?*
*The term "White" (wit, Flemish; blanche French; Weiss or Weisse, German) implies a wheat beer.*

## CURAÇAO ORANGES

THE ISLAND OF CURAÇAO, formerly a colony of the Netherlands, is known for a sour style of orange used by Dutch liqueurists and gin-distillers and Belgian brewers. During the colonial period, the Netherlands and Belgium were one country.

## DOMUS LEUVENDIGE WITTE

Leuven is the home of the popular Stella Artois, and the biggest brewing center in Belgium. It is east of Brussels, near the wheat-growing area. Leuven has its own tradition of wheat beers, upheld by the Domus brewery and pub. Within the Domus range is Leuvendige Witte, with a fresh, orange-cream aroma; a palate surging with lemon-soda flavors; and a spicy, balancing dryness. Leuven is a university city known for its student bars, among which Domus is a classic.

**Region of origin** Province of Flemish Brabant, Belgium

**Style** Belgian Wheat Beer

**Alc. content** 4.0 abw (5.0 abv)

**Ideal serving temperature** 48–50° F (9–10° C)

## L'ABBAYE DES ROCS BLANCHE DES HONNELLES

In the French-speaking part of Belgium, "white" wheat beers are identified by the word *blanche*. This example is made by a brewery named after a farm that was once a monastery. The brewery is near Montignies-sur-Roc, between Mons and Valenciennes. Montignies-sur-Roc is on two small rivers called the Honnelles. Blanche des Honnelles is fuller in color and stronger than most wheat beers, with marmalady and very honeyish flavors.

**Region of origin** Province of Hainaut, Belgium

**Style** Belgian Wheat Beer

**Alcohol content** 4.8 abw (6.0 abv)

**Ideal serving temperature** 48–50° F (9–10° C)

## HAECHT WITBIER

The older spelling of the village of Haacht, between Brussels, Leuven, and Mechelen. This company began as a dairy in the 1800s, and later added a brewery. It uses a magnificently restored 1930s' brewhouse. The company is best known for its Pilsner-style beer. It also produces this dry, grainy, Belgian white, which in aroma and flavor emphasizes the wheat rather than the fruit and spices.

**Region of origin** Province of Flemish Brabant, Belgium

**Style** Belgian Wheat Beer

**Alcohol content** 3.8 abw (4.8 abv)

**Ideal serving temperature** 48–50° F (9–10° C)

## MATER WIT BIER

The village of Mater, which was probably established by the ancient Romans, is near Oudenaarde, on the old route from Cologne to the sea. A family named Roman has for 14 generations run this beautifully kept brewery. Like the three neighboring breweries in the Oudenaarde area, it is best known for its brown beer. It also has this enjoyable white, with the fresh flavors of homemade lemonade, sherbet, and a balancing, dry spiciness.

**Region of origin** Province of East Flanders, Belgium

**Style** Belgian Wheat Beer

**Alcohol content** 4.0 abw (5.0 abv)

**Ideal serving temperature** 48–50° F (9–10° C)

## CELIS WHITE

Having established and sold the Hoegaarden brewery in Belgium, Pierre Celis moved to the United States. He settled in Austin, Texas, where he had Belgian friends, and started a beautifully appointed brewery. His Celis White is very similar to the beer he made in Belgium, but perhaps softer, less flowery, and with more fruity acidity. The Austin brewery is operated by the Celis family but owned by Miller. Celis White is also made in Belgium under license by De Smedt.

**Region of origin**
Southwest US

**Style** Belgian-style Wheat Beer

**Alcohol content**
3.9 abw (4.9 abv)

**Ideal serving temperature**
48–50° F (9–10° C)

## DE RIDDER WIECKSE WITTE

The "wick" is the neighborhood where the De Ridder brewery stands, on the Left Bank of the Meuse (in Dutch, Maas) River, in the heart of Maastricht, the historic city in Dutch Limburg. The city, surrounded by small breweries, is known for its many cafés. In the center, De Ridder is a local landmark dating from 1852. Its wheat beer has melony fruit aromas and flavors, and a dry, gingery, rooty finish. De Ridder is owned by Heineken.

**Region of origin** Province of Limburg, the Netherlands

**Style**
Belgian-style Wheat Beer

**Alcohol content**
4.0 abw (5.0 abv)

**Ideal serving temperature**
48–50° F (9–10° C)

*A cool beer*
*The label suggests a serving temperature of 43–46° F (6–8° C), and some brewers of this style might agree, but such cold temperatures kill flavor.*

## UNIBROUE BLANCHE DE CHAMBLY

The French language is in this instance not from Belgium but from Canada. In the Montreal suburb of Chambly, the Unibroue microbrewery produces Belgian-style beers of great character. The brewery's founders include Canadian rock singer Robert Charlebois. It received some initial consultancy from the Belgian brewery Riva. Blanche de Chambly is mouth-fillingly spritzy, with big, perfumy, orange and lemon notes.

**Region of origin**
Province of Quebec, Canada

**Style**
Belgian-style Wheat Beer

**Alc. content** 4.0 abw (5.0 abv)

**Ideal serving temperature**
48–50° F (9–10° C)

## MOKU MOKU BISUCUIT WEIZEN

The phrase *Moku Moku* refers to smoke screens historically used by Ninja warriors, practitioners of martial arts in the local mountains. The brewery is near Ueno, east of Kyoto and Osaka, Japan. The beer's name alludes to biscuit malt, though this Belgian term sits oddly with the German *Weizen*. The beer has an orangy color; starts with a nutty maltiness; and finishes perfumy, fragrant, and slightly smoky. An interesting hybrid from Japan.

**Region of origin**
Honshu, Japan

**Style**
Belgian-German Wheat Beer

**Alcohol content**
3.6 abw (4.5 abv)

**Ideal serving temperature**
48–50° F (9–10° C)

# BELGIAN-STYLE WHEAT BEERS

## COORS BLUE MOON BELGIAN WHITE

The world's biggest brewery is the Coors facility in Golden, Colorado. This company is best known for very light-bodied American lagers, but it also makes several specialities, including a range under the Blue Moon label. These include a good example of a Belgian white, made with a proportion of oats. This beer, with a full color for the style, has a creamy, oily, orange-zest character, moving to a dry, light finish.

**Region of origin** Southwest US

**Style** Belgian-style Wheat Beer

**Alcohol content** 4.0 abw (5.0 abv)

**Ideal serving temperature** 48–50° F (9–10° C)

## VAN EECKE WATOU'S WIT

A statue of an unnamed brewer stands in one of the main squares of Watou, West Flanders, celebrating the town's preoccupation. This little town has no fewer than three breweries. Among them, Van Eecke is known for a golden ale dedicated to the nearby hop-growing town of Poperinge (*page 137*). Van Eecke additionally produces the notably foamy, pale, dry, herbal, flowery Watou's Wit. It also has a range of complex abbey-style beers under the rubric Het Kapittel ("The Chapter").

**Region of origin** Province of West Flanders, Belgium

**Style** Belgian Wheat Beer

**Alcohol content** 4.0 abw (5.0 abv)

**Ideal serving temperature** 48–50° F (9–10° C)

## GRAND-PLACE BLANCHE

It is possible to have a beer at a pavement café in what appears to be the Grand' Place of Brussels, while actually being inside a former sake warehouse in Nagoya, Japan. The square has been recreated with astonishing accuracy by a designer of movie sets. This version of the Grand' Place is actually a brewpub, offering a flowery golden ale, a toffeeish brown ale, and a perfumy, sweetish, very fruity *blanche*, with excellent flavor development. Grand-Place is owned by the Shirayuki sake company.

**Region of origin** Honshu, Japan

**Style** Belgian-style Wheat Beer

**Alcohol content** 4.0 abw (5.0 abv)

**Ideal serving temperature** 48–50° F (9–10° C)

## GULPENER KORENWOLF

A "corn wolf" is a hamster, a creature that gathers grain in summer and stores it for the winter. The Dutch, living in a tiny and physically vulnerable country, have an affection for all that is small, industrious, and prudent. Korenwolf is a Belgian-style wheat beer with an earthy perfume and a big, fruity attack. It is full of flavor: refreshing, satisfying, and appetizing. The beer is made by the respected Gulpener brewery near the city of Maastricht.

**Region of origin** Province of Limburg, the Netherlands

**Style** Belgian-style Wheat Beer

## DE LEEUW VALKENBURGS WIT

The name De Leeuw (as in "Leo") means The Lion, a popular heraldic name for breweries. This old-established Lion Brewery is in Valkenburg, east of Maastricht, in Dutch Limburg. The brewery, in one of the few hilly parts of the Netherlands, is particularly proud of its spring water. The *wit* named after the town is soft, malty, and gently fruity, with a dryish finish. The winter *wit* is bigger, with a suggestion of fruit pancakes.

**Region of origin** Province of Limburg, the Netherlands

**Style** Belgian-style Wheat Beer

**Alcohol content** 3.8 abw (4.8 abv)

**Ideal serving temperature** 48–50° F (9–10° C)

## RIVA DENTERGEMS WIT

A river's source originally provided the water for, and inspired the name of, this long-established, family-owned brewery in Dentergem, on the borders of West and East Flanders. Riva makes a wide variety of beers, but is well known for its Belgian white. In some countries, the brew is known as Wittekop, a reference to its big, white head. The beer is dry and cleansing, with a complex spice and fruit character, developing towards a refreshing surge of sweet lemon in the finish.

**Region of origin** Province of West Flanders, Belgium

**Style** Belgian Wheat Beer

**Alcohol content** 4.0 abw (5.0 abv)

**Ideal serving temperature** 48–50° F (9–10° C)

## STEENDONK BRABANTS WITBIER

A Belgian white made by the renowned Palm brewery in Steenhuffel, to the northwest of Brussels, and marketed jointly by the people who produce the famous, strong, golden Duvel, in nearby Breendonk. The name is a marriage of the two villages. The beer is pale and milky, spicy and dry, with cinnamon in its spicing and a melony fruit character.

**Region of origin** Province of Flemish Brabant, Belgium

**Style** Belgian Wheat Beer

**Alcohol content** 3.6 abw (4.5 abv)

**Ideal serving temperature** 48–50° F (9–10° C)

## TIMMERMANS LAMBIC WIT

The typical spicing of a Belgian wheat, but applied to a *lambic*: the style of beer given a winey taste by the use of wild yeasts. The flavors are reminiscent of light toast with lemon, orange, and ginger marmalade notes (though no ginger is used). Very crisp and refreshing. The beer is made by the *lambic* brewers Timmermans, in the traditional region of that style.

**Region of origin** Province of Flemish Brabant, Belgium

**Style** White *Lambic*

**Alcohol content** 3.6 abw (4.5 abv)

**Ideal serving temperature** 48–50° F (9–10° C)

# THIRST QUENCHERS: BERLIN-STYLE WHEAT BEERS

THE LIGHTEST AND FRESHEST-tasting thirst quenchers are the local wheat beers of Berlin, which have an intentionally sharp, sourish finish derived from the use of a lactic culture as well as a more conventional yeast. *Berliner Weisse* beer is typically sweetened with essences of fruits or herbs and often served with candy-striped straws. The beer is seen especially in the summer on the terrace cafés by the lakes of Berlin.

*The beer greener*
*Woodruff adds*
*color and flavor*
*to Berlin's brew*
*(page 83).*

## BERLINER BÜRGERBRÄU WEISSBIER

This brewery, restaurant, and beer garden is beside that beautiful lake and picnic spot, the Müggelsee, in Köpenick on the eastern edge of Berlin. It dates from 1869 and is still in the original premises, which are now officially landmarked buildings. During the communist period it produced a *Pilsner*-style beer. At that time, a very intense-tasting *Berliner Weisse* for the East was made at a brewery, now closed, in the Pankow district. After reunification, the Köpenick brewery was acquired by the beer-making Häring family of Bavaria. They have greatly restored the brewery, introducing a wide range of beers, including the first new *Weissbier* in Berlin for many decades. (The city now has three *Weissbiers*, but it once had 700). This beer has a crisp, toasty aroma with a hint of hopsack; a light, smooth, firm body; and a late, lemony tartness. It is a very restrained interpretation of the style, a little stronger than the usual low-alcohol *Berliner Weissbier*.

| | |
|---|---|
| **Region of origin** | Berlin, Northern Germany |
| **Style** | *Berliner Weisse* |
| **Alcohol content** | 3.8 abw (4.8 abv) |
| **Ideal serving temperature** | 48–54° F (9–12° C) |

*The meaning of Weisse*
*As in Belgium (page 78), so in Germany, the term "white" (Weisse) is sometimes used to describe wheat beers. South German brewers also use the term Weizen ("wheat").*

## BERLINER KINDL WEISSE

One of the two principal brewing companies in Berlin is Kindl, founded in 1872 and now part of a national group with Binding of Frankfurt. The brewery is in Neukölln, a blue-collar residential district. Entered via a monastic-looking arch, it has a handsome, 1950s copper brewhouse set into marble tiles. The *Weisse*, most readily available in the summer, is firm, carbonic, and fruity, with

a cutting hit of sourness. It is at the low strength that is usually associated with this refreshing style of beer.

**Region of origin**
Berlin, Northern Germany

**Style** *Berliner Weisse*

**Alcohol content**
2.0 abw (2.5 abv)

**Ideal serving temperature**
48–54° F (9–12° C)

## SCHULTHEISS BERLINER WEISSE

The city's other big brewer, established in 1842 and now part of the national group Brau und Brunnen. Since the reunification of Germany, Schultheiss has closed its breweries in Kreuzberg and Spandau and moved production to a brewery dating from 1902, at Hohenschönhausen, in the former East Germany. Its *Berliner Weisse* has a secondary fermentation in the bottle, resulting in a

more complex character. It is flowery and pollenlike, with hints of celery and a lemony finish.

**Region of origin**
Berlin, Northern Germany

**Style** *Berliner Weisse*

**Alcohol content**
3.0 abw (3.7 abv)

**Ideal serving temperature**
48–54° F (9–12° C)

## BERLINER WEISSE & WALDMEISTER

Woodruff, the "master of the woods," is a small herb (*Galium odoratum*) which flourishes in moist soil and temperate climates. It

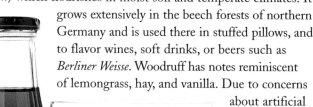

grows extensively in the beech forests of northern Germany and is used there in stuffed pillows, and to flavor wines, soft drinks, or beers such as *Berliner Weisse*. Woodruff has notes reminiscent of lemongrass, hay, and vanilla. Due to concerns

about artificial ingredients, woodruff has recently lost ground to *Himbeer* (raspberry) syrup as a flavoring for *Berliner Weisse*.

**Green party**
*The woodruff itself is natural, but additives to enhance the aroma and coloring worry some consumers.*

## BERLINER WEISSE & HIMBEER

"Beer" in this instance means "berry." The addition of raspberry syrup to *Berliner Weisse* is reminiscent of the way in which Münster *Altbier* is laced with soft fruits. Other fruits, wine, or liqueurs such as *Kümmel* are also sometimes added in Berlin. Mixtures like this may be made by the drinker or bartender, but not by the brewer, under the German Beer Purity Law. A brewer who adds such ingredients is not permitted to call the end result

beer. If brewed in Germany, a Belgian raspberry or cherry brew would have to be called a flavored alcoholic drink.

**More than saucer size**
*The king-sized champagne saucer has long been established as the most typical glass for Berliner Weisse.*

# THIRST QUENCHERS: SOUTH GERMAN WHEAT BEERS

THE MOST WIDELY AVAILABLE summer refreshers from Germany are the wheat beers associated with the area around Munich, but also made throughout Bavaria, the "rival" southern state Baden-Württemberg, and throughout the country as a whole. As well as a quenching tartness, these beers often have flavors reminiscent of apples, plums, bananas, bubblegum, and cloves, a result of the wheat's interaction with the region's local yeasts. The examples shown on these two pages are of filtered wheat beers, known as *Kristall Weizen.*

## WEIHENSTEPHANER KRISTALL WEISSBIER

The world's oldest brewery is widely believed to be at Weihenstephan (Sacred Stephen), on a hillside near Freising, 15 miles (25 km) north of Munich. Benedictine monks established a community on this hillside in at least 725 AD and were growing hops there by 768 AD. The first specific reference to brewing on the site is from 1040. Today's brewery and beer restaurant share former monastery buildings with the world's best-known university faculty of brewing. The beer is also bottled for general sale. The Weihenstephan brewery makes a wide range of products but is especially known for its wheat beers. Its *Kristall Weissbier* pours with a huge head; has a very fresh aroma; and rich, very fruity, juicy flavors. Some tasters have found suggestions of mango; there are certainly banana flavors and perhaps blackcurrant. A rival local brewery, Hofbräuhaus Freising, dating from at least the 1100s, also makes very fruity wheat beers.

| | |
|---|---|
| **Region of origin** | Upper Bavaria, Germany |
| **Style** | *Kristall Weisse/Weizen* |
| **Alcohol content** | 4.3 abw (5.4 abv) |
| **Ideal serving temperature** | 48–54° F (9–12° C) |

*The white vase*
*The vase-shaped glass is traditional for the style. The terms* Weissbier *(white beer) and* Weizenbier *(wheat beer) are used interchangeably. There is no difference.*

## CUTTING THE THIRST

THE REFRESHING character of South German wheat beers is sometimes heightened by a lemon-slice garnish. In Germany, this is more likely with the filtered type of wheat beer than the sedimented version. This custom has declined in Germany in recent years, but has become popular in the US.

## FRANZISKANER KRISTALLKLAR WEISSBIER

A Franciscan monastery brewery founded in Munich in 1363, subsequently acquired by the famous Bavarian beer-making family Sedlmayr and subsumed into their company, Spaten. Founded in 1397, Spaten uses the Franziskaner name for its wheat beers. This "crystal clear" version is very aromatic, with hay and apples in the bouquet; quenchingly fruity, with hints of sherbet lemon sweets, and developing banana flavors.

**Region of origin**
Upper Bavaria, Germany

**Style** *Kristall Weisse/Weizen*

**Alcohol content** 4.0 abw (5.0 abv)

**Ideal serving temperature**
48–54° F (9–12° C)

## MAISEL'S WEISSE KRISTALLKLAR

This Bayreuth brewery, one of several in Bavaria owned by families named Maisel, is known to some beer lovers for an ale-like speciality called *Dampfbier* (steam beer), but has

in recent years given more emphasis to its wheat beers. Its *Kristall Weisse* has a very fresh fruitiness of aroma; flavors of lemon pith or zest; and an extremely refreshing, crisp finish, like biting into an ice-cream sandwich.

**Region of origin**
Franconia, Bavaria, Germany

**Style** *Kristall Weisse/Weizen*

**Alcohol content** 4.2 abw (5.2 abv)

**Ideal serving temperature**
48–54° F (9–12° C)

***Star brewery***
*Traditionally, brewers displayed a star on the label of a new beer. This symbol of brewing is universal, but especially used in Franconia.*

## LAMMSBRÄU KRISTALL WEIZEN

Organic beers are the speciality of this brewery, which dates from at least 1628. The brewery is in the pencil-producing town of Neumarkt, in a valley 25 miles (40 km) southeast of Nuremberg. Lammsbräu gets organic barley and hops from local farmers. Its wide range of beers includes a distinctive *Kristall Weizen*, which has a very fresh hop character, a creamy malt accent, and a cherryish fruitiness.

**Region of origin**
Franconia, Bavaria, Germany

**Style** *Kristall Weisse/Weizen*

**Alc. content** 4.1 abw (5.1 abv)

**Ideal serving temperature**
48–54° F (9–12° C)

## SCHÖFFERHOFER KRISTALLWEIZEN

In Kassel, in the state of Hesse, this brewery makes a wheat beer for its parent company, the national group Binding of Frankfurt. The original brewery site was the home of Peter Schöffer, a pioneering printer from the same enterprise as Johann Gutenberg. The Schöfferhofer *Kristall Weizen* is very dry with a plummy, damsonlike fruitiness and a suggestion of grapefruit zest in the finish. Schöfferhofer is one of the more widely available examples outside Germany.

**Region of origin** Hesse, Germany

**Style** *Kristall Weisse/Weizen*

**Alcohol content** 4.0 abw (5.0 abv)

**Ideal serving temperature**
48–54° F (9–12° C)

# THIRST QUENCHERS: GERMAN-STYLE HEFEWEIZEN

THE MOST FASHIONABLE BREW with the youth in Germany in recent years has been the unfiltered, cloudy, yeast-sedimented version of the southern wheat beer. This is sometimes labelled as being *mit Hefe* (with yeast). The same style is indicated by the terms *Hefe-Weisse* or, more often, *Hefeweizen*, either hyphenated or as one word. This type of beer is often served with a morning snack of bread and veal sausages. Bavarians call it a "breakfast beer," because it is light, cleansing, and digestible.

## SCHNEIDER WEISSE

This brewery is thought to have specialized continuously in wheat beer since 1607. The present owners, the Schneider family, have been making wheat beer in their own right since 1872. They had a brewery in the street known as the Tal, in the center of Munich; after World War II they moved into their current historic brewery, north of the city at Kelheim on the Danube. The Schneider wheat beers are among the best examples of the clove-tasting, spicy, full-flavored style. The principal version, Schneider Weisse, is a darkish interpretation of the *Hefeweizen* style. It is lively, with fruity complexity, maltiness, almondy nuttiness, and clovey notes.

| | |
|---|---|
| **Region of origin** | Upper Bavaria, Germany |
| **Style** | *Hefeweizen* |
| **Alcohol content** | 4.4 abw (5.5 abv) |
| **Ideal serving temperature** | 48–54° F (9–12° C) |

**Still foaming in Munich**
*The building depicted on the label is the premises of the Munich beer restaurant. Specialities include offal dishes such as lung.*

### WEISSE: THE BEER AND THE SAUSAGE

IN MUNICH, THE SEDIMENTED STYLE of wheat beer is often served with veal sausages (*Weisswurst*) and sweet Bavarian mustard. Besides veal, the sausages may contain tiny amounts of beef and bacon, parsley, chives, and onion or lemon. This dish is never served after noon.

## UNERTL WEISSBIER

A flavorsome, traditionally made range of wheat beers is produced by the brewery of the Unertl family, in the dairy-farming town of Haag, 30 miles (48 km) east of Munich. The principal beer is in *Hefeweizen* style, turbid and full in color, but not identified as being dark. It has a juicy, toffee-apple character and a smoky, appetizing dryness. It is offered at the brewery's beer garden with bread and pork drippings (*Griebenschmalz*).

**Region of origin**
Upper Bavaria, Germany

**Style** *Hefeweizen*

**Alc. content** 3.8 abw (4.8 abv)

**Ideal serving temperature**
48–54° F (9–12° C)

## OBERDORFER WEISSBIER

One of the more widely available examples of the style in export markets. The brewery derives its name from its home town, Marktoberdorf, ("the Market of the Upper Village"), which is situated in green, rolling countryside about halfway between Munich and Lake Constance. It traces its history to a tavern in the 1500s. Oberdorfer Weissbier is lively and very light, with a perfumy, bubblegum character.

**Region of origin**
Upper Bavaria, Germany

**Style** *Hefeweizen*

**Alc. content** 3.9 abw (4.9 abv)

**Ideal serving temperature**
48–54° F (9–12° C)

## TUCHER HELLES HEFE WEIZEN

Founded as a wheat-beer brewery in 1672, and for a time owned by Bavaria's royal family. The Tucher family took over in 1855, and the brewery has had several owners since. This Nuremberg brewery again became a family business in 1994, when Inselkammer, the Bavarian brewing dynasty, took an interest. Its *Hefeweizen* has a firm background with sweet apple flavors, moving to a spicy, dry, crisp finish.

**Region of origin**
Franconia, Bavaria, Germany

**Style** *Hefeweizen*

**Alc. content** 4.2 abw (5.3 abv)

**Ideal serving temperature**
48–54° F (9–12° C)

## SCHEIDMANTEL HEFE WEISSE

Founded by the Scheidmantel family in 1834, in Coburg, seat of the family that produced many of Europe's royals. The town's fortress provides a dramatic backdrop to the brewery. Today's brewery dates from the start of the 20th century and still has the lakes that provided ice for lagering until the 1950s. Scheidmantel Hefe Weisse is smooth, orangy, and lemony.

**Region of origin**
Franconia, Bavaria, Germany

**Style** *Hefeweizen*

**Alcohol content**
4.1 abw (5.1 abv)

**Ideal serving temperature**
48–54° F (9–12° C)

# PINKUS MÜLLER HEFE WEIZEN

Such has been the success of South German wheat beers that many northern breweries have devised their own examples of this style. In Münster, the Pinkus Müller pub and brewery has a *Weizen* that is distinctly its own. The beer has a typical southern balance of wheat to barley malt, but a northern yeast character: flowery, dry, and slightly acidic. A smooth, delicate, and appetizing beer.

**Region of origin**
Münster, North Rhine-Westphalia, Germany

**Style** *Hefeweizen*

**Alc. content** 4.2 abw (5.2 abv)

**Ideal serving temperature**
48–54° F (9–12° C)

# SÜNNER HEFEWEIZEN

The northern brewery Sünner is better known for the *Kölschbier* it makes in its home town of Cologne, but it also has a *Hefeweizen*. This brew has a flowery, perfumy aroma; a smooth, soft, melony body; a light bubblegum character; and a leafy finish. The label shows the smart brewery with its battlemented gables. In the central window, the brew-kettle is clearly visible.

**Region of origin**
Cologne, North Rhine-Westphalia, Germany

**Style** *Hefeweizen*

**Alc. content** 3.8 abw (4.9 abv)

**Ideal serving temperature**
48–54° F (9–12° C)

# HERRENHÄUSER WEIZEN BIER

This Hanover brewery, opened in 1868, is known for its Pilsner-style beer, including a kosher version. Its home state of Lower Saxony may have produced sourer, more northern styles of wheat beer in the distant past, but this recent example is broadly in the southern style. It has a sweetish, spicy aroma; a smooth, faintly syrupy palate; and a lightly tart finish. A field of wheat is vividly depicted on the label.

**Region of origin** Hanover, Lower Saxony, Germany

**Style** *Hefeweizen*

**Alc. content** 4.4 abw (5.5 abv)

**Ideal serving temperature**
48–54° F (9–12° C)

# UERIGES WEIZEN

Most Düsseldorf *Altbier* breweries have long specialized in their hometown style, some to the exclusion of any other. The classic old-town brewpub *Zum Uerige* remains the bedrock of *Altbier*, but has in recent years made a concession to the fashion for wheat beers with its Ueriges Weizen. Made with the *Altbier* yeast, and thus rather northern in style, it has a good, clean, malt background, and is light, flowery, gingery, and very crisp, with a minerally dryness in the finish.

**Region of origin**
Düsseldorf, North Rhine-Westphalia, Germany

**Style** *Hefeweizen*

**Alcohol content** 3.6 abw (4.5 abv)

**Ideal serving temperature**
48–54° F (9–12° C)

## GAMBRINUS BÍLÉ

The name Gambrinus is probably a corruption of Jan Primus, the first duke of Flanders and legendary king of beer. The reference crops up all over the beer world, but Jan Primus did marry into Bohemian royalty, and this Gambrinus brewery is in Pilsen in the Czech Republic. It occupies a site adjoining the Urquell brewery. Like its neighbor, Gambrinus is known for a beer in the Pilsner style. In recent years it has also added this perfumy, peachy, tart, light wheat beer.

**Region of origin** Pilsen, Bohemia, Czech Republic

**Style** *Hefeweizen*

**Alcohol content**
4.1 abw (5.1 abv)

**Ideal serving temperature**
48–54° F (9–12° C)

## SISSONS WISE GUY WEISSBIER

Actors between roles are often to be found tending bar; Hugh Sisson was able to do so in his family's tavern in Baltimore. In 1989 a brewery was added, initially making ales and more recently this punning ("Wise") *Weisse*. The beer has a lemony fruitiness. It begins with hints of lemon curd; moves to a pithlike character; and finishes with a suggestion of cloves, nuts, smokiness, and a more grainy note. A Weihenstephan yeast is used.

**Region of origin**
Mid Atlantic US

**Style** *Hefeweizen*

**Alcohol content**
3.3 abw (4.1 abv)

**Ideal serving temperature**
48–54° F (9–12° C)

## MICHELOB HEFEWEIZEN

The world's biggest brewing company, and producer of American Budweiser, has in recent years experimented with a wide range of specialities, including dark lagers, bock beers, very hoppy ales, porters, and several wheat beers. In the last category, the one that seems to have become established is under the "super-premium" brand Michelob. This *Hefeweizen* is quite full in color; freshly aromatic; fruity and sherbety; with a suggestion of banana toffee.

**Region of origin**
Midwest US

**Style** *Hefeweizen*

**Alc. content** 4.0 abw (5.0 abv)

**Ideal serving temperature**
48–54° F (9–12° C)

## TABERNASH WEISSE

The town of Tabernash, west of Denver, Colorado, is named after a Native American chief of the Ute nation. This name also attaches to a range of beers produced in Colorado, at Longmont. One of its creators studied brewing at Weihenstephan, and later wrote a book on wheat beers. Tabernash has a good nutmeg, clovey spiciness in the aroma; is quite sweet; and develops very good fruit flavors, especially banana.

**Region of origin**
Southwest US

**Style** *Hefeweizen*

**Alcohol content**
4.4 abw (5.5 abv)

**Ideal serving temperature**
48–54° F (9–12° C)

**White mountains**
*The snow-capped mountains on the label of this "white" beer are the Rockies. They dominate this part of Colorado, which is dense with small breweries.*

# THIRST QUENCHERS: GERMAN DARK WHEAT BEERS

ONE OF THE LESSER-KNOWN but most flavorsome brew styles is the dark version of the South German wheat beer. This type of beer combines the toffeeish lusciousness of dark malts with the fruity sharpness of wheat and the spiciness of Bavarian top-fermenting yeasts. These beers are as toothsome as candy apples. Served cool, they are a quencher for late spring or early fall. They are also delicious as dessert beers, with fruity or toffeeish dishes. The beers are sometimes identified as black (*Schwarze*) or, more traditionally, dark (either *Dunkel, Dunkle*, or *Dunkles*, depending upon the grammar) wheat (*Weizen*). Often, they are served with a sediment of yeast (*Hefe*).

**Weeping Radish . . .**
*. . . is a brewery in Manteo, North Carolina, that in the fall produces an appleish, strong, dark wheat beer, at 4.8 abw (6.0 abv).*

## MÖNCHSHOF KAPUZINER SCHWARZE HEFEWEIZEN

The "Monk's Court" range of beers date from a Capuchin friary that was brewing in the 1300s in Kulmbach in northern Bavaria. Today, Kulmbach has two major breweries, Reichelbräu and EKU, under the same ownership; the latter brews the Mönchshof beers. The Schwarze Hefeweizen is a very flavorsome beer, with vanilla aromas and flavors and some banana notes, drying into treacle toffee and a hint of cloves. Kulmbach is known both for dark and strong brews, and makes a greater volume of beer per head of population than any other town in Germany. It has 30,000 people and produces 281,690,141 pints (1.6 m hectoliters) of beer per year, that is, 5,300 liters (9,390 pints) per person.

| | |
|---|---|
| **Region of origin** | Franconia, Bavaria, Germany |
| **Style** | Dark Wheat Beer |
| **Alcohol content** | 4.3 abw (5.4 abv) |
| **Ideal serving temperature** | 48–54° F (9–12° C) |

**Black is beautiful**
*"Black" lagers became fashionable in Germany when examples from the East were rediscovered after the Berlin Wall tumbled. Mönchshof had long made a black lager, and now has this almost ebony wheat beer.*

## FRANZISKANER DUNKEL HEFE-WEISSBIER

The Franciscan strand in the heritage of the Spaten brewing company is celebrated by a range of light but tasty wheat beers, including this version. Like several other brewers, Spaten-Franziskaner uses the contradictory conjunction of "dark" and "white" in its name for this style. This brew has a toffeeish malt aroma, and a creamy, grainy palate. It finishes with some spiciness, suggesting cinnamon and pepper.

**Region of origin**
Munich, Upper Bavaria, Germany

**Style** Dark Wheat Beer

**Alcohol content** 4.0 abw (5.0 abv)

**Ideal serving temperature**
48–54° F (9–12° C)

## HB SCHWARZE WEISSE

The royal family of Bavaria maintained a monopoly on the brewing of wheat beers from the 1600s to the early 1800s. The *Hofbräuhaus* (Royal Court Brewery) of Munich once specialized in the style. It has promoted its own examples since the revival of interest in wheat beers in the late 1970s. This one is very lively, with spicy (licoricelike), chewy malt flavors; treacle toffee in the middle; and a grainy, slightly tannic (green apple) finish.

**Region of origin** Munich, Upper Bavaria, Germany

**Style** Dark Wheat Beer

**Alcohol content**
4.1 abw (5.1 abv)

**Ideal serving temperature**
48–54° F (9–12° C)

## HOPF DUNKLE WEISSE

Hans Hopf, owner of this brewery, almost certainly owes his surname to the hop plant. As chance would have it, he specializes in wheat beer, a style that is usually only lightly hopped. His Dunkle Weisse has a hint of hop in the bouquet, along with some fresh pear and banana. It is a lively beer, firm and smooth, with a restrained dryness, and a quenching, refreshing finish. The brewery is located in Miesbach, which is approximately 35 miles (56 km) south of Munich.

**Region of origin**
Upper Bavaria, Germany

**Style** Dark Wheat Beer

**Alc. content** 4.0 abw (5.0 abv)

**Ideal serving temperature**
48–54° F (9–12° C)

## HERRNBRÄU HEFE-WEISSBIER DUNKEL

The Beer Purity Law was announced at Ingolstadt in 1516, now the home of the Herrnbräu brewery. At one stage it was against the law for a brewer in the town to fail to meet his quotas. Even so, a road had to be built specially to bring beer in to Ingolstadt from nearby Kelheim. Today's dark wheat beer has a lightly nutty sweetness, chocolaty flavors, and a flowery dryness reminiscent of violets.

**Region of origin** Upper Bavaria

**Style** Dark Wheat Beer

**Alc. content** 4.2 abw (5.3 abv)

**Ideal serving temperature**
48–54° F (9–12° C)

# THIRST QUENCHERS: WHEAT ALES

WHEAT GIVES A HINT of quenching tartness, and a definite crispness, even to beers made with conventional ale yeasts. Wheat ales are a new style, introduced primarily in Britain and the US in recent years. They are intended as a summery refresher that is easily drinkable but has some character. Most have a pale, gold, or bronze color and a modest alcohol content. They are often appreciated by the consumer wishing to find a more interesting step up from a light or "premium" lager.

*Pigs and pints . . .*
*. . . personify the Loaded Hog chain of brewpubs in New Zealand.*

## KING & BARNES WHEAT MASH

Once a purely local brewery in Horsham, Sussex, King & Barnes, which traces its origins to 1800, has in recent years won a far wider reputation by developing a range of bottle-conditioned speciality brews. Some are seasonal, others produced year-round. Several employ unusual grains (one of the best contains rye), others feature specific hop varieties (notably one with Liberty), or use herbs. Wheat Mash is usually available in April. The term "mash" refers to the blending of the grains with the brewing water. This beer contains 40 percent wheat (the remainder being barley malt), is hopped with the Goldings variety, and is fermented with the brewery's clean, dry, two-strain ale yeast. The result is a firm, grainy brew, as crisp as a cracker; with a late, wheaty, lemony, perfumy tartness. Other beers include an outstanding pale ale, called Festive, and a Christmas brew.

**Region of origin** Southeast England

**Style** Wheat Ale

**Alcohol content** 3.6 abw (4.5 abv)

**Ideal serving temperature** 50–58° F (10–14° C)

*Handle with care*
*The beer should be stored for a day or two before use, to let the yeast settle, and handled gently when the beer is to be served. The neck label makes this point.*

## HOPBACK THUNDERSTORM

Having been very successful with a seasonal beer called Summer Lightning, this Salisbury brewery in 1997 paid its further respects to the unpredictability of British weather by adding a wheat ale identified as Thunderstorm. This bottle-conditioned beer is made with 50 percent wheat and hopped entirely with the variety Progress. It has a light but firm, juicy malt background; the faintest hint of banana yeastiness; long, very dry, lemon-zest and juniper hop flavors; and a crisp finish.

**Region of origin**
Southern England

**Style** Wheat Ale

**Alcohol content**
4.0 abw (5.0 abv)

**Ideal serving temperature**
Store: 50–58° F (10–14° C)
Serve at 50° F (10° C)

*Nectar of the Gods*
*The ancient Roman god of drink, Bacchus, appears on all of this brewer's labels.*

## ANDERSON VALLEY HIGH ROLLERS WHEAT BEER

The wine-growing Anderson Valley, in Mendocino County, California, also has an outstanding brewery. This was established in 1987, on the site of the early 1900s Buckhorn Saloon at Boonville. A wide range of brews includes High Rollers Wheat Beer, named after the hills that seal off the valley. This beer has an emphatically fruity bouquet; a good malt background; flavors reminiscent of sweet apple juice; and a very crisp finish.

**Region of origin**
California, US

**Style** Wheat Ale

**Alcohol content**
4.2 abw (5.3 abv)

**Ideal serving temperature**
50° F (10° C)

## PYRAMID WHEATEN ALE

The name alludes to a pyramid-shaped peak in the Cascade Mountains. Pyramid and its brother brewery Thomas Kemper now share premises in Seattle, with an additional brewpub at Berkeley, California. The brewery began in Kalama, Washington, in 1984, and pioneered the idea of a wheat brew made with an ale yeast. This unusual approach was signaled in the odd name Wheaten Ale.

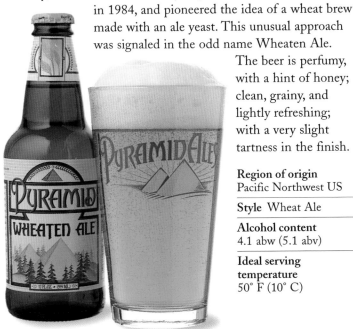

The beer is perfumy, with a hint of honey; clean, grainy, and lightly refreshing; with a very slight tartness in the finish.

**Region of origin**
Pacific Northwest US

**Style** Wheat Ale

**Alcohol content**
4.1 abw (5.1 abv)

**Ideal serving temperature**
50° F (10° C)

## SAINT ARNOLD KRISTALL WEIZEN

Two different saints called Arnold are patrons of Belgian and French beermakers, and either sits oddly with the German term

*Kristall Weizen.* What the Saint Arnold brewery offers under this name is, in fact, a Wheat Ale. It is a light, perfumy beer; firm and smooth; with hints of vanilla; a very slight, sweet-orange fruitiness; and a crisp finish. Saint Arnold, a well-regarded microbrewery, was founded in 1994, in Houston, Texas. The brewery also makes amber and brown ales.

**Region of origin** Southwest US

**Style** Wheat Ale

**Alc. content** 3.9 abw (4.9 abv)

**Ideal serving temperature**
50° F (10° C)

# THIRST QUENCHERS: FLEMISH "SWEET AND SOUR" RED ALES

THE FLEMISH PROVINCES of Belgium, particularly West Flanders, produce a range of reddish-brown ales that are curiously sharp and wonderfully refreshing. They can shock at the first encounter, but once enjoyed they are forever appreciated by the lover of characterful beer. The classic of the style, Rodenbach, has a growing following in Britain, the US, and Japan. The best of these beers contain sweet, reddish, Vienna-style barley malts, and gain color, lactic acidity, and vinegary fruitiness from long periods in magnificent ceiling-high oak tuns.

*It's wine! . . .*
*. . . announced this 1930s poster. A tannic, acidic Italian wine, perhaps?*

## RODENBACH

During Austrian rule in Belgium, the first Rodenbach arrived from the Rhineland as a military doctor, and later married into a Flemish family. In 1820, a Rodenbach bought a brewery, and the family has been involved in the present one, in Roeselare, since 1836. With nearly 300 fixed wooden vessels, it is one of the world's most unusual breweries. The basic Rodenbach is a blend of 75 percent "young" beer (matured in metal tanks for four to five weeks) and 25 percent aged brew (more than two years in wood). It emerges with a fruity perfume; passion fruit, iron, and oakiness in the palate; and a late, puckering tartness. Grand Cru, a bottling of the aged version only, is clean and sharp, with a sour-cream acidity. A version sweetened with cherry essence is called Rodenbach Alexander.

**Region of origin**
Province of West Flanders, Belgium

**Style** Flemish Red/Brown

**Alcohol content** 4.0 abw (5.0 abv)

**Ideal serving temperature** 48–55° F (9–13° C)

### THE RODENBACH DYNASTY

THIS STATUE IN ROESELARE commemorates author Albrecht Rodenbach, who wrote in Flemish. Another author in the family, Georges, preferred French. Politician Alexander was active in Belgium's independence movement. Constantine, ambassador to Greece, is buried in front of the Parthenon.

# PETRUS OUD BRUIN

In the Petrus range, this reddish-brown brew in the Flemish style is the one that at least superficially resembles the world-famous Pétrus wine. It is a complex brew: it has a tannic aroma and a very smooth palate, with a clean, toffee-like maltiness, and hints of chocolate and cinnamon-dusted pears. This is from the De Brabandere brewery, of Bavikhove, near Kortrijk (in French, Courtrai).

**Region of origin** Province of West Flanders, Belgium

**Style** Flemish Red/Brown

**Alc. content** 4.4 abw (5.5 abv)

**Ideal serving temperature** 48–55° F (9–13° C)

*Vintage Petrus*
*The wooden vessels in which this beer ages are laid horizontally. They held white wine and Calvados before being installed at the De Brabandere brewery.*

# VERHAEGHE VICHTENAAR

The Verhaeghe family, of Vichte, near Kortrijk, have been brewing since the 1500s, originally in a château farmhouse brewery. Their entry in the local style pours with a huge, rocky head. It is one of the sweeter examples, but lively and layered, with notes of Madeira, vanilla, oak, iron, and the acidity of a fresh apple. A stronger companion brew called Duchesse de Bourgogne has a similar character but with distinct chocolate and cream flavors.

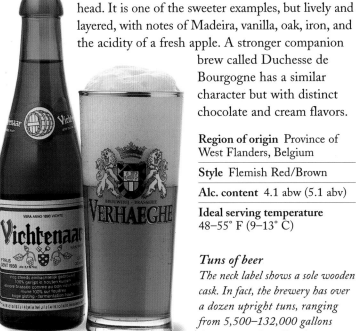

**Region of origin** Province of West Flanders, Belgium

**Style** Flemish Red/Brown

**Alc. content** 4.1 abw (5.1 abv)

**Ideal serving temperature** 48–55° F (9–13° C)

*Tuns of beer*
*The neck label shows a sole wooden cask. In fact, the brewery has over a dozen upright tuns, ranging from 5,500–132,000 gallons (250–6,000 hectoliters).*

# VAN HONSEBROUCK BACCHUS

The orgiastic name is one of several extrovert brands from the Van Honsebrouck brewery, of Ingelmunster, West Flanders. The beer has a vinegary bouquet; a touch of caramel; an oaky, woody palate; and a late, light, spritzy acidity. Wood aging is used. An East Flanders brewery, Van Steenberge, of Ertevelde, has an entry called Bios, from the Greek word for life. This has a slightly syrupy start and a late, lactic dryness.

**Region of origin** Province of West Flanders, Belgium

**Style** Flemish Red/Brown

**Alc. content** 3.6 abw (4.5 abv)

**Ideal serving temperature** 48–55° F (9–13° C)

*Leonine label*
*The black lion on the label is the symbol of Flanders. The brewery's home town was once the seat of the Count of Flanders.*

# ALKEN-MAES ZULTE

This beer was originally produced at a brewery founded in 1891, called Anglo-Belge, at Zulte, in East Flanders. Anglo-Belge originally also made vinegar and distilled spirits, and was known for its stout. It closed in 1989, and the beer is now made at the Alken-Maes brewery in Jumet, near Charleroi. The uprooted Zulte is the most caramelly example of the style, grainy, with a fruity dryness and sharpness.

**Region of origin** Province of Hainaut, Belgium

**Style** Flemish Red/Brown

**Alc. content** 3.8 abw (4.7 abv)

**Ideal serving temperature** 48–55° F (9–13° C)

*The Zulte uprooting*
*In 1977, the brewery in Zulte was acquired by Kronenbourg. In 1982 the French company bought Alken and in 1988 Maes, which had owned the Union brewery in Jumet since 1978.*

# RESTORATIVES: BLACK BEERS

THE MOST RECENT BEER FASHION in Germany has been for brews described as black (*schwarz*), a style once thought especially suitable for nursing mothers. Black beers have been rediscovered in Germany since reunification and are particularly associated with the old eastern states, especially Thuringia. The traditions of black beers and very dark lagers merged in northern Bavarian towns such as Kulmbach and Erlangen. Originally, black beers were very dark ales, and they retained their color after lager yeasts were introduced. German brewers introduced black beers to Japan more than 100 years ago, and the tradition flourishes there more strongly than ever. Typically, these beers have a bitter-chocolate character.

## SAPPORO BLACK BEER

In Japan, sake (really a rice beer rather than a wine) was joined by locally made western-style brews in the late 1800s. These beers were a result of American, Dutch, and German influence. At that time, German lagers were dark. The brewery in Sapporo opened in 1876, before registered brands existed. This national brewer has a wide range of products, including an interesting black beer, which received its first definite mention in 1892. Today's neck label boasts "Japan's oldest brand." The beer smells like a box of chocolates; has complex, long flavors reminiscent of roasting coffee and figs; and finishes with a licorice note. Sapporo's national rivals Asahi and Kirin both have black beers, and so do many of the small, new-generation breweries in Japan.

| | |
|---|---|
| **Region of origin** | Hokkaido, Japan |
| **Style** | Black Beer |
| **Alcohol content** | 4.0 abw (5.0 abv) |
| **Ideal serving temperature** | 48° F (9° C) |

### DIET OF WORDS

GERMANY'S GREATEST writer, Johann Wolfgang von Goethe (1749–1832), took an interest in beer from his student days. He sustained himself on black beer from Köstritz (*right*) when he was unable to eat during a period of illness.

## KÖSTRITZER SCHWARZBIER

The most famous black beer, made in Bad Köstritz, Thuringia. Beer was made in the castles of two local aristocrats between the 1500s and 1600s, and won a wider reputation in the 1700s. The aristocrats' emblems survived on the town's 1907 brewery, which made the local style throughout the communist period. This black brew has a spicy aroma hinting at red peppers, figs, and bitter chocolate. The same character emerges in big, expressive, smooth, long, dry, well-combined flavors.

**Region of origin**
Thuringia, Germany

**Style** Black Beer

**Alc. content** 3.8 abw (4.8 abv)

**Ideal serving temperature**
48° F (9° C)

## SCHWARZER STEIGER

A *Steiger* is someone who walks in the hills or, in this instance, patrols underground, in a mine. The excavation of silver was once important in the area of Dresden, where Steiger is an old local beer brand. Today's Schwarzer Steiger is produced by Feldschlösschen (Castle in the Fields), one of several breweries with that name. The modern brewery is on the edge of the city, but part of the original survives in the center. This beer has an aroma of violets and dark chocolate; a firm, slightly cedary palate; and a big, coffee-and-dried-figs finish.

**Region of origin**
Dresden, Saxony, Germany

**Style** Black Beer

**Alc. content** 3.8 abw (4.8 abv)

**Ideal serving temperature**
48° F (9° C)

## MÄRKISCHER LANDMANN SCHWARZBIER

The expression *Märkischer Landmann* refers to a citizen of the state of Brandenburg, which centers on Berlin. The Märkischer Landmann Schwarzbier was launched by the Berliner Kindl brewery in 1995, at the time when black brews were becoming fashionable. It has a licoricelike, malt aroma; a light, dry, grainy palate; and a slightly oaky, sappy finish.

**Region of origin**
Berlin/Brandenburg, Germany

**Style** Black Beer

**Alc. content** 4.1 abw (5.1 abv)

**Ideal serving temperature**
48° F (9° C)

## BERLINER BÜRGERBRÄU BERNAUER SCHWARZBIER

Historic Bernau, northeast of Berlin, once had 142 small breweries and its prosperity was based on its sales of beer to other towns. Now it has none, but its name has been saluted by the Berliner Bürgerbräu brewery in this black beer. Bernauer Schwarzbier is among the most truly black examples of the style, with an earthy aroma; an oily, espresso, chocolate-and-rum flavor; and a long, smooth, clingy finish.

**Region of origin**
Berlin/Brandenburg, Germany

**Style** Black Beer

**Alcohol content** 4.2 abw (5.2 abv)

**Ideal serving temperature**
48° F (9° C)

# RESTORATIVES: DUTCH "OLD BROWN" LAGERS

THE FIRST BREWS MADE WITH A LAGER PROCESS were dark brown examples, in Bavaria, and this tradition survives in all-malt, dark lagers in Germany. Derivatives are produced in many parts of the world (*pages 148–149*), but in a particularly distinctive form in the Netherlands. There, "old brown" (in Dutch, *oud bruin*) lagers are typically very sweet, caramel-tinged, and low in alcohol. They are the classic example of a dark brew as a restorative. No Dutch beer maker regards the old brown style as the peak of the art, but most of the established breweries – even major companies such as Heineken and Grolsch – maintain such a product, albeit to satisfy a small market.

## HEINEKEN OUD BRUIN

The most international of beer makers traces its history to 1592, to a brewery in the center of Amsterdam, the site of which is now a famous steak restaurant. The first Heineken became involved with the brewery in 1863, at which time white beer, *faro* (a sweetened beer broadly in the *gueuze* type), old brown, ale, and porter were being produced. Lager brewing of dark brown beers began in 1869 and today's yeast culture was introduced in 1886. Heineken still makes a conventional, dryish, dark lager, mainly for export to the US, but also has the quite different sweeter type in its home market. This Oud Bruin has a coffeeish aroma; a slightly licoricelike palate; and, as with most examples, a sweet finish.

*Secret smile*
*When the current typography of the word Heineken was designed, the shape of the letter "e" was intended to be subliminally reminiscent of a smile.*

**Region of origin**
Province of North Brabant, the Netherlands

**Style** Old Brown Lager

**Alcohol content** 2.0 abw (2.5 abv)

**Ideal serving temperature** 46–48° F (8–9° C)

### MASTER BREW

THE DUTCH MASTERS often featured beers, typically dark. The beers of the time were probably multi-grain, sweetish, spiced brews, but made with wild yeasts. The example on the right is from the Amsterdam painter Pieter Quast (1601–47).

## BRAND OUD BRUIN

A smooth and malty interpretation, with a finish reminiscent of saccharine-sweetened coffee, from this brewery in Wijlre, east of Maastricht. An antique-style beer seems very appropriate at the Netherlands' oldest brewery. A spiced beer, fermented with wild yeast, was made in the days when the brewery was a brewpub on the Lord of the Manor's estate. When the local clergyman complained that peasants preferred the pub to the pulpit, the brewery was sold to the Brand family.

**Region of origin** Province of Limburg, the Netherlands

**Style** Old Brown Lager

**Alc. content** 2.8 abw (3.5 abv)

**Ideal serving temperature** 46–48° F (8–9° C)

*The Lord's beer*
*When the Lord of the Manor owned the Wijlre brewery, he proclaimed a local monopoly on beer. This is remembered in the text on the neck label.*

## BUDELS OUD BRUIN

A hint of fruit and a creamy, grainy palate, with a toffeeish finish in this example from the brewery at Budel, near the Belgian border. Promotional literature from a dozen years ago describes the beer as "tasty, toothsome, soft, mild, gentle, kind, friendly, and suitable for a cozy, sociable drink." The English word "cozy" fails to do justice to the untranslatable Dutch *gezellig*. Comfort and safety, with a beer and friends, are important in a country so vulnerable to the sea.

**Region of origin** Province of North Brabant, the Netherlands

**Style** Old Brown Lager

**Alc. content** 2.8 abw (3.5 abv)

**Ideal serving temperature** 46–48° F (8–9° C)

*Hope and anchor*
*Like several other breweries, the one at Budel has an anchor as its emblem. This is not a maritime reference, but a biblical allusion to optimism: "Hope . . . anchor of the soul" (Hebrews vi: 19).*

## ALFA OUD BRUIN

Why Alfa? "Because we are the first – the best," said Great-grandfather Meens, an enthusiast for ancient Greek. The Meens family date from the 1600s, their farm from the 1750s, and its monasterylike brewery from 1870. Its sandstone spring produces glacial water said to be 6,000 years old. Most of the beers are all-malt, but Old Bruin is sweetened, perhaps less overtly than some: clean, very nutty, and toffeeish, with a treacly malt finish.

**Region of origin** Province of Limburg, the Netherlands

**Style** Old Brown Lager

**Alc. content** 2.0 abw (2.5 abv)

**Ideal serving temperature** 46–48° F (8–9° C)

*Animal farm*
*The neck label shows the three lions of Limburg. The crest on the main label, showing three ducks, represents the Meens family. Four generations of this family have worked in the brewery.*

## RIDDER DONKER

This brewery's parish church in Maastricht is St. Martin's, named after one of the Knights Templar (the order that protected pilgrims). *Ridder* means rider, or knight; *Donker* means dark. A suit of armor can be seen in the conference room of the brewery. The Ridder brewery was founded in 1857 by the van Aubel brothers. When there was no successor, in 1982, it was acquired by Heineken. Ridder Donker is a typical *oud bruin*, with its own soft, fluffy, licoricelike maltiness.

**Region of origin** Province of Limburg, the Netherlands

**Style** Old Brown Lager

**Alc. content** 2.8 abw (3.5 abv)

**Ideal serving temperature** 46–48° F (8–9° C)

*Donker blend*
*The back label on this beer suggests that it be used to make a sjoes, comprising half-and-half of old brown and Pilsner-style lager.*

# RESTORATIVES: MILD ALES

A "MILD" IS AN ENGLISH TERM FOR AN ALE that is only lightly hopped, and therefore lacks any obvious bitterness. The style is usually low in alcohol and inexpensive. A mild is often dark, due to the use of luscious, treacly malts. Initially it was a restorative for farm laborers, and later for industrial workers. It has survived best in the forge towns of England's West Midlands, where castings are made for the car industry. Elsewhere, mild has been half-forgotten in the post-industrial age, but some breweries are rediscovering it.

## Mild Thing

*Mild can be wild*
*A Pittsburgh brewpub, The Strip, archly dubs its nutty mild ale* Mild Thing.

*Under the volcano*
*The label shows Mount Taranaki. The volcanic peak last erupted 350 years ago, so drinkers feel reasonably secure as they restore themselves after hiking the local nature trails.*

## MIKE'S MILD ALE

A rare antipodean mild. The beer might be mild-tasting, but there is a boldness to its proclamation of style. Mike Johnson, a brewer with 12 years' experience, set up on his own in 1989. His White Cliffs brewery is on the coast at Urenui, on New Zealand's North Island. Behind the coast and to the west lies Mount Taranaki (18,200 ft/2,500 m high). From the start, Mike Johnson's flagship product has been his Mild Ale. This has a fresh, earthy aroma; a smooth body; appetizing and pronounced cookie, milk-chocolate, and malt flavors; and a very lightly roasty dryness in the finish. It shows an outstanding balance of mild malt characteristics, though it lacks somewhat in ale fruitiness.

**Region of origin**
North Island, New Zealand

**Style** Mild Ale

**Alcohol content** 3.2 abw (4.0 abv)

**Ideal serving temperature**
50° F (10° C)

### TREACLY TETLEY

TETLEY, IN LEEDS, Yorkshire, is Britain's biggest cask ale brewery. Tetley Mild is distinctively rummy, lightly treacly, and a modest 2.6 abw (3.3 abv). It contains a small amount of Demerara sugar.

## HULL MILD

A claim to fame among beer lovers, especially in North America: the original Hull brewery, based in the Yorkshire fishing and port city of Hull, employed Peter Austin, who later used its distinctively fruity yeast in new-generation breweries throughout the US and Canada. The brewery closed in the 1970s, but the name was resurrected by a microbrewery in 1989. The micro uses the same yeast to make this smooth, toasty, chocolaty, fruity, winey mild.

**Region of origin**
Northeast England, UK

**Style** Mild Ale

**Alcohol content**
2.6 abw (3.3 abv)

**Ideal serving temperature**
50–55° F (10–13° C)

## WARD'S CLASSIC YORKSHIRE ALE

A great beer-making city much diminished, Sheffield should be proud of Ward's, a classic Victorian brewery. When the Yorkshire city was also famous for coal and steel, Ward's strong mild was a much-needed restorative. It is a characterful, rummy, dryish interpretation of the style, available only on draft. Ward's Classic Yorkshire Ale is a bottled big-brother brew. It has a very lively interplay of flavors, balancing a perfumy, peachy fruitiness with distinctly nutty maltiness: satisfying, smooth, and drinkable.

**Region of origin**
Northern England, UK

**Style** Strong Mild/
Yorkshire Ale

**Alcohol content**
4.0 abw (5.0 abv)

**Ideal serving temperature**
50–55° F (10–13° C)

## BANKS'S

One of the most famous brewers of mild is Banks, in the West Midlands city of Wolverhampton. The brewery's renown derives from the quality of its mild, and the high volume of its sales. Nonetheless, fearing that the industrial image of the English Midlands might be unfashionable, a marketing genius has in recent years added the meaningless description "uniquely balanced beer," and an exhortation that the brew be served chilled. If the instruction is followed, it will flatten the creamy, oily, nut-toffee maltiness of this delicious, flavorsome brew.

**Region of origin**
Central England, UK

**Style** Mild Ale

**Alcohol content**
2.8 abw (3.5 abv)

**Ideal serving temperature**
50–55° F (10–13° C)

## MANNS ORIGINAL BROWN ALE

This style of dark, malty, sweetish, low-strength brown ale was once made by every English brewery as a bottled version of its draft mild. Few have such a product today, but this minor classic survives. Originally brewed in London, this ale is now made by Usher's in the town of Trowbridge, Wiltshire. It is light, but smooth and creamy, with flavors of chocolate-coated raisins.

**Region of origin**
Southern England, UK

**Style** Brown Ale/Mild

**Alcohol content**
2.3 abw (2.8 abv)

**Ideal serving temperature**
50–55° F (10–13° C)

# RESTORATIVES: SWEET STOUTS

WITHIN THE FAMILY OF STOUTS, the distinctly sweet style has long been regarded as what today might be called an energy drink. Some of these stouts are sweet simply because they emphasize maltiness rather than hop bitterness. Others are given sweetness and body by the use of various types of sugar – often lactose, which is extracted from milk. Having also the coffeeish and chocolaty flavors of toasted or roasted malt, they are the beer world's counterpart to cream liqueurs. In recent years, several Japanese and American breweries have introduced new examples of this old style of beer.

*Stout from the sea*
*The Roman god of the sea, Neptune, arises like a strong man from a garland of malt and hops on Lacto's label.*

## FARSONS LACTO TRADITIONAL STOUT

As its name suggests, this stout contains lactose. It is a classic example of a beer marketed as a restorative. Lacto Traditional Stout also has added vitamin B. It is made in a palm-fringed, 1950s brewery by Farrugia and Sons ("Farsons"), on the Mediterranean island of Malta, where it is popular among nursing mothers. The stout is also traditionally used there as an ingredient in Christmas puddings, and its sales soar in November. An important malt in this brew is the dark, sweetish style typically used to make mild ales. Crystal malt is also employed, perhaps contributing to the nutty, polished oak aroma. The beer is light-bodied, but creamy and smooth, with rich flavors suggesting ginger, dark chocolate, and currants. It has a slightly yogurty finish.

**Region of origin** Malta

**Style** Sweet Stout

**Alcohol content** 2.7 abw (3.4 abv)

**Ideal serving temperature** 55° F (13° C)

### STOUT PUNCH

THE USE OF SUGAR in some beers derives from colonial times. Cane grown in the former British Caribbean has left people there with a sweet tooth. A local drink is made with stout, rum, condensed milk, and an egg. Jamaica's Dragon Stout (5.6 abw/7.0 abv) is sweetish, creamy, and raisiny.

# MACKESON STOUT

The world's most widely-known sweet stout was developed with the help of a dietician in 1907. It was originally made by the Mackeson brewery in the small English port of Hythe, Kent. After several changes of ownership, the product came into the hands of the national brewer Whitbread. Mackeson Stout contains lactose, and a milk churn is shown on the label.

The beer is light, smooth, and creamy, with hints of evaporated milk and coffee essence, and a liqueurish finish.

**Region of origin**
Southeast England, UK

**Style** Sweet Stout

**Alcohol content**
2.4 abw (3.0 abv)
Export version
4.0 abw (5.0 abv)

**Ideal serving temperature**
55° F (13° C)

# GUERNSEY MILK STOUT

"Milk Stout" was a popular colloquialism after World War II. The UK Ministry of Food eventually deemed it misleading, but such legislation does not apply on the Channel Islands. With their reputation for dairy cattle, it seems appropriate that they still have a Milk Stout. Disappointingly, this does not contain lactose. It nonetheless has a deliciously creamy flavor, drying in a chewy, licorice-toffee finish.

**Region of origin**
Guernsey, Channel Islands

**Style** Sweet Stout

**Alcohol content**
2.6 abw (3.3 abv)

**Ideal serving temperature**
55° F (13° C)

*Polo pint*
*The trademark of the brewery is a polo pony, reflecting a past owner's enthusiasm.*

# CSARDA SWEET STOUT

*Csarda* is Hungarian for inn. Travels in Europe inspired a Japanese clothing manufacturer to open a brewery making a range of beers stretching from a Pilsner and wheat beer to a bitter and this sweet stout, which contains lactose. It has a yogurty aroma and milky, peaches-and-cream flavors, but is beautifully balanced. The Csarda brewery and country-style restaurant is in the heart of downtown Yokohama.

**Region of origin**
Japan

**Style** Sweet Stout

**Alcohol content**
4.0 abw (5.0 abv)

**Ideal serving temperature**
55° F (13° C)

*Dancing beer*
*The label image reflects the traditional costume of a dancer at a Hungarian inn, or Csarda.*

# YOUNGER OF ALLOA SWEETHEART STOUT

A famous old name in Scottish brewing, George Younger, is kept alive in this product. Among several different Younger breweries, the Alloa brewery was acquired and then closed by Tennent, of Glasgow, in the 1960s. Tennent, in turn, is owned by Bass. Aptly, Sweetheart Stout is the most sugary example of the style: with vanilla, caramel, and medicinal notes. In a style that is typically low in alcohol, this example is especially modest.

**Region of origin**
Scotland, UK

**Style** Sweet Stout

**Alcohol content**
1.6 abw (2.0 abv)

**Ideal serving temperature**
55° F (13° C)

# WINTER WARMERS: BOCK BEERS

THE STRONG LAGERS (AND COMPARABLY STRONG WHEAT BREWS) identified as Bock are sometimes intended specifically for spring, but more often they are understood as winter warmers. Some are launched each year in October or November; others appear at Christmas, New Year's, or February; and several are available all year round. These beers are rich and malty, sometimes sweet, and sustaining. The Bock tradition is German, but it has also spread to nearby countries, notably the Netherlands and Norway. It is also widely followed in the parts of the US and Canada settled by German-speaking peoples, and even in some parts of Australia. In the southern hemisphere, it probably tastes best in June or July.

Painting by Robin Collier

## BURRAGORANG BOCK BEER

As the Aboriginal-sounding name suggests, this is an Australian beer. It is produced near Burragorang Lake, in Picton, 50 miles (80 km) southwest of Sydney, and is possibly the biggest-tasting beer in Australia. In 1978, the first application to license a microbrewery in Australia was made by Geoff Scharer, a fourth-generation Australian from a family who originated from Zürich, Switzerland. In 1987, Scharer finally made beer, advised by the late Otto Binding, Germany's microbrewery pioneer. Made with three malts and German Spalt hops, Burragorang Bock Beer pours with a huge head; has a silky body; a perfumy, appetizing, malt character; suggestions of molasses toffee; and a resiny hop balance. The brewery also has a very hoppy, Pilsner-style brew.

**Region of origin**  New South Wales, Australia

**Style**  Bock

**Alcohol content**  5.1 abw (6.4 abv)

**Ideal serving temperature**  48° F (9 °C)

### IT'S THE WATER

THE DEPICTION OF THE Burragorang Valley on the Burragorang Bock Beer label shows a tract of land owned by the brewery's proprietor. The Valley is the main source of Sydney's water. The painting was commissioned by the Water Board from artist Robin Collier.

## KNEITINGER BOCK

A charitable foundation benefiting orphans and sick children has operated this family brewery in the town of Regensburg, Bavaria, since the death, in 1991, of the last Kneitinger. The brewery dates from 1530, and had been in the Kneitinger family since 1876. The brewery and its adjoining original inn are a registered landmark. The inn taps the first cask of a new Bock on the first Thursday in October. Kneitinger Bock is very rich and layered in its complex malt character, with a faint smokiness.

**Region of origin**
Regensburg, Bavaria, Germany

**Style** Bock

**Alcohol content**
4.8 abw (6.0 abv)

**Ideal serving temperature**
48° F (9° C)

## AUGUST SCHELL DOPPEL BOCK

The German-accented August Schell brewery, in New Ulm, Minnesota, has in recent years done much to rediscover its heritage. In addition to a tawny, rummy Bock (4.6 abw; 5.8 abv), there is now this well-balanced *Doppel*. It has an appetizing balance of hop and malt in the aroma; a smooth, medium body; clean, syrupy notes in the palate; and an underpinning of dryness and hoppiness in the finish. The *Doppel* is available from January to March.

**Region of origin** Midwest US

**Style** Double Bock

**Alc. content** 5.4 abw (6.8 abv)

**Ideal serving temperature**
48° F (9° C)

## BRICK BOCK

Jim Brickman founded this sizeable new-generation brewery in the old beer and whiskey town of Waterloo, Ontario, in 1984. Although its Bock recipe has been varied from one year to the next, its typical characteristics include a very malty aroma; a light but firm palate; and a depth of dark-malt flavors, developing licorice, rooty, peaty, burned, whiskeyish notes. The beer is said to be matured for three months.

**Region of origin**
Province of Ontario, Canada

**Style** Bock

**Alcohol content**
5.6 abw (7.0 abv)

**Ideal serving temperature**
48° F (9° C)

*Seal of strength*
*Some Brick Bock bottlings have an attractive wax seal.*

## AASS BOCK

Aass (pronounced like the first syllable of "awesome") means "summit" in Norwegian: here it is a family name. This old brewery in Drammen, near Oslo, produces a good example of a Norwegian Bock: it has a sweet, licorice-toffee, malt aroma and palate, and is smooth and creamy. It is made with a double-decoction mash, a long boil, and six months' maturation. It is sometimes served with marzipan cake, a Norwegian favorite.

**Region of origin**
Norway

**Style** Bock

**Alcohol content**
5.2 abw (6.5 abv)

**Ideal serving temperature**
48° F (9° C)

## JOPEN BOK BIER

The word *Jopen* was used in Haarlem, once a great brewing city in the Netherlands, to describe a size of barrel. This "four-grain" beer is made from barley, wheat, rye (all malted), and raw oats, and is top-fermented and bottle-conditioned. Although developed in Haarlem, it is produced at the Schaapskooi Trappist brewery. To experience its fragrant, orangy aroma is like biting into the fruit itself. The beer is lightly syrupy and malty in the palate, with spicy, dry flavors (but no spices are used).

**Region of origin**
Province of North Holland, the Netherlands

**Style**
Top-fermenting Bock

**Alcohol content**
4.4 abw (5.5 abv)

**Ideal serving temperature**
48° F (9° C)

## AMSTEL HERFSTBOCK

The Amstel is the river that gives Amsterdam its name. The Amstel brewery used to stand on the river, a few blocks from Heineken. The bigger company took over its local rival in 1968, but the Amstel name survives on a distinct range of products, now produced in South Holland and North Brabant. These range from Amstel Light to this very malty, October Bock. This beer has a licorice-toffee aroma; smooth, pleasantly medicinal "cough sweet" flavors; and an aromatic finish.

**Region of origin**
Province of North Brabant, the Netherlands

**Style** Bock

**Alcohol content**
5.6 abw (7.0 abv)

**Ideal serving temperature**
48° F (9° C)

## HEINEKEN TARWEBOK

One of the most distinctive, flavorsome, and complex beers made by Heineken is this wheat Bock. No fewer than four types of barley malt are used, along with 17 percent wheat malt. The result is a silky-smooth beer, with suggestions of cream, coffee, chocolate, prunes, and rum. This Dutch interpretation of the style does not have the phenol smokiness or bubblegum flavors that might be found in a typical German *Weizenbock*.

**Region of origin**
Province of North Brabant, the Netherlands

**Style** Wheat Bock

**Alcohol content**
5.2 abw (6.5 abv)

**Ideal serving temperature**
48–50° F (9–10° C)

## SCHNEIDER AVENTINUS

When the famous Schneider family were brewing in Munich, their bottling hall was on a street called Aventinstrasse, which provided an ideal name for this "double" *Weizenbock*. With its alcoholic warmth and layers of malty complexity, balanced by clovey spiciness, figgy, raisiny fruitiness, sparkle, and champagnelike acidity, Aventinus is a truly remarkable beer.

**Region of origin** Munich, Upper Bavaria, Germany

**Style** Wheat Double Bock/*Weizenbock*

**Alcohol content**
6.1 abw (7.7 abv)

**Ideal serving temperature**
48–50° F (9–10° C)

# BOCK BEERS

## COUGAN'S BOCK

An astonishingly drinkable, Irish-sounding Bock that can be found far from Germany, in a brewery and pub (actually it is more a neighborhood bar) called Cougan's, in Phoenix, Arizona. Cougan's is owned by the fashionable brewpub chain, Hops! Talented brewer and beer historian Daniel Rothman created this lively brew, with its rocky head; deep amber color; malty fruitiness of aroma; cookielike flavors; and leafy, hoppy, balancing dryness.

**Region of origin** Southwest US

**Style** Bock

**Alcohol content** 4.7 abw (5.9 abv)

**Ideal serving temp.** 48° F (9° C)

## DENISON'S BOCK

The Denison's brewery at the Growler's Pub, in Toronto, Ontario, produces a full range of German styles, in consultation with Prince Luitpold of the Kaltenberg brewery in Bavaria. These include a ruby-colored Bock that pours with a big head; has a nutty, syrupy, creamy aroma and flavor; developing a deep, peppery dryness towards a lively finish. There is also a tawny *Dunkler Weizenbock* with a toffeeish, fruity palate, finishing with a touch of clove.

**Region of origin**
Province of Ontario, Canada

**Style** Bock

**Alcohol content** 5.2 abw (6.5 abv)

**Ideal serving temp.** 48° F (9° C)

## DOCK STREET ILLUMINATOR

Wry twists on the Salvator tradition are offered by many North American breweries, with names such as Hibernator, Terminator, and Liberator. This enlightening example, Illuminator, from the Dock Street brewery and pub in Philadelphia, is a dark amber Double Bock: creamy, with vanilla notes, and pruney flavors.

**Region of origin** Northeast US

**Style** Double Bock

**Alcohol content** 5.8 abw (7.2 abv)

**Ideal serving temp.** 48° F (9° C)

## FORDHAM CALVINATOR

Benjamin Fordham was an immigrant from London who made English-style ales in the earliest days of Annapolis, Maryland. The brewery named after him is at a 1740s tavern called the Ram's Head. Despite its English heritage, the brewery makes German styles, produced according to the Purity Law. Its Calvinator has a deep, ruby color; a huge, rocky head; a perfumy, malt aroma; a very smooth body; and lively, assertive malt flavors, finishing with a powerful hop bitterness. The name? "Calvinists would like beer if they tasted ours."

**Region of origin** Northeast US

**Style** Double Bock

**Alcohol content** 6.0 abw (7.5 abv)

**Ideal serving temp.** 48° F (9° C)

## GORDON BIERSCH BLONDE BOCK

This California-based chain of brewery restaurants produces beers in classic German styles. Its Blonde Bock is bright gold in color, with a malty aroma; has barley-sugar notes and whiskeyish flavors; a light, flowery finish; and a late hit of warming alcohol. Try it as a dessert beer or the last beer on a winter's night.

**Region of origin** California, US

**Style** Bock

**Alcohol content**
5.6–5.8 abw (7.0–7.2 abv)

**Ideal serving temp.** 48° F (9° C)

## GROLSCH HERFSTBOK

The well-known Dutch brewer has in its wide range several variations on the Bock theme. This "Harvest" Bock for late autumn and early winter has a very attractive, tawny, reddish color; a big, well-retained, rocky head; a fresh, malty aroma; a very sweet but nutty and appetizing palate; and a pleasantly medicinal, warming finish.

**Region of origin** Eastern Netherlands

**Style** Bock (*Bok*)

**Alcohol content** 5.2 abw (6.5 abv)

**Ideal serving temp.** 48° F (9° C)

## HOSTER'S CAPTIVATOR

In the lively brewing town of Columbus, Ohio, Hoster's was once a famous name. It bids to be so again, having been revived in 1989. A wide range of mainly German styles is produced. The Captivator has an attractive garnet color; a smooth, syrupy, textured palate; and a complex of satisfying flavors, drying into light smokiness, leafy hoppiness, and warming alcohol.

**Region of origin** Midwest US

**Style** Double Bock

**Alcohol content** 6.8 abw (8.5 abv)

**Ideal serving temp.** 48° F (9° C)

## SPECULATOR

This Double Bock is spiced with ginger, cloves, cinnamon, nutmeg, and pepper: the spices typically used in the Dutch national cookie *speculaas*. The beer is cerise to black in color, with a big, warm, dusty, spicy, cherryish aroma. It has a smooth palate, with bitter-cherry, rooty, licoricelike flavors; and a menthol, herbal finish. It is made by the North Holland Foundation of Alternative Brewers.

**Region of origin**
North Holland, the Netherlands

**Style** Double Bock (*Dubbel Bok*)

**Alcohol content** 6.8 abw (8.5 abv)

**Ideal serving temp.** 48° F (9° C)

## WÜRZBURGER HOFBRÄU SYMPATOR

The winemaking town of Würzburg banned brewing "for ever" in 1434, but to no avail. In the 1600s, when the vineyards could not quench the thirsts of the military in the 30 Years War, the local bishop decreed that the town should have a brewery, which was sited in the royal armory. The brewery later became a private business, and its present buildings date from 1882. The Sympator has a deep, chestnut color; a creamy, well-retained head; a brandyish aroma; and very clean, complex, malty flavors, and fudgy notes.

**Region of origin**
Franconia, Bavaria, Germany

**Style** Double Bock (*Doppelbock*)

**Alcohol content** 6.3 abw (7.9 abv)

**Ideal serving temp.** 48° F (9° C)

# WINTER WARMERS: SPICED BEERS

**B**EFORE HOPS BECAME THE BREWER'S FAVORITE HERB, many of the spices used in beer were those that bring the hot flavors of sunny lands to a more wintry world. Ginger, nutmeg, cinnamon, and cloves are mentioned in laws concerning brewing in the seventh century AD, and were no doubt used long before that. None of these has ever totally vanished from the brewery, and all have enjoyed a revival in recent years. Some of today's spiced beers are even intended to be tasted warm, as mulled ales.

**Cherry Christmas**
*The typical Liefmans tissue comes in Christmassy colors for this brew, but Glühkriek might better be enjoyed with winter sports. The Ardennes are less suitable than the Alps, Aviemore, or Aspen.*

## LIEFMANS GLÜHKRIEK

Anyone who has skiied in the Alps has been offered *Glühwein* – a "glow wine," served warm and spiced, typically with cloves and cinnamon. The German prefix *Glüh* is used by the otherwise Flemish-speaking Belgian brewery Liefmans to promote the same notion. This beer, based on the cherry brew Liefmans Kriek, contains the same two spices, but also anise. The cinnamon seems most obvious in the aroma, with ironlike, medicinal flavors giving way to sweet, sugared-almond notes, balanced by fruity acidity and a clovey finish. The aromas increase and the sweetness diminishes if the beer is mulled. It is intended to be heated as though it were hot chocolate. This is best done in a double boiler (*bain-marie*), though any pan, or even a microwave, can be used.

**Region of origin**
Province of East Flanders, Belgium

**Style** Spiced Cherry Beer

**Alcohol content** 5.2 abw (6.5 abv)

**Ideal serving temperature** 158° F (70° C)

### SAINTLY PLEASURES

**T**HE BEERS OF THE St. Peter's brewery are available in London at a tavern named after the Priory of St. John of Jerusalem. Behind the 1800s shopfront of the Jerusalem Tavern is a building from the early 1700s. The name is much older. There was a Jerusalem Coffee House in the 1600s and an earlier tavern in the 1300s.

# UNIBROUE QUELQUE CHOSE

The Belgian company that owns Liefmans was originally a consultant to this very adventurous Quebecois brewery. Unibroue has some truly remarkable beers, and this is one of them. Liefmans Glühkriek and Quelque Chose have much the same base beer, but the latter is blended with a paler, stronger brew, with a complex malt specification including some whiskey malt. The resultant beer is therefore stronger, but it also seems lighter-bodied, fruitier, and tarter.

**Region of origin**
Province of Quebec, Canada

**Style** Spiced Cherry Beer

**Alc. content** 6.4 abw (8.0 abv)

**Ideal serving temperature**
158° F (70° C)

*Something else . . .*
*"Is it a wine or a beer, or something else?" people asked. "It's something else! Really something!!" replied the brewer.*

# MÅRTEN TROTZIG'S ÖL

The brewery Sofiero is in the small Swedish town of Laholm, and is named after the castle at nearby Hälsingborg. It originally made nontaxable, low-alcohol, "country" beers, but in 1988 decided to brew something stronger. Mårten Trotzig was a trader who imported wines, beers, and spices, including ginger, to Sweden in the 1600s. The beer that takes his name is a ginger-spiced, bronze lager: aromatic, light, firm, and rounded, with a very dry finish.

**Region of origin**
Sweden

**Style** Spiced Lager

**Alcohol content**
4.5 abw (5.6 abv)

**Ideal serving temperature**
48–50° F (9–10° C)

*Beer from the wood*
*The wooden drinking vessel shown on the label is a powerful symbol of the deeply forested Baltic countries.*

# ST. PETER'S SPICED ALE

The 13th-century St. Peter's Hall is a manor house, near Bungay, Suffolk, England. It was acquired in 1995 by an expert on marketing, with an enthusiasm for the drinks industry, and turned into a brewery, bar, and restaurant. A wide range of beers has been produced, one of the most assertive being this dark ale spiced with cinnamon and apple. It has a deep ruby color; a very aromatic, dark-chocolate bouquet; an oily, smooth body; a palate suggesting mocha, nuts, and port; and a very dry, tannic finish.

**Region of origin**
Eastern England, UK

**Style**
Spiced Dark Ale

**Alcohol content**
5.2 abw (6.5 abv)

**Ideal serving temp.**
50–55° F
(10–13° C)

# GROLSCH WINTERVORST

"Winter Frost" is a distinctive and flavorsome strong ale in a "Four Seasons" range from this Dutch brewer. Wintervorst is spiced with clover, honey, and orange peel. It pours with a big, rocky, well-retained head; an aromatic, malty bouquet; rich, sweet, appetizing, licoricelike flavors; a lightly oily, soothing, smooth body; and a gently herbal, flowery finish.

**Region of origin**
Eastern Netherlands

**Style** Spiced Ale

**Alcohol content**
6.0 abw (7.5 abv)

**Ideal serving temperature**
48° F (10° C)

*Vorst of both worlds*
*"Frost" and "first" sound as similar in Dutch as in English. The wintry king (the "first" person) on the label and glass depicts this wordplay.*

# WINTER WARMERS: OLD ALES

FLAVORSOME, OFTEN DARK BROWN ALES, usually malt-accented, sweet, and relatively full-bodied but only medium-to-strong in alcohol, are typically regarded as winter warmers. Brews in this style are most often described as old ales. This can imply an old style of beer, or it can suggest a longer-than-usual aging. One or two brews labeled "old ale" are much stronger, and can be matured in the bottle. A great many beers in this style have the term "Old" or "Winter" in their brand names, and some are also identified as barley wines: the styles blur into each other. The purist might argue that old ales are typically the darker, less potent of the two, and frequently available on draft; while barley wines are stronger brews more often found in the bottle.

*Ale halo*
*Amid Australia's sea of bland, sweet lagers, Tooheys Old emphasizes its status as an ale by declaring, on the neck label, that it is made with top-fermenting yeast.*

## TOOHEYS OLD BLACK ALE

Irish-Australian brothers founded the Tooheys brewery in Sydney, in the mid-1800s. It became known as the city's "Catholic" brewery and still thrives as part of the national group Lion Nathan. Tooheys has maintained the tradition of an old ale, which was at one stage brewed north of Sydney in the city of Newcastle, where it was popular with miners. Toohey's Old has a modest alcohol content and light but smooth body. The flavors are very gentle, but there are touches of bitter-chocolate, cream, and oloroso sherry spiciness, nuttiness, and fruitiness. It finishes toasty and dry and has more complexity than its local rival, from the Tooth's brewery. The latter, established in 1835 by an Englishman, became Sydney's "Protestant" brewery. Tooth's is now owned by the national group Fosters.

**Region of origin**
New South Wales, Australia

**Style** Old Ale

**Alcohol content** 3.5 abw (4.4 abv)

**Ideal serving temperature** 50° F (10° C)

### OLD WOOD

THE FAMOUS OLD ALE brewery, Theakston, in North Yorkshire, England, uses wooden casks for some local deliveries. It employs two coopers to maintain (and occasionally build) casks. Some of the wood used is up to 80 years old.

## MARSTON'S OWD RODGER

Who was "Owd" (Old) Rodger? The renowned Marston's brewery, in Burton, England, does not know, except that his name has been used since at least the 1950s, and perhaps even before that. Several such beers are named after long-gone brewers, drinkers, cellarmen, bartenders, or local characters. Owd Rodger is the stronger style of old ale and has a warming alcohol note. It pours with a dense head, leaving good lacework; has an almost purple color; a licorice aroma; a rooty palate; a lightly creamy body; and a juicy, fruity, portlike finish.

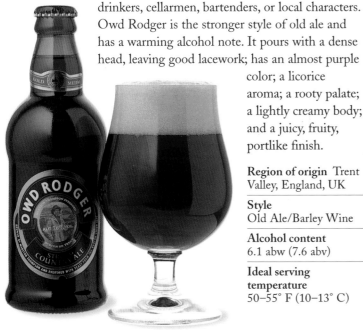

**Region of origin**  Trent Valley, England, UK

**Style**
Old Ale/Barley Wine

**Alcohol content**
6.1 abw (7.6 abv)

**Ideal serving temperature**
50–55° F (10–13° C)

## YOUNG'S WINTER WARMER

This seasonal brew from the famous London brewery has had several names, including Old Ale, but adopted the identity Winter Warmer in the early 1970s. It is a registered name in the UK, but has been copied in the US. Young's Winter Warmer is drinkable, light and smooth in body, and deceptively powerful. It has pronounced cookielike, malt flavors, developing to raisiny fruitiness; with a faintly smoky, dry finish.

**Region of origin**
London, England, UK

**Style**  Old Ale

**Alcohol content**
4.0 abw (5.0 abv)

**Ideal serving temperature**
50–55° F (10–13° C)

## THEAKSTON OLD PECULIER

The best-known example of an old ale as a dark brown, full-bodied, sweet, malty brew, medium-to-strong, and widely available on draft, is Old Peculier from Theakston. The tiny 1870s brewery, in Masham, North Yorkshire, England, is now owned by Scottish Courage. Old Peculier (reviving a medieval spelling) has a notably soft and oily body; flavors reminiscent of milk chocolate; and a raisiny, blackcurrant dryness in the finish. It is a soothing and sustaining brew.

**Region of origin**
Northern England, UK

**Style**  Old Ale

**Alcohol content**
4.5 abw (5.6 abv)

**Ideal serving temperature**
55° F (13° C)

## GRANITE BREWERY PECULIAR

Inspired by Theakston's Old Peculier, but opting for a more conventional spelling, this Canadian beer is similar in style but slightly paler in color and lighter in body. It pours with a lively, bubbly head; has a fresh, minty, hop aroma; very nutty, creamy, toffeeish, satisfying flavors; and an appetizing, leafy dryness in the finish. The beer was first made in the Granite brewpub in rocky Nova Scotia. There are two breweries there, in Halifax, and a third in Toronto, Ontario.

**Region of origin**
Ontario, Canada

**Style**
Old Ale/Strong Ale

**Alcohol content**
4.5 abw (5.6 abv)

**Ideal serving temperature**
50–55° F (10–13° C)

## HIGHGATE & WALSALL OLD ALE

The most famous of specialized mild ale producers is this 100-year-old English brewery in the West Midlands, owned for many years by Bass, but now independent. A beer that is only gently hopped, and malt-accented, like a mild, but with more alcohol, is a classic approach to an old ale or winter warmer. This November and December brew is a fine example. It has a

hint of passion fruit in the bouquet; touches of iron, oak, and well-done toast in the palate; and a toffeelike, comforting finish.

**Region of origin**
Central England, UK

**Style** Old Ale

**Alcohol content**
4.1 abw (5.1 abv)

**Ideal serving
temperature**
50–55° F (10–13° C)

## SARAH HUGHES DARK RUBY

Mrs. Hughes made this beer in the 1920s in a tiny tower brewery and pub at Sedgeley, near Dudley, in England's West Midlands. In those days beers were stronger, and its potency might once have passed as a mild. The brewery closed in 1957, but Mrs. Hughes' grandson restored it in 1987. This bottle-conditioned beer is fruity, toasty, rich, and complex, with some winey notes. The pub, The Beacon, is a real Victorian delight.

**Region of origin**
Central England,
UK

**Style** Old Ale

**Alcohol content**
4.8 abw (6.0 abv)

**Ideal serving
temperature**
50–55° F (10–13° C)

*Dudley drafts*
*Mrs. Hughes appears
on Dark Ruby's label.
There is a tradition
of tiny breweries
around Dudley.*

## WADWORTH OLD TIMER

This classic English country brewery in Devizes, Wiltshire, makes two beers broadly in the old ale style. One, called Farmer's Glory, is in the mode of a mild with extra alcohol (3.6 abw; 4.5 abv), and is intended as a compensation when summer fails to be sunny. It is malty and sweetish, but with a touch of dry hop. Old Timer is creamier, with a fresh, vanilla-pod, nutty maltiness that is both appetizing and satisfying in winter.

**Region of origin**
West of England, UK

**Style** Old Ale

**Alcohol content**
4.8 abw (6.0 abv)

**Ideal serving
temperature**
50–55° F (10–13° C)

*Old time brewing*
*Old Timer is traditional
in almost every
painstaking detail
of production.*

## ROBINSON'S OLD TOM

Many breweries have a cat to keep mice away from the barley malt. Perhaps such a cat inspired a brewer at Robinson's, near Manchester, to draw a tomcat's face in his log when he made a batch of this malty beer in 1899. This beer has been known as Old Tom since at least that time. In those days, most breweries would have called it simply Old Ale or Barley Wine. Old Tom has

a huge roundness of flavors, suggestions of cherry brandy, and a distinctive dryness in the finish.

**Region of origin**
Northwest England,
UK

**Style**
Old Ale/Barley Wine

**Alcohol content**
6.8 abw (8.5 abv)

**Ideal serving
temperature**
50–55° F (10–13° C)

# OLD ALES

## PITFIELD DARK STAR

An enduring legend among British beers, Dark Star, from the pioneering Pitfield microbrewery, in London, won the overall championship at the 1987 Great British Beer Festival. A decade later, it was judged best of all the Champion Beers of Britain over 25 years of the festival. By then it was being produced at the Evening Star brewery and pub in Brighton, Sussex, where it is still made. It is a beautifully rounded old ale, with licoricelike malt notes, hints of apple fruitiness, and a dryish, warm finish.

**Region of origin**
Southeast England, UK

**Style** Old Ale

**Alcohol content** 4.0 abw (5.0 abv)

**Ideal serving temperature**
50–55° F (10–13° C)

## FULL SAIL WASSAIL WINTER ALE

Windsurfers on the Columbia River provided a name for this well-established new-generation brewing company in Oregon. It has a microbrewery at the confluence of the Hood and Columbia Rivers, and a brewpub in nearby Portland. Not only is Full Sail Wassail Winter Ale a triumphant combination of alliteration and rhyme, it is also an awesome ale, pungent and powerful. It has a garnet color; a spicy aroma; an oily texture; and an intensely dry, sappy, brandyish finish.

**Region of origin**
Pacific Northwest US

**Style** Old Ale

**Alcohol content** 5.2 abw (6.5 abv)

**Ideal serving temperature**
50–55° F (10–13° C)

## KALAMAZOO THIRD COAST OLD ALE

The Eccentric Ale of this Michigan brewer is available only on the premises. It is Kalamazoo's most powerful winter warmer, spiced with – among other ingredients – snuff, saw palmetto berries, and roasted locust pods (they are poisonous unless roasted). The more widely available Third Coast Old Ale, burgundy in color, has a remarkable balance of syrupy sweetness; coffeeish acidity; spicy, fragrant hop; and leafy dryness.

**Region of origin** Midwest US

**Style** Old Ale

**Alcohol content** 6.4 abw (8.0 abv)

**Ideal serving temperature**
50–55° F (10–13° C)

## PALVASALMI REAL ALE BREWERY "VALTE"

This new-generation brewery and tasting room is run by two sisters at Saarijärvi, near Jyväskylä, a regional capital in central Finland. In the 17th century, the town was called Palvasalmi, which means a channel between two lakes. The brewery uses the English term Real Ale in its name. The beer called Valte is named after a dark-haired gipsy. The brew is burgundy-to-black, with a molasses aroma; a rummy palate; and a smoky finish.

**Region of origin** Finland

**Style** Old Ale

**Alcohol content** 4.2 abw (5.2 abv)

**Ideal serving temperature**
50–55° F (10–13° C)

## PETONE OWD JIM

An English-sounding "owd" ale produced in New Zealand, by a German. Manfred Graff, from Nuremberg, made beer in various countries before marrying a New Zealander and settling there. He built his own brewery in a 1950s shoe factory in Petone, near Wellington. He uses an *Altbier* yeast. Owd Jim, which is primarily consumed in winter, has a ruby color; a hint of molasses; a toffeeish palate; and a creamy, grainy finish.

**Region of origin**
North Island, New Zealand

**Style** Old Ale

**Alcohol content** 4.0 abw (5.0 abv)

**Ideal serving temperature**
50–55° F (10–13° C)

## RENWICK HURRICANE PREMIUM PURE MALT BEER

In the winemaking Marlborough district of New Zealand, where hurricanes hardly ever happen, former London cabbie and ship's steward Bill Penfold set up a pub, the Cork and Keg, and this small brewery, at Renwick. His Hurricane Premium Pure Malt Beer is in the style of an old ale, with a dark orange-to-chestnut color; suggestions of dark chocolate and vanilla; and a pleasantly medicinal finish.

**Region of origin**
South Island, New Zealand

**Style** Old Ale

**Alcohol content** 3.8 abw (4.8 abv)

**Ideal serving temperature**
50–55° F (10–13° C)

## SHAKESPEARE KING LEAR OLD ALE

One of the earliest new-generation breweries in New Zealand is at the Shakespeare, a turn-of-the-century pub near the waterfront in Auckland. The business is run by former New Zealand All Black rugby union player, Ron Urlich. All the beers are named after Shakespearian characters. King Lear Old Ale is very big indeed, with a dense head; an ebony color; a full body; textured maltiness; very distinct chocolate and rum flavors; a dryish, roasty finish; and a lingering warmth.

**Region of origin**
North Island, New Zealand

**Style** Old Ale

**Alcohol content** 6.0 abw (7.5 abv)

**Ideal serving temperature**
50–55° F (10–13° C)

## SUMMIT WINTER ALE

This highly regarded new-generation brewery is in Saint Paul, state capital of Minnesota. Founder Mark Stutrud was a therapist to substance abusers before establishing the brewery in 1986. Summit produces a wide range of ales, made with a British yeast. Its Winter Ale has a ruby color; a smooth, firm body that is nonetheless light on the tongue; a cookielike maltiness; and dryish, lively flavors reminiscent of vanilla, coffee, and cherries.

**Region of origin** Midwest US

**Style** Old Ale/Winter Ale

**Alcohol content** 5.0 abw (6.2 abv)

**Ideal serving temperature**
50–55° F (10–13° C)

# WINTER WARMERS: WHISKEY-MALT BEERS & STRONG SCOTTISH ALES

ALTHOUGH SCOTLAND MAKES BEERS of all colors and strengths, its most famous brews are dark, rich ales potent enough to fight the country's gusty, snowy weather. An example similar to an English barley wine is usually known in Scotland as a *wee* ("small") *heavy*. The romance of Scotland and the renown of its distilled spirits have in recent years inspired brewers in other countries to use peat-dried malts like those typically employed in whiskey. These represent a style in their own right (*page 116*). Some North American brewers use similar peated malts in Scottish-style ales (*page 117*).

**Winged warmer**
*This enamel long pre-dates Nussdorf's whiskeyish brew.*

## MITCHELL'S OLD 90/- ALE

The spread of the Scottish people has done much to introduce their beer styles to a wider world. Alexander Angus Mitchell was from Blairgowrie in Perthshire. He fought in the famous Highland regiment the Black Watch in the wars between the British and Dutch farmer (*Boer*) settlers in Southern Africa at the turn of the century. He married locally, and his grandson Lex founded the Mitchell's brewery, in Knysna, Western Cape, in 1984. The term 90/-, on his Scottish ale, refers to the old British unit of currency, the shilling. Traditionally, a "Ninety Shilling" was a strong ale. This unfiltered, unpasteurized example is spiced with cinnamon. It has an aroma reminiscent of Scotch whiskey; a malty palate; and a dry, slightly tart finish.

| | |
|---|---|
| **Region of origin** | South Africa |
| **Style** | Strong Scottish Ale |
| **Alcohol content** | 5.6 abw (7.0 abv) |
| **Ideal serving temperature** | Store at 41° F (5° C)  Serve at 50° F (10° C) |

## THE LADY OF TRAQUAIR

THE ENERGY OF Catherine Maxwell Stuart has done much to promote interest in the beers made at her family's castle, Traquair House. A *quair* is a winding stream. The house is alongside a stream running into the Tweed River. Lady Catherine is seen here with brewer Ian Cameron.

## BROUGHTON OLD JOCK

To Americans, the name of this drink sounds unsavory, but Scotsmen are called "Jock" (or, in Glasgow, "Jimmie") the way people in B-movies are called "Mack." This alcoholic manifestation might variously be regarded as an old ale, barley wine, or, in the more typically Scottish parlance, a wee heavy. It has more hop aroma than many Scottish ales; an appetizing, smooth, tasty maltiness; and a soothing, whiskeyish, warm finish.

**Region of origin**
Scottish Borders, UK

**Style**
Strong Scottish Ale

**Alcohol content**
5.4 abw (6.7 abv)

**Ideal serving temp.**
50–55° F (10–13° C)

## BORVE ALE

A hugely distinctive, characterful, complex beer from a tiny brewery in a former school at the hamlet of Ruthven, near Huntley, in the Grampian mountains. Borve Ale is matured in casks that have previously been used to age first Bourbon, then Scotch whiskey. It emerges with an oaky, "hopsack" aroma; a relatively light but clingy body; orangy flavors; and a big finish that is charcoal-like, peppery, and even salty.

**Region of origin**
Highlands, Northern Scotland, UK

**Style**
Strong Scottish Ale

**Alcohol content**
8.0 abw (10.0 abv)

**Ideal serving temperature**
50–55° F (10–13° C)

*Gaelic Ale*
*The Scottish Gaelic text on the label says "Brought to life on the Isle of Lewis."*

## TRAQUAIR HOUSE ALE

Beer from the castle at Traquair was first mentioned in 1566. The brewery was revived in 1965, by the 20th Laird ("Lord") of Traquair, Peter Maxwell Stuart. It is now managed by his daughter, Lady Catherine. The brewery's principal product has a lightly oaky aroma; touches of fresh earthiness, pepperiness, and nutty maltiness in the palate; and some woody, rooty tartness in the finish.

**Region of origin**
Scottish Borders, UK

**Style**
Strong Scottish Ale

**Alcohol content**
5.8 abw (7.2 abv)

**Ideal serving temp**
50–55° F (10–13° C)

*Label lore*
*The back label declares that Traquair's main gates will remain closed until a Stuart returns to the British throne.*

## GORDON HIGHLAND SCOTCH ALE

The Christmas beer under the Gordon name has this year-round counterpart with a marginally less hefty alcohol content but a big, fresh, rich maltiness and toasty balance. Both are made for the Belgian market by Scottish Courage. A similar beer, slightly less strong (5.8 abw; 7.3 abv) but with all the richness of a fruit-filled chocolate praline, was launched in the British market in 1998 under the name McEwan's No. 1 Champion Ale.

**Region of origin**
Southern Scotland, UK

**Style**
Strong Scottish Ale

**Alcohol content**
6.9 abw (8.6 abv)

**Ideal serving temperature**
50–55° F (10–13° C)

## HOEPFNER BLUE STAR

This beer was first brewed, in 1996, on New Year's Eve, a very important day for the Scots. It does not identify itself as being Scottish in style, but is in character very similar to the various whiskey-malt brews. The beer contains a proportion of beech-smoked malt, and has a subtly sappy dryness in the finish. It is oily, malty, and lightly nutty, with a touch of flowery elegance. Blue Star is produced by Hoepfner of Karlsruhe, Germany.

**Region of origin**
Baden-Württemberg, Germany

**Style** Smoked *Altbier*

**Alc. content** 4.4 abw (5.5 abv)

**Ideal serving temperature**
48° F (9° C)

## NUSSDORFER OLD WHISKY BIER

Having Anglicized his name for "Sir Henry's," a vaguely Irish stout, Baron Henrik Bachofen von Echt next turned his Vienna brewery to a Scottish theme with this satisfyingly malty brew. Among whiskey-malt beers, this example has notably lively, fruity, complex flavors. Though the smokiness is very restrained, it is just enough to provide a good, balancing dryness.

**Region of origin**
Austria

**Style**
Whiskey-malt *Altbier*

**Alcohol content**
4.9 abw (6.1 abv)

**Ideal serving temperature**
48° F (9° C)

## PELFORTH AMBERLEY

This *bière aromatisée au malt à whisky* is made by Pelforth in Lille, France. Amberley is smooth, firm, and dry. Among European examples of the style, it has perhaps the most obvious late smokiness. Whiskey-malt beer was pioneered in Alsace, France, by the lightly grainy-peaty Adelscott. There is a companion brew of a much darker style called Adelscott Noir. These beers are produced at the Adelshoffen brewery.

**Region of origin**
Northern France

**Style** Whiskey-malt Lager

**Alcohol content**
5.6 abw (7.0 abv)

**Ideal serving temperature**
48° F (9° C)

## MAC QUEEN'S NESSIE

The mythical monster Nessie is said to live in a Scottish loch, not a lake in the Alps, but its fame captures the imagination far and wide. The beer called Nessie is made by the castle brewery of Eggenberg, in lake country at Vorchdorf, between Salzburg and Linz, Austria. This incarnation of Nessie is a deep gold or bronze rather than the full "red" extravagantly promised on the label, but there is a real heftiness of malt in both the aroma and palate, with a late dryness and faint smokiness.

**Region of origin** Austria

**Style** Whiskey-malt Lager

**Alcohol content**
5.8 abw (7.3 abv)

**Ideal serving temperature**
48° F (9° C)

*Monstrously royal*
*Just in case Nessie is not sufficiently Scottish-sounding, the brewery has invented the company name, Mac Queen's.*

# WHISKEY-MALT BEERS & STRONG SCOTTISH ALES

## BELHAVEN WEE HEAVY

Oily, creamy, grainy, toasty, nutty (suggesting almond), and fruity (pineapple perhaps) . . . this has all the richness and flavor of a classic wee heavy, though it is less strong than some. Despite this, it is headily alcoholic and a good winter brew. Belhaven sometimes produces a stronger (6.4 abw; 8.0 abv) draft-only version under the name 90/-. There is also a less potent (4.8 abw; 6.0 abv) bottled wee heavy under the Fowler's name, brewed for the Bass subsidiary, Tennent's. This is pleasant enough, but a shadow of the beer produced by the long-gone Fowler's of Prestonpans.

**Region of origin**
Southern Scotland, UK

**Style** Wee Heavy

**Alcohol content** 5.2 abw (6.5 abv)

**Ideal serving temperature**
55° F (13° C)

## FISH POSEIDON OLD SCOTCH ALE

The Fish brewery, in Olympia, Washington, produces this hugely assertive, peated Scottish ale. An unusually large proportion of the malt used, about eight percent, is peated. While many such beers employ only a lightly peated malt, this contains the heavily kilned style. The result is a remarkable blend of sweetish, treacle-toffee maltiness; earthy chewiness; and woody smokiness.

**Region of origin** Northwest US

**Style** Strong Scottish Ale

**Alcohol content** 6.4 abw (8.0 abv)

**Ideal serving temperature**
55° F (13° C)

## MASH AND AIR SCOTCH ALE

Britain's first American-style brewpub opened in Manchester in 1997, with a London branch the following year. "Mash" refers to the infusion of grains in the making of beer, not to the food. "Air" was inspired by the building, a former textile mill towering over Manchester's nightlife quarter. One of the most characterful among the early beers was the Scotch Ale, very smooth and silky, developing some medicinal warming notes, and with a slightly smoky finish. Chocolate malt is used, along with Maris Otter, and hops from both England and Washington State.

**Region of origin**
Northwest England, UK

**Style** Strong Scottish Ale

**Alcohol content** 4.8 abw (6.0 abv)

**Ideal serving temperature**
50–55° F (10–13° C)

## MOUNT HOOD PITTOCK WEE HEAVY

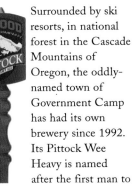

Surrounded by ski resorts, in national forest in the Cascade Mountains of Oregon, the oddly-named town of Government Camp has had its own brewery since 1992. Its Pittock Wee Heavy is named after the first man to reach the summit of Mount Hood (1,239 ft/378 m), in 1857. Henry L. Pittock was a businessman, writer, and mountaineer. This beer contains oats, peated malt, and East Kent Goldings, and has a relatively cool fermentation and maturation. It is a delicious brew, garnet-to-brown in color, with the aroma of cherry nougat; a fudgy palate, with lots of flavor development; and a caramel dryness in the finish.

**Region of origin** Northwest US

**Style** Wee Heavy

**Alcohol content** 6.4 abw (8.0 abv)

**Ideal serving temperature**
55° F (13° C)

## ORKNEY SKULLSPLITTER

Many skulls were said to have been split by a Viking ruler of Orkney in the ninth century. During renovations of the island's cathedral in 1919, a split skull was found sealed into a pillar. This beer, if taken in excess, seems to promise an eternal sleep. The Orkney brewery's Skullsplitter is a wee heavy. It has a raisiny, sweet aroma; a very creamy taste, developing flavors like a Dundee fruit cake dunked in port; and a toasty finish.

**Region of origin**
Orkney Islands, Scotland, UK

**Style** Strong Scottish Ale/Wee Heavy

**Alcohol content** 6.8 abw (8.5 abv)

**Ideal serving temperature**
55° F (13° C)

## PYRAMID SCOTCH ALE

A thistle in front of Egyptian pyramids makes an odd conjunction on this Scotch Ale from Seattle. The neck label light-heartedly proposes it as a drink after caber-tossing (the Highland sport in which pine trunks are thrown). The beer is made with a proportion of peated malt and some roasted barley. It has a cerise-to-burgundy color; a creamy, chocolate aroma; coffee-essence flavors; and a perfumy, smoky, portlike, oaky, dryish, warming finish.

**Region of origin** Northwest US

**Style** Strong Scottish Ale

**Alcohol content** 4.8 abw (6.0 abv)

**Ideal serving temperature**
55° F (13° C)

## UNIBROUE RAFTMAN

Lumberjacks who cut timber and rafted it down the St. Lawrence River were always willing to settle their differences over a beer, according to the neck label of this woody tasting brew. It is, in fact, a peat-smoked *bière au malt de whisky*, and perhaps the most assertive example of this style. It has an orangy, resiny aroma; a light, firm, malty middle; and an oaky, sappy, smoky finish. Raftman is one of the many individualistic beers from Unibroue, of Chambly, near Montreal.

**Region of origin**
Province of Quebec, Canada

**Style** Peat-smoked Ale

**Alcohol content** 4.4 abw (5.5 abv)

**Ideal serving temperature**
55° F (13° C)

## VERMONT PUB AND BREWERY WEE HEAVY

Lager expert and beer writer Greg Noonan established this brewery with his wife Nancy, who now runs it. The brewery, in Burlington, Vermont, has a wide range of very individualistic beers. Its Wee Heavy has a tawny-to-red color; a rich, fruity, syrupy maltiness; and a peppery, warming finish. The beer varies slightly each winter, its original gravity matching the year (e.g., 1098 for 1998). Classic "vintages" have popped up in some states at very high strengths.

**Region of origin** Northeast US

**Style** Wee Heavy

**Alcohol content** 6.4 abw (8.0 abv)

**Ideal serving temperature**
55° F (13° C)

# WINTER WARMERS: BALTIC PORTERS AND STOUTS

THE MOST WINTRY BEERS OF ALL are the extra-strong, almost tarlike porters and stouts originally made in Britain for export to the cold countries of the Baltic and Scandinavia. Because these beers were favored by the royal court in St. Petersburg, names such as Russian Stout and Imperial Stout are often used. In these hugely rich beers, the typical roastiness of stout develops into a burnt currant fruitiness with a warming embrace of alcohol.

**A Great Beer**
*Catherine II is mentioned on the label, which is partly rendered in Russian. The beer is a last vestige of a 200-year-old export trade.*

## COURAGE IMPERIAL RUSSIAN STOUT

Britain's biggest brewing company, Scottish Courage, is the current owner of this label. Behind it lies a powerful beer that is produced only occasionally and vintage-dated. Courage inherited the product from the now-defunct Barclay's brewery in London. That brewery exported the beer to the Baltic during the time of Empress Catherine II. With her encouragement, British-style porter, the most sophisticated beer of the day, was introduced to the Russian Empire. Today's Courage Imperial Russian Stout is winey, sherryish, raisiny, woody, and sappy. The most recent vintages have been made at Courage's subsidiary brewery, John Smith's, in Tadcaster, Yorkshire. That brewery's neighbor and independent rival, Samuel Smith's, produces an imperial stout that is slightly less strong but richer, more creamy, and peppery.

**Region of origin** London, England, UK

**Style** Imperial Stout

**Alcohol content** 8.0 abw (10.0 abv)

**Ideal serving temperature** 55–64° F (13–18° C)

### IMPERIAL THIRSTS

EMPRESS CATHERINE II was also known as Catherine the Great. Her appetites matched her name: she was said to breakfast on vodka-laced tea and a caviar omelette. A letter still exists from a later empress, Alexandra Feodorovna, thanking a British supplier for 5,000 bottles of stout donated to local hospitals.

## SINEBRYCHOFF PORTER

When Nikolai Sinebrychoff founded this brewery (also known as "Koff") in Helsinki in 1819, the city was under Russian rule. Koff has brewed porter from the start, apart from a period of prohibition in Finland in the early part of the 20th century. Porter was reintroduced for the 1952 Olympics. This brew is lively and flavorsome: dry, smooth, oily, coffeeish, and flowery, with fresh wood notes. It is rich and warming in the finish.

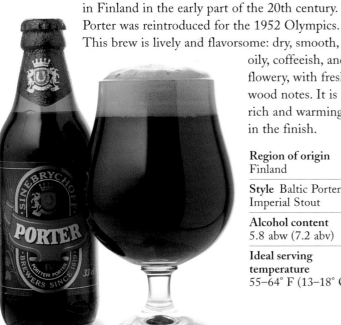

**Region of origin**
Finland

**Style** Baltic Porter/Imperial Stout

**Alcohol content**
5.8 abw (7.2 abv)

**Ideal serving temperature**
55–64° F (13–18° C)

## BALTIKA PORTER

The capital of imperial stout is home to this beer from the Baltika brewery, established in St. Petersburg as recently as 1990. Baltika Porter is soft, starting with a cereal-grain sweetness, but in the end proving to be lightly dry, with some whiskeyish notes. A fruitier, winier imperial porter is made by the nearby Vienna brewery. A firmer, spicier, more warming example comes from Stepan Razin, the city's oldest brewery, founded in 1795.

**Region of origin**
St. Petersburg, Russia

**Style**
Baltic Porter/Imperial Stout

**Alc. content** 5.6 abw (7.0 abv)

**Ideal serving temperature**
55–64° F (13–18° C)

## OKOCIM PORTER

The district of Okocim is in the town of Brzesko, to the east of Cracow, Poland. The brewery there was founded in 1845 and makes a porter in the northerly, Baltic tradition. It has a soothing, almost medicinal character, with hints of cinnamon, drying in a cedary, appetizing finish. Other Polish strong porters include a notably smooth example from the town of Zywiec and a more raisiny interpretation from the Elblag brewery.

**Region of origin**
Province of Galicia, Poland

**Style** Strong Porter/Imperial Stout

**Alcohol content**
6.5 abw (8.1 abv)

**Ideal serving temperature**
55–64° F (13–18° C)

*Imperial helmet?*
*This grandiose mug was designed to mark one of the brewery's anniversaries.*

## NORTH COAST OLD RASPUTIN RUSSIAN IMPERIAL STOUT

Grigori Rasputin was a mystic who influenced the royal family prior to his assassination. He is celebrated with some irony in this rich, buttery, toffeeish, rummy imperial stout. Along with an excellent dry stout called Old No. 38, it is produced by the North Coast brewery, in the one-time whaling port of Fort Bragg, California. Founded in 1987, the brewery began life in an old Presbyterian church and mortuary.

**Region of origin**
California, US

**Style** Imperial Stout

**Alcohol content**
7.1 abw (8.9 abv)

**Ideal serving temperature**
55–64° F (13–18° C)

# NIGHTCAP BEERS: BARLEY WINES

BARLEY WINE IS A TERM USED in the English-speaking world for the strongest of ales. They are beers, but some of them are as strong as wines and do have winey flavors. These derive from the behavior of ale yeasts at high strengths, often over long periods of fermentation and maturation. Some American brews in this style use wine yeasts, which are capable of creating more alcohol. Barley wines are best enjoyed in a small goblet, with a book at bedtime or a late-night movie.

## ELDRIDGE POPE
## THOMAS HARDY'S ALE

The ultimate book-at-bedtime beer. This brew is named after the novelist and poet Thomas Hardy, who wrote admiringly of the Eldridge Pope beer. In 1968, a festival to celebrate Hardy was held in his home town of Dorchester, and this beer was launched as a commemorative brew. Thomas Hardy's Ale is a beer that will mature in the bottle. When young, it can be as rich, creamy, and meaty as beef broth. There may also be apple-wood smokiness. After about five years, it develops Madeira flavors, and samples left to mature for 25 years have proven lean, warming, and elegant.

**Region of origin** West of England, UK

**Style** Barley Wine/Old Ale

**Alcohol content** 9.6 abw (12.0 abv)

**Ideal serving temperature**
Store: 55° F (13° C)
Serve: 55–64° F (13–18° C)

### ONE FOR THE LIBRARY

As THOMAS HARDY'S is typically stored for bottle-aging, the presentations on both left and right may be seen. In the 1980s, the beer was served at the National Theatre, London, to celebrate a play about the brewery by David Edgar.

THOMAS HARDY'S ALE VINTAGE 1997

In 'The Trumpet-Major' Hardy wrote of Dorchester's strong beer "It was of the most beautiful colour that the eye of an artist in beer could desire; full in body, yet brisk as a volcano; piquant, yet without a twang; luminous as an autumn sunset;..."

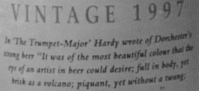

# BASS NO 1

This may have been the first barley wine to have been widely marketed, but that is not the reason for the name. Bass had several brewhouses even at the start of the 20th century, and this beer was produced in Number One. Today, it is made only occasionally at the Bass museum in Burton, but it is commercially available. It is firm, smooth, oily, oaky, and at first tasting shockingly bitter, but strangely addictive.

**Region of origin**
Trent Valley, England, UK

**Style** Barley Wine

**Alcohol content**
8.4 abw (10.5 abv)

**Ideal serving temperature**
Store at 55° F (13° C)
Serve at 50–55° F (10–13° C)

# WHITBREAD GOLD LABEL

Traditionally, barley wines were full in color, with the rich, treacly flavors that come from dark malts. Gold Label was the first pale one, launched in 1951, by a brewer that later became part of the Whitbread national group. It has an amber or bronze color, but its flavors speak of pale malts. Gold Label has a firm creaminess, with shortbread flavors, developing to a fruity, spicy dryness with hints of apricot and aniseed. Originally made in Sheffield, Yorkshire, this beer now comes from a brewery near Blackburn, Lancashire.

**Region of origin**
Northern England, UK

**Style** Barley Wine

**Alcohol content**
8.7 abw (10.9 abv)

**Ideal serving temperature**
50–55° F (10–13° C)

# COTTAGE NORMAN'S CONQUEST

Chris Norman, an airline pilot, took early retirement and started a brewery with his wife Helen in 1993. It was not quite in a cottage, but was initially in a garage at their house at Little Orchard, West Lydford, Somerset. Two years later, their barley wine was judged Champion Beer at the Great British Beer Festival. For a big beer, it is remarkably appetizing, with fresh cinnamon, sultana, and apple aromas. It has a clean, creamy palate and a spicy, peppery, balancing dryness.

**Region of origin**
West of England, UK

**Style** Barley Wine

**Alcohol content**
5.6 abw (7.0 abv)

**Ideal serving temperature**
Store 55° F (13° C)
Serve at 50–55° F (10–13° C)

# YOUNG'S OLD NICK

Once, every regional brewery in England had its own barley wine. Many have since dropped this style on the grounds that it is a minor speciality, but the London brewery Young's – a famously stubborn enterprise – has remained loyal to the style. This example is a rich, toffeeish brew, with a banana-liqueur finish. As the label suggests, this is one to enjoy in front of the fire before retiring for the night.

**Region of origin**
London, England, UK

**Style** Barley Wine

**Alcohol content**
5.4 abw (6.8 abv)

**Ideal serving temperature**
55° F (13° C)

***The old devil***
*An "old" ale in name, Old Nick is strong enough to wear the neck-label barley wine.*

# HERTOG JAN GRAND PRESTIGE

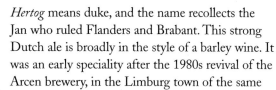

*Hertog* means duke, and the name recollects the Jan who ruled Flanders and Brabant. This strong Dutch ale is broadly in the style of a barley wine. It was an early speciality after the 1980s revival of the Arcen brewery, in the Limburg town of the same name. The beer has a dense head; a garnet color; a spicy malt aroma; a surprisingly light, soft body; and a sweetish, very slightly meaty, portlike finish.

**Region of origin**
Province of
Limburg, the
Netherlands

**Style** Barley Wine

**Alcohol content**
8.0 abw (10.0 abv)

**Ideal serving temperature**
55° F (13° C)

# CHELSEA OLD TITANIC

Had it completed its voyage, the Titanic would have docked at Pier 59 on New York's Hudson River. That is now a yacht marina and the site of the Chelsea brewery and pub (this part of Manhattan is known as Chelsea). The brewery's barley wine, named with black humor, might be enjoyed with an epic novel, but not one that prompts nightmares. It has a whiskeyish aroma; a malty, warming palate; and a toasty finish.

**Region of origin**
Northeast US

**Style** Barley Wine

**Alcohol content**
6.4 abw (8.0 abv)

**Ideal serving temperature**
55° F (13° C)

*Not to be iced*
*Icebergs loom on the label, but this ale is to be served at a natural cellar temperature.*

# ANCHOR OLD FOGHORN

Any vessel sailing into misty San Francisco Bay might welcome a warning foghorn. So would any drinker of discernment. This brew led the way in the introduction of barley wines by small American brewers, in 1975, and remains a leader in quality. It has a soft, oily, apricot-citrus character in both its big bouquet and juicy palate, and an intense, flowery dryness. The beer has between nine and ten months on dry hops. It is big yet complex, and even subtle. Drink it with a Jack London novel.

**Region of origin**
California, US

**Style** Barley Wine

**Alcohol content**
7.0 abw (8.7 abv)

**Ideal serving temperature**
55° F (13° C)

*Late warning*
*The maritime name of this big beer came later than that of the famous brewery.*

# BIG TIME OLD WOOLY

Mammoths might have been more common in icy Alaska than in rainy Washington State, but the hairy pachyderm makes an appropriate symbol for this big, strong winter warmer. The Big Time pub and brewery in Seattle is noted for beers with extravagant names and flavors to match. This one has beautifully combined aromas and flavors of fragrant hop, grapefruit zest, and layered maltiness. It is smooth and hoppy enough to be dazingly soporific.

**Region of origin**
Pacific Northwest
US

**Style** Barley Wine

**Alcohol content**
8.0 abw (10.0 abv)

**Ideal serving temperature**
55° F (13° C)

*Prehistoric nip*
*Old Wooly is vintage-dated, and unusual in that it develops with age.*

# BARLEY WINES

## BOULDER CREEK DIZZY LIZZY

A dryish but well balanced, astonishingly drinkable barley wine is among the British-accented beers from this Californian brewery and pub in the logging town of Boulder Creek, in the Redwood Hills north of Santa Cruz. Dizzy Lizzy starts soft and slightly syrupy, with a very clean maltiness; seems to slim down to quite a lean, firm, nutty character; then dries into a rounded finish with some flowery hoppiness. It is made mainly from pale ale malt, with a touch of crystal malt, and some brown sugar in the brew kettle.

**Region of origin** California, US

**Style** Barley Wine

**Alcohol content** 8.5 abw (10.6 abv)

**Ideal serving temperature** 55° F (13° C)

## BRIDGEPORT OLD KNUCKLEHEAD

A celebrated barley wine from the pioneering brewery and pub in Portland, Oregon. An assertive, delicious, juicy maltiness is cut by grassy, peppery hop flavors, and rounded in a warming finish. A bottling is released in November, and each year's label features a different local celebrity. One year, the mayor of Portland was asked if he would like to be the next Knucklehead; "It's a lot better than being Bud," he replied.

**Region of origin**
Pacific Northwest US

**Style** Barley Wine

**Alcohol content** 7.3 abw (9.1 abv)

**Ideal serving temperature** 55° F (13° C)

## MARIN "OLD DIPSEA"

In laid-back Marin County, across the water from San Francisco, this brewery and pub at Larkspur Landing makes many flavorsome specialities. The jokingly named "Old Dipsea" has an attractive, bright amber color, and a herbal hop accent in its aroma, flavor, and long dryness. This emphatic hop character is balanced by a firm, lean, juicy maltiness. It is very drinkable.

**Region of origin** California, US

**Style** Barley Wine

**Alcohol content** 7.6 abw (9.5 abv)

**Ideal serving temperature** 50–55° F (10–13° C)

## PIKE OLD BAWDY

A house of ill repute once occupied the Seattle building that became the first site of the Pike Brewery, hence Old Bawdy as a name for its robust barley wine. This is an unusual example of the style in that it contains a proportion of peated malt and is aged in oak. The beer has a peaty brown color and a sweetly malty aroma, becoming earthy and oaky, and finishing with a suggestion of a salty Scotch whiskey. A bedtime beer for someone who might otherwise favor a Laphroaig or Lagavulin.

**Region of origin**
Pacific Northwest US

**Style** Barley Wine

**Alcohol content** 8.0 abw (10.0 abv)

**Ideal serving temperature** 55° F (13° C)

## RICHBRAU POE'S TELL TALE ALE

The Gothic horror stories of Edgar Allan Poe may not be best for bedtime reading, but they do go well with this unusual beer. Poe worked briefly in Richmond, Virginia, as assistant editor of the *Southern Literary Messenger*. This beer comes from Richbrau, a brewery and pub in that town. The brew is aged in casks that previously held red wine, and that is reflected in its character. It has a pinkish russet color; a cellar aroma; a surprisingly light body with a firm, malty background; and an oaky, extraordinarily winey finish.

**Region of origin** Mid Atlantic US

**Style** Barley Wine

**Alcohol content** 8.0 abw (10.0 abv)

**Ideal serving temperature** 50–55° F (10–13° C)

## SIERRA NEVADA BIGFOOT ALE

Probably the world's hoppiest barley wine, especially in its bouquet. A remarkably aromatic interpretation of the style, with flavors that seem to explode on the tongue. Typically lemon-grassy, citric, grapefruity, tangerinelike American hop notes, and plenty of bitterness, combine with a huge maltiness and a crisp, clean yeast character in a big, bottle-conditioned brew that develops great complexity.

This is a world classic from the respected Sierra Nevada brewery in Chico, California.

**Region of origin** California, US

**Style** Barley Wine

**Alcohol content** 8.0 abw (10.0 abv)

**Ideal serving temperature** 50–55° F (10–13° C)

## SMITHWICK'S BARLEY WINE

A little-known speciality from the ale brewery in Kilkenny, Ireland. This barley wine, already of modest strength for the style, is often served in a mix with the regular Smithwick's Ale. The barley wine has a distinctly Burgundyish color; a full body; and notes of chocolate, toffee, Turkish delight, and fruit.

**Region of origin** Republic of Ireland

**Style** Barley Wine

**Alcohol content** 4.4 abw (5.5 abv)

**Ideal serving temperature** 50–55° F (10–13° C)

## WOODFORDE HEADCRACKER

Whimsically aggressive name for a "very strong pale ale" (or barley wine) from Woodforde, a very successful new-generation brewery in Norfolk, England. This beer is relatively light but smooth; starting malty, developing to a dry, medicinal, peppery hoppiness; and finishing with a marmalady fruitiness.

**Region of origin** Eastern England, UK

**Style** Barley Wine/Strong Pale Ale

**Alcohol content** 5.6 abw (7.0 abv)

**Ideal serving temperature** 50–55° F (10–13° C)

# APERITIFS: EXTRA-DRY PILSNER LAGERS

MANY GOLDEN LAGERS call themselves Pilsners (sometimes spelled Pilsener or abbreviated to Pils), but this term should be reserved only for a truly hoppy example: this means a flowery bouquet and an appetizingly dry finish. The bitterness of the best examples arouses the gastric juices and awakens the appetite. All borrow their designation from the world's first golden lager, which was made in 1842 in the Bohemian city of Pilsen, in the Czech Republic.

## PILSNER URQUELL

The term *Urquell* means "original source" in German, the official language of Bohemia when it was a part of the Austrian empire. Bohemia now forms, with Moravia, the Czech Republic. In Czech, the beer is called Plzeňský Prazdroj. This is the original Pilsner, copied throughout the world, often by lesser, blander beers. Its golden color was a novelty at the time when glass vessels were replacing stoneware steins and pewter tankards, but the beer's fame was also due to its quality. The famous Bohemian Saaz hop imparted the flowery, spicy aroma and bitter finish; the equally renowned Moravian barley malt provided a soft, delicious balance. Both characteristics have diminished slightly in recent years, but Pilsner Urquell is still one of the world's great beers.

*The Pilsner glass*
*Tall, conical glasses are often used to present Pilsner-style beers. This shape helps to sustain the sparkle.*

**Region of origin**
Pilsen, Bohemia, Czech Republic

**Style** Pilsner

**Alcohol content** 3.3 abw (4.4 abv)

**Ideal serving temperature** 48° F (9° C)

### TRIUMPHAL BREW

WITH ITS MAGNIFICENT, Napoleonic-looking arches, the Pilsner Urquell brewery reflects the pride inspired by its famous beer. In the former Austrian Empire, Germany and Scandinavia, several great breweries have similar architectural features . . . like Victorian industrial buildings in Britain.

## MORAVIA PILS

Although the name honors the Czech barley-growing region, it is the export of Bohemian hops down the Elbe River that seems to have inspired the especially assertive Pilsners of North Germany. Moravia Pils is one of the best-known examples. It has a flowery, minty aroma; a light, firm, clean, dry maltiness; a big hit of hop bitterness; and a gently dry finish. The Moravia brewery in Lüneburg is owned by Holsten.

**Region of origin**
Lower Saxony, Germany

**Style** Pilsner

**Alcohol content**
3.8 abw (4.8 abv)

**Ideal serving temperature**
48° F (9° C)

## JEVER PILSENER

The town of Jever (pronounced "yayver") is in the German part of Friesland, a region that also straddles Denmark and the Netherlands. The people of Friesland are reputed to have a taste for food and drink with strong flavors. Jever Pilsener is famous among beer lovers worldwide for its bitterness. It pours with the blossoming head favored on German Pilsners, and has a tingling, almost rough dryness on the tongue.

**Region of origin**
Northern Germany

**Style** Pilsner

**Alcohol content**
3.9 abw (4.9 abv)

**Ideal serving temperature**
48° F (9° C)

## RADEBERGER PILSNER

The King of Saxony was supplied with beer from this brewery in Radeberg, northeast of Dresden. The area, with its own history of hop-growing, is close to the Czech region of Bohemia. The brewery dates from 1872, and its Pilsner survived as a speciality during East Germany's 40-odd years of communism. Radeberger Pilsner is aromatic, with earthy hop flavors, a firm body, and a crisp, dry finish.

**Region of origin** Saxony, Germany

**Style** Pilsner

**Alcohol content** 3.8 abw (4.8 abv)

**Ideal serving temp.** 48° F (9° C)

*Head fit for a king*
*Radeberger pours with a huge head, half-filling its elegant flute glass.*

## WERNESGRÜNER PILS LEGENDE

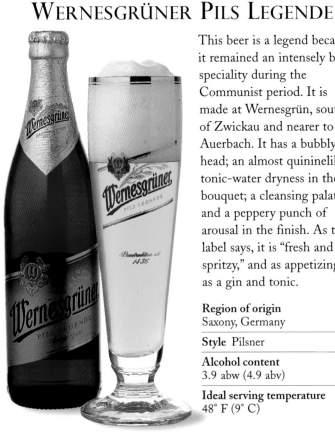

This beer is a legend because it remained an intensely bitter speciality during the Communist period. It is made at Wernesgrün, south of Zwickau and nearer to Auerbach. It has a bubbly head; an almost quininelike, tonic-water dryness in the bouquet; a cleansing palate; and a peppery punch of arousal in the finish. As the label says, it is "fresh and spritzy," and as appetizing as a gin and tonic.

**Region of origin**
Saxony, Germany

**Style** Pilsner

**Alcohol content**
3.9 abw (4.9 abv)

**Ideal serving temperature**
48° F (9° C)

## DAS FEINE HOFMARK WÜRZIG HERB

As the road from Nuremberg approaches the Czech border, the Das Feine Hofmark brewery sits on a hillside at Loifling, near Cham. It produces its *würzig* (aromatic) Pilsner in two versions. The *mild* is beautifully flowery, with a gently perfumy dryness; but this *herb* ("bitter") version of the beer is a touch firmer in its dry finish.

**Region of origin**
Bavaria, Germany

**Style** Pilsner

**Alcohol content**
4.5 abw (5.6 abv)

**Ideal serving temperature**
48° F (9° C)

## HOEPFNER PILSNER

The family name derives from "hop farmer," though the member who founded this brewery in Karlsruhe, Germany, was a priest. The brewery was established in 1798, has seen six generations of Hoepfners, and is now in an 1898 building that looks like a castle. Hoepfner Pilsner is very well hopped, but the bitterness is balanced by a mint-creme aroma and light, marshmallow maltiness. Its complexity may owe something to the use of traditional open fermenters.

**Region of origin**
Baden-Württemburg, Germany

**Style** Pilsner

**Alc. content** 3.8 abw (4.8 abv)

**Ideal serving temperature**
48° F (9° C)

## ST. GEORGEN KELLER BIER

In Germany, Pilsner beers are normally filtered; this beer is not, and therefore it is, strictly speaking, a *Kellerbier* (taken from the cellar while still hazy). Nonetheless, it is of a typical Pilsner strength, with a superbly appetizing, fresh, flowery, hop character. The hop is balanced by a lightly nutty maltiness and a yeasty acidity in the finish. The beer is made by St. Georgen at Buttenheim in Bavaria, near the great brewing town of Bamberg.

**Region of origin**
Franconia, Bavaria, Germany

**Style** *Kellerbier/* Unfiltered Pilsner

**Alcohol content**
3.9 abw (4.9 abv)

**Ideal serving temperature**
48° F (9° C)

***A seasonal saint***
*St. George's Day sometimes marked the season's last brew.*

## CHRISTOFFEL BLOND

One of the world's hoppiest Pilsner-style beers, made at Roermond in Dutch Limburg, near the German border. The town's saint is St. Christopher. This new-generation brewery was founded in 1986 by Dutch brewer Leo Brand. Its Blond beer has spicy, piny, hop aromas; very lively flavors; and an appetizingly robust bitterness in the finish. In the Netherlands, the term Pils often indicates a bland beer; the brewery avoids this description.

**Region of origin**
Province of Limburg, the Netherlands

**Style** Pilsner

**Alcohol content**
4.0 abw (5.0 abv)

**Ideal serving temperature**
48° F (9° C)

# CON DOMUS

A beer with Domus? The student clientele of the Domus brewery and pub in Leuven, Belgium, is no doubt amused by the sexy pun, but the beer is perfectly serious. It has a flowery, oily, hop aroma; a rich malt background; and a spicy, minty finish. It is very dry indeed and an excellent aperitif. A cheekily assertive Pilsner-style beer made in the shadow of the town's Stella Artois brewery.

**Region of origin** Province of Flemish Brabant, Belgium

**Style** Pilsner

**Alcohol content** 4.0 abw (5.0 abv)

**Ideal serving temperature** 48° F (9° C)

***Hoppy students***
*The Catholic University of Leuven, dating from 1425, and boasting Erasmus and Mercator among its alumni, awards doctorates in brewing science.*

# STOUDT'S PILS

Not a stout brewery – the family name is spelled with a "d" and is originally German. Mrs. Carol Stoudt runs this brewery, in Adamstown, Pennsylvania, and has won awards for many styles of beer. Her Pils ("assertively hopped with Saaz," according to the label) is one of America's best examples. It has an excellent hop character in its aroma, flavor, bitterness, and finishes with a very late, lingering, lemony dryness. The brewery adjoins a steak restaurant and a Sunday antique market.

**Region of origin**
Northeast US

**Style** Pilsner

**Alcohol content** 3.6 abw (4.5 abv)

**Ideal serving temperature** 48° F (9° C)

# DOCK STREET BOHEMIAN PILSNER

The Dock Street brewery and pub in Philadelphia produces two Pilsner-style brews: a regular Bohemian and an occasional German version. Bohemian Pilsner is softly aromatic, with a sweet, malt background and a crisply hoppy finish. The signature hop is the Bohemian variety Saaz. The German version is firmer and drier, and features Tettnang hops.

**Region of origin**
Northeast US

**Style** Pilsner

**Alcohol content** 4.1 abw (5.1 abv)

**Ideal serving temperature** 48° F (9° C)

# VICTORY PRIMA PILS

The stylized hop on the label is appropriate for this very bitter Pilsner made in Downingtown, Pennsylvania, by the Victory brewery and pub. It has a "fresh sea air" aroma of Saaz hops; almost gritty hop flavors; a lean malt background; and a firm, bitter finish. This Pilsner was inspired by the very hoppy example of the style made by the Vogelbräu brewery and pub in Karlsruhe, Germany.

**Region of origin** Northeast US

**Style** Pilsner

**Alc. content** 4.3 abw (5.4 abv)

**Ideal serving temperature** 48° F (9 °C)

***Pennsylvania prime***
*The state of William Penn was once the heart of German brewing in the US. It bids to be so again.*

# APERITIFS: DRY ABBEY BEERS

AMONG THE TRAPPIST ABBEYS of Belgium and the Netherlands, only Orval restricts itself to just one beer: an intensely dry, amber, strong ale that is a superb aperitif. The abbey of Chimay has three principal beers, with a distinctly dry speciality in the middle of its range. The abbey of Westmalle has a golden "single" for the monks to drink with their meals; a stronger, sweeter, dark "double;" and a yet more potent, pale, fruitily-dry aperitif "triple." Terms such as single, double, and triple date from times before widespread literacy and correspond to the strength of the beer.

**A touch of glass**
*The Orval glass was designed by Henri Vaes, the abbey's architect.*

## ORVAL

The abbey's name derives from *Vallée d'Or* (Valley of Gold). Legend has it that a countess lost a gold ring in a lake there, and vowed that she would establish a monastery if it were ever returned. A trout appeared from the waters with her gold ring in its mouth, and she was as good as her word. Monks have occupied the site in the Ardennes, since 1070. Today's 1930s abbey is an architectural gem, and the beer a classic. It gains its color from its own specification of malt, and is dry-hopped. The hopsack aroma derives from the use of a semiwild yeast (*Brettanomyces*), which adds a light, firm body and fresh acidity of finish.

**Region of origin**
Province of Luxembourg, Belgium

**Style** Abbey (Authentic Trappist)

**Alcohol content** 5.0 abw (6.2 abv)

**Ideal serving temperature**
Store at around 57° F (14° C)
Serve no colder than 50° F (10° C)

### ON GOLDEN POND

THE COUNTESS WAS MATILDA of Tuscany (*c.* 1046–1115), wife of the Duke of Lorraine. Her husband was assassinated by the Duke of Flanders, and she was mourning him when she founded the "Valley of Gold." She is depicted here by the Belgian artist Camille Barthélémy (1890–1961).

# CHIMAY CINQ CENTS

The best-known of the Trappist abbey breweries dates from the mid-1800s. It became known for dark, sweet brews, but in the 1960s decided to add a drier beer to its range. This version was originally known by the white cap on the bottle, but an additional champagne-style presentation was added to celebrate the 500th anniversary of the nearby town of Chimay. Cinq Cents has a remarkably fluffy body; a light but firm hit of malt; and an intense, late, junipery dryness.

**Region of origin**
Province of Hainaut, Belgium

**Style** Abbey (Authentic Trappist)

**Alc. content** 6.4 abw (8.0 abv)

**Ideal serving temperature**
Store: around 57° F (14° C)
Serve: at least 50° F (10° C)

*It's a corker*
*Chimay beers in the original bottles do not seem to gain quite the softness in maturation imparted by this larger, corked version.*

# WESTMALLE TRAPPIST

The Westmalle abbey dates from 1794. This pale beer was added to its range of beers in the period following World War II.

Westmalle Trappist has become a classic, much imitated for its orangy-gold color; its combination of high strength and drinkability; and its complex of appetizing aromas and flavors. A sea-air freshness in the nose, from Saaz hops; herbal, sagelike notes; and an orange-zest fruitiness are just some of the elements.

**Region of origin** Province of Antwerp, Belgium

**Style** Abbey (Authentic Trappist) Triple

**Alcohol content**
7.2 abw (9.0 abv)

**Ideal serving temperature**
Store at around 57° F (14° C). Serve no colder than 50° F (10° C)

# BOSTEELS TRIPEL KARMELIET

A Belgian Carmelite abbey reputedly made a three-grain beer at Dendermonde in the 1600s. This inspired the Bosteels brewery, in nearby Buggenhout, to create, in 1997, a *tripel* made from barley, wheat, and oats. Each is used both raw and malted, and the beer is also heavily spiced. Tripel Karmeliet is a brew of some finesse and complexity: with a wheaty lightness, sweet lemons, an oaty creaminess, and a spicy, medicinal dryness.

**Region of origin** Province of East Flanders, Belgium

**Style** Abbey Triple

**Alcohol content**
6.4 abw (8.0 abv)

**Ideal serving temperature**
Store at around
57° F (14° C)
Serve no colder than
50° F (10° C)

# VILLERS TRIPPEL

Villers-la-Ville is a ruined Cistercian Abbey southeast of Brussels that brewed in 1215. Today the abbey is remembered in a range of beers made in Liezele, near Puurs, north of the city. The brewery dates from 1727, and three of its past owners were mayors of the town. Villers Trippel is very fruity, with suggestions of apples, apricots, and honey. It is one of the drier examples of this style produced outside monasteries, but not especially complex.

**Region of origin** Province of Antwerp, Belgium

**Style** Abbey Triple

**Alcohol content**
6.8 abw (8.5 abv)

**Ideal serving temperature**
Store at around 57° F (14° C). Serve no colder than 50° F (10° C)

# APERITIFS: STRONG GOLDEN ALES

**T**HE FLOWERIEST OF APERITIF BEERS are the Belgian-style strong golden brews originally inspired by the classic, Duvel. The flowery character of these ales arises from hop varieties normally used in lagers – and from aromas created during the fermentation of such strong brews. Their distinctive character shines through because, despite their strength, these beers are lean in body: pale malts and highly fermentable sugars are used, and there is a maturation in the bottle. The Belgians regard beers in this style as an elegant aperitif, even where wine is to be served with the lunch or dinner. They can also be served after the meal, chilled, like the "white alcohol" brandies of Alsace.

**Belgium's devil**
*In local lore, the devil shown above is said to haunt hop-growers. The image is from the Hopduvel, a famous beer café in Ghent.*

## MOORTGAT DUVEL

The strange case of a dark brown beer that turned to gold. When British beers were fashionable in Belgium, the family-owned Moortgat brewery, at Breendonk, north of Brussels, produced a Scottish ale, using McEwan's yeast. The brewery later decided to restyle this, keeping the Scottish yeast and ale fermentation, and the high strength, but using pale malts to meet a tide of golden lagers. The beer is hopped with the Styrian Goldings variety (often used in English ales) and Saaz (typically preferred in lagers). An elaborate sequence of warm and cold fermentation and maturation lasts for well over three months and sometimes more than four. "The Devil of a Beer!" someone in the brewery observed of the first experimental batch, hence the Flemish corruption *Duvel* (pronounced "doovl"). The brew is extremely fragrant, and has flavors reminiscent of orange zest, pear brandy, green apples, and the lightest touch of smooth, stony dryness.

**Region of origin**
Province of Antwerp, Belgium

**Style** Belgian-style Strong Golden Ale

**Alcohol content** 6.8 abw ( 8.5 abv)

**Ideal serving temperature** 50° F (10° C)

## LOUWAEGE HAPKIN

Named after an ax-wielding Count of Flanders, Boudewijn Hapkin. (All beers in this style have names that are in some way diabolical.) In complexity, Hapkin perhaps comes closest to Duvel. This beer has a very perfumy aroma; a soft maltiness; a clean, smooth fruitiness; a persistent bead; and a spritzy, very dry finish. Hapkin is made by the family-owned Louwaege brewery, at Kortemark, southwest of Bruges.

**Region of origin**
Province of West
Flanders, Belgium

**Style** Belgian-style
Strong Golden Ale

**Alcohol content**
6.8 abw (8.5 abv)

**Ideal serving
temperature**
50° F (10° C)

## ALKEN-MAES JUDAS

Deceitful? Well, deceptively potent, true to style. Judas is from the Belgian national brewer Alken-Maes, and has a fruity dryness; a sweet-orange palate; and a dry finish. Julius – winier, spicier, and drier – is its national rival from Interbrew (Artois). The makers of Judas suggest a serving temperature of 43–46° F (6–8° C) and Julius 41–43° F (5–6° C). At these temperatures, all that can be tasted is the sensation of cold.

**Region of origin**
Province of Antwerp,
Belgium

**Style** Belgian-style
Strong Golden Ale

**Alcohol content**
6.8 abw (8.5 abv)

**Ideal serving
temperature**
50° F (10° C)

## ARCEN HET ELFDE GEBOD

The name means "The Eleventh Commandment." This ordination is: "Enjoy!" and refers to food and drink. Het Elfde Gebod is a bright Dutch beer, more restrained in alcohol than its competitors, with a perfumy apple aroma; some banana and honey notes in the palate; and a teasing interplay of sweetness and dryness. The beer was originally produced by Breda/ Oranjeboom, and is now made by the Arcen brewery, which long ago made Skol.

**Region of origin**
Province of Limburg,
the Netherlands

**Style** Belgian-style
Strong Golden Ale

**Alcohol content**
5.6 abw (7.0 abv)

**Ideal serving
temperature**
50° F (10° C)

## JEANNE D'ARC BELZEBUTH

"Beelzebub" is from the ancient Greek and Hebrew for the Devil, or his alternate the "Lord of the Flies." He is graphically shown on the label of this beer, from a French brewery with the combustible name Jeanne d'Arc. This immensely strong, bright beer is said to be all-malt (that is, not to contain other sugars). It is smooth, almost fluffy, starting candyish, with peppery alcohol flavors perhaps contributing to a spicy, surprising dryness. Belzebuth is less thick than might be expected at its strength, but is very heady.

**Region of origin**
Northern France

**Style** Belgian-style Strong
Golden Ale

**Alcohol content**
12.0 abw (15.0 abv)

**Ideal serving temperature**
50° F (10° C)

# APERITIFS: INDIA PALE ALES

Many drinkers have encountered the term "IPA" without realizing that the initials stand for "India Pale Ale." When pale ales became fashionable, the British Empire in India was at its height, and a special version of the style was made for the British colonial rulers. India Pale Ales were stronger than usual so that they could continue fermenting during the long sea journey. Hops, being a preservative, were used especially heavily, and that made the beer bitter. In most British examples, the bitterness is no longer extreme, but US revivalists (such as the Steelhead brewery and café at Eugene, Oregon) make some of the world's driest, and most appetizing, beers.

*Bombay Bomber . . .*
*. . . is made by Teri*
*Fahrendorf at Steelhead.*

**Bravura bitterness**
*The name 1812 is*
*whimsically intended*
*to suggest an "overture"*
*of hop aroma.*

## EMERSON'S 1812 INDIA PALE ALE

Not from India, but certainly round the Horn. This new-generation brewery is in the New Zealand city of Dunedin (the old name for Edinburgh). It makes some of New Zealand's best beers. Emerson's 1812 India Pale Ale is very appetizingly aromatic, with a spicy hop bouquet. There is also a great deal of hop flavor, rather than pure bitterness. The hop notes are set against a light, smooth, juicy, malt background. The flavors are beautifully combined, and the finish is fresh, dry, and faintly lemony. The inspiration for the brewery was a visit by George Emerson, a bio-chemist, to Edinburgh in 1983. He traveled with his son Richard, 18 at the time, who later established the business. Richard, who is almost entirely deaf, has nonetheless been a voluble publicist for his products.

**Region of origin**
South Island, New Zealand

**Style** India Pale Ale

**Alcohol content** 3.9 abw (4.9 abv)

**Ideal serving temperature** 54° F (12° C)

### THIRST CLIPPER

Pale ale was perfected by brewers like Allsopp and Bass in Burton, from the 1820s. Burton is in the middle of England, but was linked by canal and river to the sea. India Pale Ales were shipped to Calcutta to quench the thirsts of British plantation owners there. The clippers came back with tea.

## BURTON BRIDGE EMPIRE PALE ALE

Although pale ale is said to have been first produced in London, the style was made famous by the great breweries of Burton, helping this small town in the Midlands to become Britain's beer capital. New-generation brewery Burton Bridge has sought to revive the tradition of strong, hoppy IPA in Britain. There is a distinct "hopsack" aroma and taste to this lively, leafy, peppery, orangy, and bitter brew.

**Region of origin**
Trent Valley, England, UK

**Style** India Pale Ale

**Alcohol content**
6.0 abw (7.5 abv)

**Ideal serving temperature**
50–55° F (10–13° C)

## COBBOLD IPA

Coastal, barley country brewery, in Ipswich, England. The enterprise was founded by country gentry, and traces its history to 1723, but was reborn as a microbrewery in a management buyout in 1990. The IPA pours with a very well-retained head; has a good English, slightly peppery, hop aroma; a smooth, light body; a light palate, with a touch of clean apple; and a firm hit of dryness in the finish. There is some appetizingly lingering bitterness.

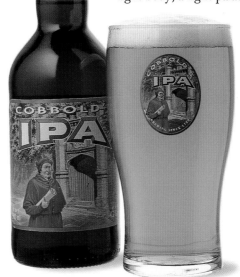

**Region of origin**
Eastern England, UK

**Style** India Pale Ale

**Alcohol content**
3.4 abw (4.2 abv)

**Ideal serving temperature**
50–55° F (10–13° C)

## McNEILL'S DEAD HORSE INDIA PALE ALE

Cellists Ray and Holiday McNeill run a brewery and pub in a former police station in Brattleboro, Vermont. Their beers are wonderfully appetizing, despite off-putting names. Dead Horse IPA is aromatic, with long, oily, hop flavors; a firm, malt background; and a cedary, dry finish. It is dry-hopped with East Kent Goldings. This is one of the best IPAs on the East Coast (Brooklyn's East India Pale Ale being another fine manifestation), but the US is dense with outstanding examples.

**Region of origin**
Northeast US

**Style** India Pale Ale

**Alcohol content**
4.6 abw (5.8 abv)

**Ideal serving temperature**
50–55° F (10–13° C)

## BIG TIME BHAGWAN'S BEST INDIA PALE ALE

Several American breweries use jocular names for their IPAs. Big Time, in Seattle, pays wry tribute to Bhagwan Shree Rajneesh, who established a commune in nearby Oregon in the 1980s. The beer has the grapefruit-zest American hop aroma typical in many northwestern beers; perfumy, sweet-orange flavors; a light, soft body; and a lemony, stony, appetizingly dry finish.

**Region of origin**
Pacific Northwest US

**Style** India Pale Ale

**Alcohol content**
4.6 abw (5.8 abv)

**Ideal serving temperature**
50° F (10° C)

## BRAINS IPA

"It's Brains You Want," says the slogan. The brewery, founded in 1713, was acquired by Samuel and Joseph Brain in 1882, and is still owned by the family. It is in the center of Cardiff, capital of Wales. The brewery's principal beers are known for their maltiness, but its IPA has a hoppy fragrance. It then presents a lightly malty, sweetish background flavor, before returning to the hop in an appetizing finish, with suggestions of orange zest and lemon rind.

**Region of origin**
South Wales, UK

**Style** India Pale Ale

**Alcohol content**
3.6 abw (4.5 abv)

**Ideal serving temperature**
50–55° F (10–13° C)

*Dragon's brew*
*Many IPAs have symbols of India on the label, but Brains prefers the red dragon of Wales.*

## MARSTON'S INDIA EXPORT

In the town of Burton, at the heart of India Pale Ale country, the Marston's brewery has since 1992 produced this revivalist example. It has a fine bead; a delicate aroma, with only the faintest hint of the typical Burton sulfur; a lightly oily, malt background; a light, very clean, refreshing, sweet apple palate; and a delicate touch of acidity and dryness in the finish. Like many British manifestations, it could do with a little more hop.

**Region of origin**
Trent Valley, England

**Style** India Pale Ale

**Alcohol content**
4.4 abw (5.5 abv)

**Ideal serving temperature**
50–55° F (10–13° C)

## BOSTON BEER WORKS BACK BAY INDIA PALE ALE

The excellent selection of brewpubs has become a tourist attraction in Boston, Massachusetts. The Boston Beer Works, an industrial-chic bar near the Fenway Park home of the Red Sox, has some very assertive products, in a rotating selection of 30–40 brews. Its IPA, named after the Back Bay area of Boston, has a fresh, leafy bouquet, with suggestions of lemon pith; a light, clean, malt background; a quick development into a woody, hop dryness; and a robustly bitter, appetizing finish.

**Region of origin**
Northeast US

**Style** India Pale Ale

**Alcohol content**
5.2 abw (6.5 abv)

**Ideal serving temperature**
50–55° F (10–13° C)

## CATAMOUNT 10 IPA

This pioneering new-generation brewery, established in 1987 in White River Junction, Vermont, launched an IPA to mark its tenth year. The beer has a fine bead; the complex hop bouquet is spicy, piney, and grapefruity; the body is firm; the palate is fresh, with a tingling hit of orange zest developing to flavors reminiscent of tangerine icing on a sponge cake; and a balancing minty, herbal dryness.

**Region of origin**
Northeast US

**Style** India Pale Ale

**Alcohol content**
5.0 abw (6.2 abv)

**Ideal serving temperature**
50–55° F (10–13° C)

# MAGIC HAT BLIND FAITH IPA

"The idea of opening a brewery? We pulled it out of a hat," said one of the founders. Magic Hat first fired its kettle in 1994. The brewery has a purple ceiling, with moons and stars suspended as mobiles. It is in the "alternative" city of Burlington, Vermont. Blind Faith IPA has a light but firm, crisp body; very good, spicy, hop flavors; a smooth, toffeeish, malt background; and the hops and malt round out beautifully in the finish.

**Region**
Northeast US

**Style** India Pale Ale

**Alcohol content**
4.9 abw (6.1 abv)

**Ideal serving temperature**
50–55° F (10–13° C)

# PARK SLOPE INDIA PALE ALE

Where the borough of Brooklyn, New York City, slopes towards its elegant Prospect Park, a district of imposing brownstones has become a "village" of food shops and cafés. An 1890s bakery there was turned into a pub and brewery in 1994. The pub still operates, but with a brewery on a separate site nearby. Its IPA is perfumy, with sweet apple flavors; well balanced and drinkable; with lingering hop notes and a crisp finish.

**Region of origin**
Northeast US

**Style** India Pale Ale

**Alcohol content**
4.8 abw (6.0 abv)

**Ideal serving temperature**
50–55° F (10–13° C)

# BRIDGEPORT INDIA PALE ALE

One of the many fruity, dry, bitter India Pale Ales made in the Pacific Northwest. This bottle-conditioned brew, from Portland, Oregon, has a lemony, grapefruity, resiny aroma; an oily palate, with suggestions of vanilla pod and orange peach sorbet; and a rush of intense minty, woody, cedary bitterness in the finish. No fewer than five hop varieties are used: Cascade, Chinook, Golding, Crystal, and Northwest Ultra.

**Region of origin**
Pacific Northwest US

**Style** India Pale Ale

**Alcohol content**
4.4 abw (5.5 abv)

**Ideal serving temperature**
50–55° F (10–13° C)

# GRANT'S INDIA PALE ALE

The first new-generation brewery in the US to use the term India Pale Ale was Grant's, in Yakima, capital of the Washington State hop-growing region. Grant's thus began the revival of this classically hoppy style. Grant's IPA is unusually pale, with a firm, dry, slender body. It has a great deal of floral hop flavor; a fresh apple fruitiness; and a powerful, lingering, very

dry, bitter finish. The hop varieties used are Galena and Cascade, and the beer is said to have 50 units of bitterness.

**Region of origin**
Pacific Northwest US

**Style** India Pale Ale

**Alcohol content**
3.4 abw (4.2 abv)

**Ideal serving temp.**
50–55° F
(10–13° C)

# APERITIFS: EXTRA-HOPPY ALES

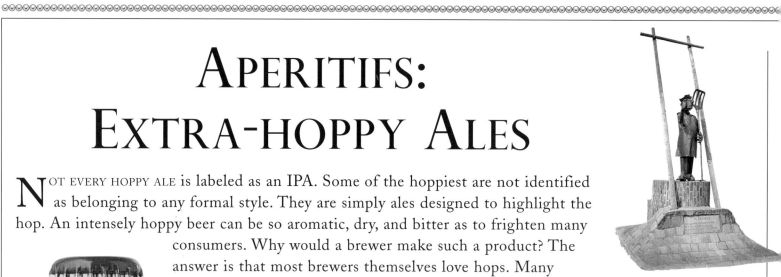

Not every hoppy ale is labeled as an IPA. Some of the hoppiest are not identified as belonging to any formal style. They are simply ales designed to highlight the hop. An intensely hoppy beer can be so aromatic, dry, and bitter as to frighten many consumers. Why would a brewer make such a product? The answer is that most brewers themselves love hops. Many would like to make their beers far hoppier than the marketing department advises. The beers on these two pages are expressions of brewers' hoppiest ambitions.

*Framed by hop poles*
*"The Brewer" statue in*
*Watou, near Poperinge*
*in West Flanders, Belgium.*

## ANCHOR LIBERTY ALE

This world classic has its origins in a pilgrimage made in the early 1970s by Anchor's owner Fritz Maytag to several great English ale breweries, among them Young's of London. Inspired by the hoppy ales of England, he began to work on a brew that would highlight American varieties of hop. His Liberty Ale was first produced in 1975, to commemorate Paul Revere's ride of 1775. (Revere rode from Boston to Lexington, Massachusetts, to warn the American patriots that the British were coming to seize their weapons; thus started the War of Independence.) Anchor Liberty is hugely aromatic, though its perfumy bouquet is complex and rounded. The body is surprisingly light, but smooth and oily. The palate gradually develops cleansing, lemon-rind, angelica, appetizing flavors, building to an intense finish as dry as a Martini.

**Region of origin** West US

**Style** American Ale

**Alcohol content** 4.9 abw (6.1 abv)

**Ideal serving temperature** 50° F (10° C)

*Taking a Liberty*
*The American eagle seems to have made a nest from barley and hops on the label of Anchor Liberty. The hops are of the variety Cascade, from Washington State.*

# TUPPERS' HOP POCKET ALE

Bob Tupper is a history teacher who gives lectures on beer at a famous bar, The Brickskeller, in Washington, DC. He and his wife Ellie, an editor, designed this beer, which is produced by the local Old Dominion brewery. It has a flowery aroma; a crisp, cedary, malt background; and wood-bark bitterness in its big, lingering finish. A hop "pocket" is the long sack in which pressed hops are packed. It looks like a boxer's punchbag: this beer hops and hits with the best.

**Region of origin**
Mid Atlantic US

**Style** American Ale

**Alcohol content**
4.8 abw (6.0 abv)

**Ideal serving temperature**
50° F (10° C)

# YOUNG'S SPECIAL LONDON ALE

London beermaker John Young has a Belgian-born wife, and once made a superbly hoppy English ale for her local brewery near Liège. The product survives in Britain as Young's Special London Ale, though it can today be easier to find in the US. The drily aniseedy, spicy English hop is extremely powerful, but cushioned by a malty creaminess and a lively, fruity, yeast character, with suggestions of banana and orange zest. The fruitiness softens the final, peppery punch of hop bitterness.

**Region of origin**
London, England, UK

**Style** English Ale/
Strong Pale Ale

**Alcohol content**
5.1 abw (6.4 abv)

**Ideal serving temperature**
50° F (10° C)

# POPERINGS HOMMEL BIER

Situated near to the World War I graves of Ypres, the town of Poperinge is the center of a small hop-growing region. Although the word hop is used in Flemish, there is also a local variation, *hommel*, from the Latin *humulus*. This beer, highlighting the local hops, is made by the Van Eecke brewery in nearby Watou. It is a bottle-conditioned ale with a roselike floweriness, honeyish notes, orange-zest hop flavors, and a late spicy, cumin-seed dryness.

**Region of origin**
Province of West
Flanders, Belgium

**Style**
Strong Golden Ale

**Alcohol content**
6.0 abw (7.5 abv)

**Ideal serving
temperature**
50° F (10° C)

# BUSH 7%

The name facilitates a wordplay in French. "Bush Sept" sounds like "Bouchette," implying a mini-mouthful. Only in Belgium could a beer of such potency (actually, 7.5 percent) be deemed small, but this is a lower-strength version of the regular 12 percent Bush. The drop, in gravity as well as alcohol, diminishes the maltiness, and allows the yeasty floweriness (perhaps violets) to come through, and the minty, peppery hop. There is also added coriander.

**Region of origin** Province of
Hainaut, Belgium

**Style** Strong Golden Ale,
with spice

**Alc content** 6.0 abw (7.5 abv)

**Ideal serving temperature**
50° F (10° C)

*Fit for a king*
*Bush 7% is sold as Clovis in the US, after the King of the Franks.*

# BEER AND FOOD

CHOOSE THE RIGHT BEER AND YOU HAVE ONE of the world's great aperitifs – more effective in this respect than even dry sherry or champagne. Although wine is a fine accompaniment to good food, many dishes are better illuminated by beer: starters such as asparagus, scrambled eggs, smoked salmon, or sausages; spicy dishes and many ethnic foods; and chocolate desserts are just a few examples. Some of these are among the items that might be found in a *brasserie* – French for brewery, but the term has come to mean a certain style of restaurant. The first brasseries were taverns attached to breweries. Their eclectic approach to dining is mirrored in contemporary lunch spots from London to New York and Tokyo to Sydney. Small wonder that interesting selections of beer are increasingly nudging the wine list.

# BEERS WITH APPETIZERS & SOUPS

IN THEIR HOME COUNTRIES, several styles of beer are typically served with specific snacks or appetizers, often featuring cheese and sausages. This is notably true of two similar-sounding traditional styles: Germany's *Gose*, associated with Leipzig and nearby towns; and Belgium's *gueuze*, from the Brussels area. *Gueuze* suits such appetizers in the way that fino sherry goes with *tapas*, and is often served with steamed mussels or with the classic Belgian dish *waterzooi*, a soup or stew made with fish or chicken.

***Savory start***
*The more acidic styles of beer are in perfect harmony with the sharper, more lactic cheeses.*

## CANTILLON GRAND CRU BRUOCSELLA 1900

The Cantillon family arrived in Brussels, "Bruocsella" in Latin, in 1900. This beer has a toasty aroma and start, with suggestions of Madeira drying into fino sherry, fresh apple, and lemon notes. It is the perfect accompaniment to sharp cheeses and the lighter soups.

**Region of origin**
Province of Flemish Brabant, Belgium

**Style** *Lambic*

**Alcohol content** 4.0 abw (5.0 abv)

**Ideal serving temperature** 55° F (13° C)

## GEUZE BOON

This spelling of *gueuze* is preferred by Frank Boon. Being a *gueuze*, this beer is a blend of young and old *lambics* that ferments in the bottle, causing carbonation and sparkle. It has great finesse: a soft floweriness of aroma, hinting at rhubarb; a momentary gingery sweetness; and a long, dry, oaky, faintly salty finish.

**Region of origin**
Province of Flemish Brabant, Belgium

**Style** *Gueuze-lambic*

**Alcohol content** 5.6 abw (7.0 abv)

**Ideal serving temperature** 55° F (13° C)

## GEUZE GIRARDIN

From an aristocrat's estate brewery, now run by the Girardin family. The brewery at St. Ulriks-Kapelle in the traditional region of *gueuze* production grows its own wheat, and still has a mill that grinds the grain between stones. Gueuze Girardin is elegant, lean, and complex; perfumy and dry; with unfolding flavors of cedar, hay, and acacia honey.

**Region of origin**
Province of Flemish Brabant, Belgium

**Style** *Gueuze-lambic*

**Alcohol content** 4.0 abw (5.0 abv)

**Ideal serving temperature** 55° F (13° C)

## EVERY BEER LOVER'S DREAM WOMAN

THE LADY DEPICTED in the postcard (*right*) is a good prospect for marriage. She has a curvaceous figure, comprising bottles of *Gose* beer, her legs are glasses of the brew, and she is rich, judging from the bag of money in her hand. *Gose* beer features, too, in her punning name:

Fräulein Gosella. With her, "anything goes," according to her motto, *Gosi van Duti*, a play on the title of Mozart's famous opera. Male fantasies have changed little over the ages. The card is from a whimsical collection of eight published between 1896 and 1905. The artist is unknown.

### GOSE OHNE BEDENKEN

The German town of Goslar, Lower Saxony, is said to have given its name to this style of wheat beer, which was once popular in Leipzig. The style has recently been revived by Goslar's Ohne Bedenken taproom and beer garden. *Gose* is a wheat beer, lightly spiced with salt. It is flavored with coriander and emerges with a citric palate. Traditionally, it is matured in flasks with a narrow neck so that the yeasty head acts as a bung to foster carbonation.

*Gose* is often served with Camembert cheese, sometimes with a digestif of *Allasch*, an almond-flavored version of the caraway liqueur *Kümmel*.

**Region of origin** Lower Saxony, Germany

**Style** *Gose*

**Alcohol content** 3.8 abw (4.8 abv)

**Ideal serving temperature** 48–50° F (9–10° C)

### *Belgian broth*
*This chicken* waterzooi *includes cream, shallots, leeks, carrots, and bay leaves among its ingredients.*

## LINDEMANS CUVÉE RENÉ

Because *lambic* beers can be quite dry, many of the more popular labels are sweetened. While this is true of the regular Lindemans products, Cuvée René is in a drier style. Owner René Lindemans gives his name to a delicious, full-flavored beer: foamy and lively, with the nuttiness of a Palo Cortado sherry. It has a soft, rounded sweetness; then a long, drying finish.

**Region of origin**
Province of Flemish Brabant, Belgium

**Style** *Gueuze-lambic*

**Alcohol content** 4.0 abw (5.0 abv)

**Ideal serving temperature** 55° F (13° C)

# BEERS WITH SHELLFISH

THEY MAY BE FAMOUSLY sociable beers, but in Britain and Ireland, porters and stouts have both been partners to oysters since Georgian and Victorian times. The very combination speaks of Charles Dickens dining in a chop-house. In those days, porter was the everyday beer, and oysters were so plentiful as to be a cheap snack, often served free in pubs. Oysters can be very expensive today, but dry porters and stouts are also delicious accompaniments to mussels, clams, scallops, and crustaceans.

### GUINNESS EXTRA STOUT

The world's most famous dry stout. Irish country brewer Arthur Guinness set up in Dublin in 1759. Among the many versions of Guinness, the 6.0 abw (7.5 abv) Foreign Extra Stout has a particular tangy acidity. The bottled Extra Stout sold in Ireland best highlights the oaky dryness that is distinctive to Guinness.

**Region of origin** Republic of Ireland

**Style** Dry Stout

**Alcohol content** 3.4 abw (4.2 abv)

**Ideal serving temperature**
50–55° F (10–13° C)

### BEAMISH IRISH STOUT

A stout from what was once Cork city's "Protestant" brewery, founded in 1792, on a site even older than that. As its competitors have become sweeter, in deference to "modern" tastes, Beamish Irish Stout has seemed by comparison drier. The beer is toasty, with buttery, creamy, and peppery notes in a late, lingering, dry finish.

**Region of origin** Republic of Ireland

**Style** Dry Stout

**Alcohol content** 3.4 abw (4.3 abv)

**Ideal serving temperature**
50–55° F (10–13° C)

### MURPHY'S IRISH STOUT

From what was Cork city's "Roman Catholic" brewery, named after a well consecrated to Our Lady. Murphy's brewery was established in the 1850s, and has on occasion produced an oyster stout, made by adding a broth of the shellfish to the brew kettle. Its regular stout is mildly dry, with soda-bread graininess and a hint of peat.

**Region of origin** Republic of Ireland

**Style** Dry Stout

**Alcohol content** 3.2 abw (4.0 abv)

**Ideal serving temperature**
50–55° F (10–13° C)

***Pepper and salt***
*The peppery intensity of the drier porters and stouts counterpoints the sea-salt flavors in a mixed shellfish platter.*

## AN APHRODISIAC IN THE GLASS

DINERS AND DRINKERS who feel that only champagne is a fit accompaniment to oysters might enjoy a Black Velvet. This classic cocktail blends champagne half and half with stout. Guinness Foreign Extra Stout (*left*) is used for its power and strength. Its richness requires a very dry champagne as a balance. Some brewpubs offer stout with a whole oyster in the glass as a "mixed drink." A handful of stouts are actually produced with oysters as an ingredient, imparting a salty, gamy note. Murphy's has on occasion made an example. So has Bushy's, on the Isle of Man.

### MARSTON'S OYSTER STOUT

This bottle-conditioned beer, from the famous Marston's brewery of Burton, England, does not contain oysters, but is offered by the brewery as a perfect accompaniment to the shellfish. Among the stouts shown here, it has the fruitiest of flavors, with hints of onion or shallot, and a firm, woody, cedary background.

**Region of origin** Trent Valley, England, UK

**Style** Dry Stout

**Alcohol content** 3.6 abw (4.5 abv)

**Ideal serving temperature**
50–55° F (10–13° C)

### ELGOOD'S FLAG PORTER

Taste the sea in this porter? It is fermented in part with a yeast recovered from bottles of porter found in an 1825 shipwreck on the bed of the English Channel. Flag Porter is produced by the Elgood's brewery of Wisbech, Cambridgeshire. The beer is lively and fruity, with woody, sooty, leathery, oily notes. It is perfect with the gamier varieties of oyster.

**Region of origin** Eastern England, UK

**Style** Porter/Dry Stout

**Alcohol content** 4.0 abw (5.0 abv)

**Ideal serving temperature**
50–55° F (10–13° C)

### COOPERS BEST EXTRA STOUT

Most Australian breweries have a stout in their range, and the famously traditionalist Coopers, of Adelaide, makes a most characterful example. Coopers Stout is woody, oily, and strong, but very drinkable with the oysters and mussels of the South Seas.

**Region of origin** South Australia

**Style** Dry Stout

**Alcohol content** 5.4 abw (6.8 abv)

**Ideal serving temperature**
50–55° F (10–13° C)

# BEERS WITH SALADS & STARTERS

BROWN ALES MAY SOUND MACHO but, being the nuttiest of all beers, they provide an appetizing accompaniment to a salad or vegetable *hors d'oeuvre*. This is not a fitting role for a sweet brown ale – it applies really only to the stronger styles typical of the US and around Newcastle, England. In Europe, seasonal asparagus is often served with beer as a starter or light meal. Hoppy, fruity, strong amber or golden ales in the Belgian style provide a tastier complement than the blander lagers often offered.

**Classic combo**
*In season, asparagus is celebrated in continental Europe, often with scrambled eggs or ham (or both).*

## UNIBROUE MAUDITE

This bottle-conditioned brew is inspired by the Belgian strong golden ale, Duvel, and is made by Unibroue of Chambly, near Montreal. Maudite is a darkish interpretation of the style; fruity, spiced (with suggestions of orange zest, coriander, and pepper), and dry. It is a flavorsome beer to accompany crudités or roasted peppers.

**Region of origin**
Province of Quebec, Canada

**Style** Strong, spiced Belgian-style Ale

**Alcohol content** 6.4 abw (8.0 abv)

**Ideal serving temperature**
50–55° F (10–13° C)

## ROMAN SLOEBER

Sloeber, "joker" in Flemish, is made at Mater, near Oudenaarde, Belgium. This complex beer pours with a massive head; is aromatic, smooth, firm, and malty; with a dry, orange-zest finish, in part deriving from Styrian hops. Big enough in flavor to accompany a robust antipasto.

**Region of origin**
Province of East Flanders, Belgium

**Style** Strong Belgian Ale

**Alcohol content** 6.0 abw (7.5 abv)

**Ideal serving temperature** 50° F (10° C)

## CELIS GRAND CRU

When revivalist Pierre Celis set up the Hoegaarden brewery in Belgium, he made a strong golden ale, with orange zest and coriander, hints of peach and honeydew melon, called Grand Cru. When he moved to Austin, Texas, he created the similar Celis Grand Cru. The beer is spicy, with a suggestion of sorrel, but less delicate, grassier, and more lemony. Either is delicious with asparagus.

**Region of origin** Southwest US

**Style** Strong, spiced Belgian-style Ale

**Alcohol content** 7.0 abw (8.8 abv)

**Ideal serving temperature**
45–50° F (7–10° C)

## BROWN BEERS AND BIG BRIDGES

SALADS ARE LESS TRADITIONAL than leek puddings (with beef suet) in Newcastle, a northern English city associated in the public mind with coal and heavy engineering even in the post-industrial era. Over the years its Newcastle Brown Ale has used variations on a label design featuring the city's symbol, the "New" Tyne Bridge. Big bridges are a muscular symbol for beers thought by consumers to be full-bodied and strong. While Newcastle Brown Ale actually has a modest alcohol content (*see below*), its transatlantic counterpart, Brooklyn Brown Ale, is bigger in both its nutty, hoppy flavors and its alcohol content (4.4 abw, 5.5 abv).

### NEWCASTLE BROWN ALE

The most popular bottled ale in Britain, with a macho image and a great student following. This paler, drier style of brown ale was launched in 1927 by a head-brewer whose not-quite appropriate name was Colonel Porter. If it is not excessively chilled or gulped, this beer has a surprisingly nutty, flowery, winey delicacy.

**Region of origin**
Northeast England, UK

**Style**  Brown Ale

**Alcohol content**  3.8 abw (4.7 abv)

**Ideal serving temperature**  50° F (10° C)

*Walnut brown*
*The nuttiest of beers deserves a salad to match. This one features walnuts, crispy bacon, and mixed leaves.*

### BOSTON BEER WORKS BEANTOWN NUT BROWN ALE

The baked bean, prepared with salt pork and molasses (and sometimes beer), is a traditional Boston dish; hence the name Beantown. This beer might go well with such a simple dish. It starts sweetish, with a cherryish fruitiness, but dries out, with hints of cedar and cinnamon. It has a smooth texture, lightish body, and satisfying flavors.

**Region of origin**  Northeast US

**Style**  Brown Ale

**Alcohol content**  4.4 abw (5.5 abv)

**Ideal serving temperature**  50° F (10° C)

### VAUX DOUBLE MAXIM

Newcastle's neighbor is Sunderland, a city which makes marine engines and beer, and which has a fiercely rival soccer team. Sunderland's Vaux brewery has a brown ale called Double Maxim, named after a type of machine gun used by Captain Ernest Vaux in the Boer War. The beer is quite pale, but assertive in its nutty, fruity, dry flavors.

**Region of origin**
Northeast England, UK

**Style**  Brown Ale

**Alcohol content**  3.8 abw (4.7 abv)

**Ideal serving temperature**  50° F (10° C)

# BEERS WITH PICKLES AND PÂTÉS

EVEN WINE LOVERS TEND TO recommend beer with dishes such as pickled herrings, but which brew? Beers with a long maturation in unlined wood gain varying degrees of sourness (and sometimes ironlike flavors) that can stand up to vinegary dishes. Some of the best are made near North Sea ports with a tradition of serving herring. Another starter course might be a terrine or pâté, or foie gras. Grape lovers might suggest a rich wine, classically a Sauternes. Beer lovers could try an extra-strong Bock.

*Sweet treat*
*The custom of serving sweetish dessert wines with goose liver shocks the uninitiated. Try a similarly luscious strong beer with this game pâté.*

### SAM ADAMS TRIPLE BOCK

Sauternes wines are said to be scented, intensely sweet and oily, and to become Madeiralike with time. This beer has a minty aroma, chocolaty maple and vanilla flavors, and all the fatness and power of such a wine. Californian "champagne" yeast ferments the brew, which might better be described as barley wine; it is not a Bock. Try it with a rich, nutty terrine.

**Region of origin**  Northeast US

**Style**  Barley Wine

**Alcohol content**  14.0 abw (17.5 abv)

**Ideal serving temperature**  48° F (9° C)

### EKU 28

"The strongest beer in the world," boasts the slogan on the glass. The initials EKU indicate in German the First United Brewery of Kulmbach, a great brewing town. The figure 28 represents the beer's original gravity (in German degrees), not alcohol. Such a high gravity makes it syrupy, but its complex, tangerine flavors are surprisingly fresh and clean.

**Region of origin**
Franconia, Bavaria, Germany

**Style**  Double Bock/Strong Lager

**Alcohol content**  8.8 abw (11.0 abv)

**Ideal serving temperature**  48° F (9° C)

### SCHLOSS EGGENBERG URBOCK 23°

The castle brewery of Eggenberg, at Vorchdorf, between Salzburg and Linz, Austria, dates from the 1100s. Its Urbock has an original gravity of 23; a bubbly, well-retained head for such a strong beer; a shimmering gold color; a light creaminess, with hints of lemon, pink grapefruit, melon rind, and perhaps cinnamon.

**Region of origin**  Austria

**Style**  Double Bock

**Alcohol content**  7.7 abw (9.6 abv)

**Ideal serving temperature**  48° F (9° C)

## BEER FROM THE WOOD

IN A WINERY OR BRANDY distillery, the ceiling-high wooden tuns at Rodenbach might not seem exceptional. In a brewery, they are far more unusual. No brewery has remotely as many as Rodenbach, where they fill 11 halls. The vessels vary in size from 2,200 to 13,200 gallons (100 to 600 hectoliters), and the veterans among them are more than 150 years old. They are made from oak, variously from the Vosges region of France and from Poland. They are maintained by a team of three permanent coopers who work with numbered staves, hoops, reeds, and beeswax. Other breweries in the region have wooden tuns, but far fewer of them, to make the local reddish-brown, sourish ale.

## RODENBACH GRAND CRU

While Rodenbach's regular ale is a blend of old and young beers, Grand Cru is a straight bottling of the long-matured, stronger component. It is aged in vast oak tuns for over two years. The result is a lively bouquet, with vanilla oakiness that extends into the palate; passion-fruit flavors; and a clean, sharp, acidity.

**Region of origin** Province of West Flanders, Belgium

**Style** Flemish Red Ale

**Alcohol content** 4.8 abw (6.0 abv)

**Ideal serving temperature** 50° F (10° C)

*Acid attack*
*It takes a very iron-tasting, acidic beer to cope with vinegary dishes. The three on the left are perky enough to deal even with pickled herrings.*

## GREENE KING STRONG SUFFOLK

Many English breweries once aged beer in wooden tuns, blending old with new for equilibrium: Greene King is the last to do so. The beer's key ingredient is a strong ale matured in wooden tuns for one to five years. The beer is less sour than those made across the North Sea, but iron-tasting, sappy, peppery, and winey.

**Region of origin** Eastern England, UK

**Style** Old Ale

**Alcohol content** 4.8 abw (6.0 abv)

**Ideal serving temperature** 50–55° F (10–13° C)

## DOCK STREET GRAND CRU

The Dock Street brewery and pub in Philadelphia intends this occasional brew as a tribute to Rodenbach. It succeeds magnificently, though it is less aggressively acidic. Dock Street Grand Cru is aged in wine casks; has firm, plant-stem flavors, with a hint of sloe gin; and a cherryish, sweet-and-sour finish.

**Region of origin** Northeast US

**Style** Flemish Red Ale

**Alcohol content** 6.0 abw (7.5 abv)

**Ideal serving temperature** 50° F (10° C)

# BEERS WITH SAUSAGES

THE GERMANS DO MORE with beer than serve it with sausages (and often sauerkraut), but no combination of brew and food crosses borders so readily: from the brasseries of Paris to the German restaurants of Chicago to the brewpubs of Tokyo. The lightest of German-style brews does the trick with a veal *Weisswurst*, but anything meatier, coarser, smokier, or more spicy deserves a bigger brew: a Munich-style dark lager, with its subtle combination of malty richness and burnt flavors.

**Baroque dazzler**
*The interior of the monastery at Weltenburg has won the admiration of such distant critics as present-day artist Jeff Koons.*

## WELTENBURGER KLOSTER BAROCK-DUNKEL

The oldest "cloister" (monastery) brewery in the world, tracing its history to the 600s and its brewing to at least 1050. Weltenburg is on the Danube, near Kelheim. The Barock Dunkel ("Dark") beer is light-bodied and smooth, with a very good malt character suggesting cookies or crackers. It has a toasty, smoky, roast-malt finish.

**Region of origin**
Upper Bavaria, Germany

**Style** Munich Dark Lager

**Alcohol content** 3.6 abw (4.5 abv)

**Ideal serving temperature** 48° F (9° C)

## STAROPRAMEN DARK

This Czech brewery, a classic of the mid-1800s, is close to the center of Prague. Staropramen ("Old Spring"), is widely known for its golden lager, but it also produces a dark version. This is light-bodied, but soft and smooth; with malty licorice or aniseed notes; and an underlying flowery hop.

**Region of origin**
Bohemia, Czech Republic

**Style** Dark Lager

**Alcohol content** 3.7 abw (4.6 abv)

**Ideal serving temperature** 48° F (9° C)

**The best Wurst**
*The plate includes* Bierschinken *(ham sausage with pistachios). Green beans are typically served with beer in Japan.*

## HACKER-PSCHORR ALT MUNICH DARK

Composer Richard Strauss was the son of Josephine Pschorr, and he dedicated one of his most famous works, *Der Rosenkavalier,* to the family that financed him. Hacker-Pschorr's "Old" Munich Dark has a creamy aroma and flavor, with notes of cinnamon, and a lightly syrupy body. Try it with veal sausages.

**Region of origin**
Munich, Upper Bavaria, Germany

**Style** Munich Dark Lager

**Alcohol content** 4.2 abw (5.2 abv)

**Ideal serving temperature** 48° F (9° C)

## PASTRAMI ON RYE

DARK LAGERS ARE NOT the only beers to go well with sausages and *charcuterie*. The spicier type of sausage made with pepper or fennel, or pastrami, may find a better balance with the minty, bittersweet character of rye beers. Historically, country brewers in Russia and Finland used rye. In 1988, a brewery owned by the aristocratic German family Thurn und Taxis launched a beer made with rye and wheat. This is called Roggen ("rye") Bier. It is grainy, slightly smoky, fruity, and spicy, with a bittersweet rye character (4.0 abw; 5.0 abv). An ale called Rye Beer is made by King & Barnes, of Horsham, England. This is packed with oily, grainy, spicy flavors (4.4 abw; 5.5abv).

### SILLAMÄE MÜNCHEN

Made in Estonia, in a microbrewery established in 1993, in the Russian-speaking town of Sillamäe, once a defense industry center. München is German for Munich. The beer is a remarkable dark lager, so assertive and strong that it could equally be regarded as a Bock. It has a rich, malty aroma; a surprisingly light and smooth drinkability; and a clean, toasted-nut dryness; developing to a juicy, warming finish.

**Region of origin** Estonia

**Style** Munich Dark Lager/Bock

**Alcohol content** 5.2 abw (6.5 abv)

**Ideal serving temperature** 48° F (9° C)

### TABERNASH MUNICH

Tabernash, a town west of Denver, Colorado, is named after a Native American chief of the Ute nation. It gives its name in turn to a Denver microbrewery that specializes in German beers. One of the brewery's founders studied at Weihenstephan (*page 84*). Tabernash Munich is very smooth, with some fruity maltiness and toastiness. It has a well-rounded finish, with a hint of hoppy dryness.

**Region of origin** Southwest US

**Style** Munich Dark Lager

**Alcohol content** 3.9 abw (4.9 abv)

**Ideal serving temperature** 48° F (9° C)

### SAGRES DARK

Outside of the main beer countries, many breweries have both golden and dark lagers in their ranges. This is true in Spain and Portugal, for example. Portugal's two biggest breweries both have dark lagers. The brew shown here, Sagres, has a toffeeish, caramel character, while its rival Cristal Preta has more of a fresh-bread, malty note.

**Region of origin** Portugal

**Style** Munich Dark Lager

**Alcohol content** 3.4 abw (4.3 abv)

**Ideal serving temperature** 48° F (9° C)

# BEERS WITH SMOKED FOODS

O NCE, OPEN FIRES were widely used to dry the grains in the malting process. Another technique that imparts a smoky flavor is the use of hot rocks to heat the brew, dating from the days of wooden vessels, which could not be set over a flame. Beers made by these two methods, including some newcomers, are an unusually appropriate accompaniment to smoked or grilled foods.

### CHRISTIAN MERZ SPEZIAL RAUCHBIER

The heartland of smoked beer is the German region of Franconia, especially the town of Bamberg. Beechwood from nearby forests is used to smoke the malt. This bottled *Märzen*-style *Rauchbier* ("Smoked Beer") has a molasses aroma; a clean, dry, creamy palate; and a fragrant smokiness in the big finish. It is perfect with Bavarian smoked ham.

**Region of origin**
Franconia, Bavaria, Germany

**Style** *Bamberger Rauchbier*

**Alcohol content** 4.2 abw (5.3 abv)

**Ideal serving temperature** 48° F (9° C)

*Holy protection*
*This plaque, outside Christian Merz, warns that Heinrich the Holy protects the brewery.*

*Taking the pulse*
*Here is smoked ham, as eaten in Bavaria, with English pease pudding (a purée of peas) in place of the customary German* Erbseneintopf.

### AECHT SCHLENKERLA RAUCHBIER

Dating from 1678, the Schlenkerla tavern is an institution in Bamberg, and is noted for regional food. Schlenkerla is the most widely known *Rauchbier*. It has a firm beechwood smokiness from its aroma through its palate to a clean, dry, long finish.

**Region of origin**
Franconia, Bavaria, Germany

**Style** *Bamberger Rauchbier*

**Alcohol content** 3.8 abw (4.8 abv)

**Ideal serving temperature** 48° F (9° C)

### BOSCOS FLAMING STONE

An American pioneer of stone beer. The Boscos brewery and restaurant was opened in 1992 in the suburbs of Memphis, Tennessee. Colorado granite is heated in a wood-burning pizza oven in the making of Boscos Flaming Stone, which is based on a wheat ale. It has a pale color; a toffeeish, nutty palate; and a very late development of a refreshing, slightly sour, smoky dryness.

**Region of origin** South US

**Style** Stone Beer

**Alcohol content** 3.8 abw (4.8 abv)

**Ideal serving temperature** 50° F (10° C)

# WHERE THERE'S SMOKE THERE'S BEER

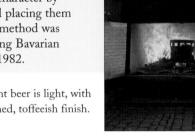

IN THE MORE WIDELY produced type of smoked beer, the grains are smoked during the malting process. Among this type, the long-established style is the *Rauchbier* of Bamberg. This is a smoked lager. Newer variations, such as the Smoked Porter (*left* and *below*) of Alaska, and the Smoked Ale of Japan, are made in the same way but with top-fermenting yeasts. Stone beers, such as Rauchenfelser Steinbier, apply the smoky, more caramelly, character by heating rocks (*right*) and placing them in the brew kettle. This method was revived by the enterprising Bavarian brewer Gerd Borges in 1982.

## RAUCHENFELSER STEINBIER

This wheat beer was first made near Coburg and is now produced near Augsburg. Hot rocks are craned into the brew kettle to bring it to the boil. The brew caramelizes around the rock. The caramel later induces a secondary fermentation in the lagering vessel. The resultant beer is light, with a clean, softly burned, toffeeish finish.

**Region of origin**
Upper Bavaria, Germany

**Style** Stone Beer

**Alcohol content** 3.9 abw (4.9 abv)

**Ideal serving temperature** 48° F (9° C)

## ALASKAN BREWING CO. SMOKED PORTER

A pioneer of smoked beers in North America. The brewery, in Juneau, state capital of Alaska, is opposite a fish smokery. The malt is smoked there, over alder. This big, complex, unfiltered brew was launched in 1988. It starts oily, with hints of bitter chocolate and burned fruits, then explodes with smokiness.

**Region of origin** Pacific Northwest US

**Style** Smoked Porter

**Alcohol content** 4.8 abw (5.9 abv)

**Ideal serving temperature**
50–55° F (10–13° C)

## MOKU MOKU SMOKED ALE

This brewery's name is a reference to the use of smoke screens by Ninja warriors. The ale is earthy and oily, with a late surge of fresh smoke. Scottish peated malt is used. The brewery is part of a cooperative that also smokes ham and makes sausages; these can be tasted, with the beer, in its restaurant in Ayama, near Ueno.

**Region of origin** Kansai, Honshu, Japan

**Style** Smoked Ale

**Alcohol content** 4.0 abw (5.0 abv)

**Ideal serving temperature**
50–55° F (10–13° C)

# BEERS WITH FISH

LIKE THE CHARDONNAYS of the wine world, the more delicate examples of Pilsners and other dry, clean-tasting, golden lagers are perfect with fish. The comparison is apt in more than just the color: their fresh, flowery palates highlight the flavors of fish without dominating them. In Bavaria, a local Pilsner might accompany pike-perch caught near Munich; in the Rhineland, Bitburger Pils is often served with local trout; and in the Czech Republic, Budweiser Budvar is offered with carp from the Bohemian lakes.

## BITBURGER PREMIUM PILS

This brewery in Bitburg claims to be the first in Germany to have used the term Pilsner, in 1883. Its Pils is very light, soft, and clean. It appears at first to be accented towards a clean, sweet maltiness, but finishes with a firm, elegantly rounded, hoppy dryness. Some of the malting barley is grown locally; so is a proportion of the hops. In early days, the lagering cellars were cooled with ice from the Eifel lakes.

**Region of origin**
Rhineland-Palatinate, Germany

**Style** Pilsner

**Alcohol content** 3.7 abw (4.6 abv)

**Ideal serving temperature** 48° F (9° C)

## CRISTAL ALKEN

Names such as "crystal" have been used by several brewers of golden lager. This particularly fine example is brewed in the town of Alken, and was the first Belgian Pilsner, launched in 1928. True to its name, Cristal tastes at first almost like spring water; then comes a clean hit of hoppy dryness; and a refreshing, crisp finish.

**Region of origin**
Province of Limburg, Belgium

**Style** Pilsner

**Alcohol content** 3.8 abw (4.8 abv)

**Ideal serving temperature** 48° F (9° C)

*Pils and pike*
*An elegant Pilsner deserves a stylish meal, such as these quenelles of pike. In Belgium, the fish might be cod or sole.*

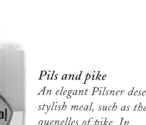

## HALLERTAU AUER PILS

Germany's best-known hop-growing region is Hallertau, just to the north of Munich. In the heart of the region, in the village of Au, there has been a castle brewery since 1590. Today, it produces a lively, bubbly Pilsner with a fresh aroma; textured malt character; and well-combined flavors of leafy, dry hop. A hop-country classic.

**Region of origin**
Upper Bavaria, Germany

**Style** Pilsner

**Alcohol content** 3.9 abw (4.9 abv)

**Ideal serving temperature** 48° F (9° C)

## BIRTH OF THE BUDWEISER BEERS

THE CITY OF BUDWEIS in Bohemia was known for beer as early as the 1300s. One of its two present breweries, Budweiser Bürgerbräu, founded in 1795, was among the pioneers of golden lager in 1853. The second of today's breweries, Budweiser Budvar (*right*), dates from 1895. By then, Adolphus Busch, a German-American, was in Missouri already marketing a beer inspired by the city of Budweis.

### BUDWEISER BUDVAR

In the Czech Republic, only beers from Pilsen may use the name of that city. While they emphasize the hop, their rivals from Budweis (in Czech, České Budějovice) lean towards a light maltiness. The beers from both the Czech Budweiser breweries are bigger in malt and hop (but not alcohol) than their US namesake.

**Region of origin**
Bohemia, Czech Republic

**Style** Golden Lager

**Alcohol content** 4.0 abw (5.0 abv)

**Ideal serving temperature** 48° F (9° C)

### FREEDOM PILSENER

British brewers generally regard lager as a style to be made cheaply for drinkers who respond less to flavor than advertising. One of the few British lagers made with any seriousness is Freedom Pilsener, from a London microbrewery established in 1995. This beer has been variable, but at its best has a smooth maltiness and late dry, flowery hoppiness.

**Region of origin** London, England, UK

**Style** Pilsner

**Alcohol content** 4.0 abw (5.0 abv)

**Ideal serving temperature** 48° F (9° C)

### CREEMORE SPRINGS PREMIUM LAGER

Creemore Springs is a ski resort north of Toronto. In 1987, its 1890s hardware store was turned into a microbrewery. Its Premium Lager has a deliciously fresh malt aroma; a smooth, clean, textured, lightly nutty body; and an elegant balance of hoppy dryness.

**Region of origin**
Province of Ontario, Canada

**Style** Golden Lager/Pilsner

**Alcohol content** 4.0 abw (5.0 abv)

**Ideal serving temperature** 48° F (9° C)

# BEERS WITH CHICKEN

THE BRONZE, SWEETISH, MALTY, medium-strong lagers traditionally brewed in March (in German, *März*) and matured through the summer, are typically served at the *Oktoberfest* with spit-roasted chicken. The combination works because the reddish, Vienna-style malts employed have a spicy sweetness that goes well with meats such as chicken. In recent years, many beers in this style have become lighter in character. Today, some of the richest *Märzen* and *Oktoberfest* lagers are made in the US.

### CATAMOUNT OCTOBERFEST

This Vermont microbrewery makes a beautifully balanced *Oktoberfest*, lighter in color and body than many American examples, but fuller than most German ones. The beer is made with Munich malt, Northern Brewer and Tettnang hops, and a lager yeast.

It has a fresh, appetizing aroma; starts very smooth and dryish; has a long development of flavors, with a spicy maltiness; and finishes crisply.

**Region of origin**  Northeast US

**Style**  *Märzen-Oktoberfest* Lager

**Alcohol content**  4.2 abw (5.3 abv)

**Ideal serving temperature**  48° F (9° C)

### OLD DOMINION BREWING CO. OCTOBERFEST

The *Oktoberfest* made at this lager-oriented micro near Washington, DC, has a malty smoothness, firmness, and nuttiness. Among the malts used is a Vienna type, and its contribution is evident in the beer's "barley sugar" sweetness and spiciness. The overall malt character is very good. There is a late, herbal, fragrant hop balance.

**Region of origin**  Mid-Atlantic US

**Style**  *Märzen-Oktoberfest* Lager

**Alcohol content**  4.6 abw (5.8 abv)

**Ideal serving temperature**  48° F (9° C)

***Chicken and barley***
*It does not have to be October. Year-round, malty lagers are a perfect partner to chicken. In Germany, chicken is as much the national fast food as the sausage.*

### PENN OKTOBERFEST

Some of America's finest German-style lagers are made by the Penn brewery and pub established in the old German quarter of Pittsburgh, Pennsylvania, in 1986. Its wide range of classic styles includes this *Oktoberfest*. The beer has a deliciously fresh malt aroma; a smooth, lightly sweet, appetizingly nutty palate; and a spicily dry hop finish.

**Region of origin**  Northeast US

**Style**  *Märzen-Oktoberfest* Lager

**Alcohol content**  4.6 abw (5.8 abv)

**Ideal serving temperature**  48° F (9° C)

## PULLING FOR VARIETY

O NCE, THE BARS OF THE US boasted tap handles announcing only familiar names such as Budweiser, Miller, and Coors. Today, more demanding beer lovers flock to the inelegantly named "multi-tap" bars and restaurants. As each new microbrewery seeks to attract attention, tap handles can become elaborate, inventive, and witty in their design, but a forest of them can also be confusing. The tap handle on the right is a model of simplicity and clarity, perhaps because the Gordon Biersch beers are most readily found in their own brewery-restaurants, where they do not have to fight the clamor of competition.

### GORDON BIERSCH MÄRZEN

Some of the best beer-friendly food in the US is found in the small chain of brewery-restaurants founded in Palo Alto, California, in 1988 by Dan Gordon and the restaurateur, Dean Biersch. Gordon is a brewing graduate of Weihenstephan, Bavaria.

Their *Märzen* has a bronze-red color; a light but smooth body; a spicy, fruity, malt character; and a dry, whiskeyish finish.

**Region of origin**  California, US

**Style**  *Märzen-Oktoberfest* Lager

**Alcohol content**  4.6 abw (5.8 abv)

**Ideal serving temperature**  48° F (9° C)

### INDEPENDENCE FRANKLINFEST

Benjamin Franklin helped draft the Declaration of Independence in Philadelphia in 1776. The Independence Brewery was founded there 219 years later. Franklinfest lager has a depth of malt aroma and spicy flavor; is light and smooth; with a clean, sweet finish.

**Region of origin**  Northeast US

**Style**  *Märzen-Oktoberfest* Lager

**Alcohol content**  4.4 abw (5.5 abv)

**Ideal serving temperature**  48° F (9° C)

### THOMAS KEMPER OKTOBERFEST

Among new-generation American breweries, Thomas Kemper was an early lager producer in 1984. The Kemper beers now share a pub and brewery in Seattle with Pyramid. This beer forms a rocky head; has a peachy aroma; a nutty malt character, becoming grainy then creamy; and a late balance of flowery hop dryness.

**Region of origin**  Pacific Northwest US

**Style**  *Märzen-Oktoberfest* Lager

**Alcohol content**  4.5 abw (5.6 abv)

**Ideal serving temperature**  48° F (9° C)

# BEERS WITH PORK

WHAT COULD BE HEARTIER than an Irish red ale (even if the color is closer to chestnut or amber) with boiled bacon and cabbage, or with loin of pork, perhaps? The love of bacon, ham, and roasts is not merely a question of Irish tradition: there is also in Irish ales a sweetness, a creaminess, and sometimes a slight butteriness, which highlights the flavor of such dishes. The buttery quality derives from the malts used and the production techniques, and sometimes the yeasts, employed.

### HEINEKEN KYLIAN

A beer of complicated parentage, including George Killian Lett's Ruby Ale and its Pelforth version (*bottom*). Heineken Kylian starts quite austere, with a firm, clean maltiness, but develops a restrained fruitiness and nutty sweetness as it warms. It is very drinkable. Try it in winter before a Dutch pea soup and ham.

**Region of origin**
The Netherlands/France

**Style** Irish Red Ale

**Alcohol content** 5.2 abw (6.5 abv)

**Ideal serving temperature** 50° F (10° C)

### MACARDLES TRADITIONAL ALE

The Macardle and Moore brewery is opposite Harp, in Dundalk, roughly equidistant between Dublin and Belfast, close to the border that divides Ireland: The brewery was built in 1863 to serve both cities, and has been owned by Guinness since the 1950s. Its ale is dark, toasty, and nutty, with a faint chocolate-cookie dryness.

**Region of origin** Republic of Ireland

**Style** Irish Red Ale

**Alcohol content** 3.2 abw (4.0 abv)

**Ideal serving temperature** 50° F (10° C)

*Down-home brew*
*Irish ales are increasingly popular abroad, but not yet fully appreciated in Ireland. They are a hearty match for local dishes such as roast pork.*

### PELFORTH GEORGE KILLIAN'S

A 15th-century Irish friary brewery inspired this beer. The brewery closed in 1956, but owner George Killian Lett licensed its Ruby Ale to Pelforth of France. The Pelforth version has a malty aroma and flavor, and faintly smoky dryness. A weaker version, lighter in flavor but fuller in color, is made by Coors of Colorado.

**Region of origin** Northern France

**Style** Irish Red Ale

**Alcohol content** 5.2 abw (6.5 abv)

**Ideal serving temperature** 50° F (10° C)

## THE ST. FRANCIS ABBEY BREWERY

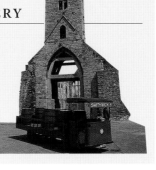

THE WORLD HAS AT LEAST a dozen breweries inside the walls of abbeys, but one country does it the other way around: Ireland has an abbey site inside a brewery in the historic town of Kilkenny. The largely-intact 13th-century abbey church of St. Francis (*right*) stands alongside the commercial Kilkenny brewery, which was established in 1710. Gradually, the abbey has been surrounded by brewery buildings. The brewer's house and a former maltings date from the 19th century, and the brewhouse from the 1960s.

### KILKENNY IRISH BEER

The Kilkenny brewery in Ireland, founded by John Smithwick, has been owned since 1965 by Guinness. Under the Smithwick's name, the brewery produces a toffeeish, buttery ale, with a touch of burned toast in the finish (3.2 abw; 4.0 abv). This is primarily sold in Ireland. Elsewhere in the world, a slightly stronger, drier, nuttier interpretation is sold as Kilkenny Irish Beer.

**Region of origin** Republic of Ireland

**Style** Irish Red Ale

**Alcohol content** 4.0 abw (5.0 abv)

**Ideal serving temperature**
48–50° F (9–10° C)

### BIG ROCK MCNALLY'S EXTRA ALE

Ed McNally's forbears left Ireland during the potato famine. He launched the Big Rock brewery, in Calgary, Canada, in 1985. His Extra Ale, a strong brew in the Irish style, has a flowery aroma and a maltiness reminiscent of toasted raisin bread.

**Region of origin**
Province of Alberta, Canada

**Style** Irish Red Ale

**Alcohol content** 5.6 abw (7.0 abv)

**Ideal serving temperature**
50–55° F (10–13° C)

### MCGUIRE'S OLD STYLE IRISH ALE

Irish-American Bill McGuire Martin has brewed this pioneering red ale in Pensacola, Florida, since 1989. On tap it has a perfumy aroma; a hint of butteriness and plummy sweetness; and a grip of malt in the finish. The bottled version, Irish Old Style Ale, is produced in Louisiana. It is paler, lighter, and drier, but still very tasty.

**Region of origin** Southeast US

**Style** Irish Red Ale

**Alcohol content** 3.6 abw (4.5 abv)

**Ideal serving temperature** 50° F (10° C)

# BEERS WITH LAMB

THE STRONG BIÈRES DE GARDE (beers to keep) of Northern France were originally farmhouse ales intended to be matured in the bottle. The tradition of presenting them in champagne bottles has grown in recent years, though most are now matured in lagering cellars. The local malts sometimes contribute a suggestion of aniseed, and there may be an earthy note from the cellar in these small, old breweries. The flavors of these beers marry beautifully with the Channel coast's lamb dishes.

### DUYCK JENLAIN

The name Duyck is from the part of Flanders that extends into France, and the farm-style brewery is just across the Belgian border at the hamlet of Jenlain, south of Valenciennes. The beer pours with a huge head; has a smooth, syrupy start; with orangy, spicy, dry flavors in the finish. It is a very good example of the style.

**Region of origin** Northern France

**Style** *Bière de Garde*

**Alcohol content** 5.2 abw (6.5 abv)

**Ideal serving temperature**
50–55° F (10–13° C)

### CASTELAIN CH'TI BRUNE

The brewery is near Lens, and *Ch'ti* refers to northern miners. Ch'ti Brune has a rich body, port flavors, and a vanilla-like nuttiness. It is good with a rich lamb stew. Ch'ti Blonde is syrupy, with fresh, apricot aromas and flavors, and a dry, smooth, nut-malt finish: try it with lamb chops.

**Region of origin** Northern France

**Style** *Bière de Garde*

**Alcohol content**
(Both versions) 5.1 abw (6.4 abv)

**Ideal serving temperature**
50–55° F (10–13° C)

*Cuisine du nord*
Bières de garde *are from a region with more interesting cuisine than is generally realized. This rack of lamb is served on a potato galette.*

### JEANNE D'ARC AMBRE DES FLANDRES

Joan of Arc was born nearby in the Champagne region. The brewery that honors her was established by the van Damme family, in 1898, at Ronchin, near Lille. The beer has a peppery start; a grainy, figgy palate; and a big, dry finish. Jeanne d'Arc also produces a malty golden brew, Grain d'Orge (6.4 abv; 8.0 abv).

**Region of origin** Northern France

**Style** *Bière de Garde*

**Alcohol content** 5.1 abw (6.4 abv)

**Ideal serving temperature**
50–55° F (10–13° C)

## A REVOLUTIONARY BEER

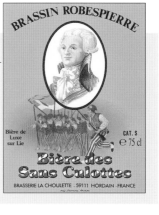

BRASSIN ROBESPIERRE is a strong, very smooth, full-bodied, soothing, but eminently drinkable golden *bière de garde*. It is a bigger version of the regular Bière des Sans Culottes (*below*), and honors French revolutionary Maximilien Robespierre, whose maternal grandfather was a brewer. These beers are produced by husband and wife Alain and Martine Dhaussy in their farmhouse brewery at Hordain, south of Lille and near Valenciennes. The brewery is named La Choulette, after a local sport that was a forerunner of lacrosse.

### LA CHOULETTE AMBRÉE

Ambrée is the principal beer from the La Choulette brewery. It pours with a big head and is very aromatic; has a spicy, aniseedy aroma and palate; and a slightly oily texture. It is a very good example of the style, and is an excellent beer with spicy foods. The brewery also produces a *framboise* version of the beer.

**Region of origin**  Northern France

**Style**  *Bière de Garde*

**Alcohol content**  6.0 abw (7.5 abv)

**Ideal serving temperature**
50–55° F (10–13° C)

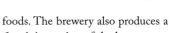

### LA CHOULETTE BIÈRE DES SANS CULOTTES

"Without culottes" refers to the ragged-trousered poor of the French Revolution. Among events leading up to the revolution was a beer tax. Sans Culottes is golden, with a toasty, yeasty, champagnelike aroma, and a similar "house character" to the Ambrée: oily and aniseedy, but less rich in spiciness and body, with a drier, elegantly bitter finish.

**Region of origin**  Northern France

**Style**  *Bière de Garde*

**Alcohol content**  5.6 abw (7.0 abv)

**Ideal serving temperature**  50° F (10° C)

### SAINT SYLVESTRE 3 MONTS

The St. Sylvestre farmhouse brewery is situated among hop gardens near Hazebrouck in the Flemish-French countryside between Dunkirk and Lille. It makes a very lively, winey, fruity, yeasty, golden beer, with a robustly dry finish and great length called 3 Monts. It brews darker beers for Christmas and spring.

**Region of origin**  Northern France

**Style**  *Bière de Garde*

**Alcohol content**  6.8 abw (8.5 abv)

**Ideal serving temperature**  50° F (10° C)

# BEERS WITH BEEF

IN THE DAYS WHEN PORTER WAS KING, the term "pale ale" was coined to describe the translucent copper or bronze brews perfected in the English town of Burton. In both their color and their dryish, complex flavors, these are the beer world's answer to claret, the subtle red wine of Bordeaux. The more assertive new-generation pale ales of America might even be compared with the fresh, fruity cabernets of the New World. These are the beers to serve with roast beef, prime rib, or a steak.

## MARSTON'S PEDIGREE

The most subtle and complex of pale ales or bottled bitters, due in part to Burton's hard water but more to the unique method of fermentation. The brew circulates through halls of huge oak barrels linked in a "union" (a Victorian system long abandoned by other breweries). This system makes for a lively, cleansing fermentation, producing a beer of light, malty, nutty dryness and subtle, apple fruitiness.

**Region of origin**
Trent Valley, England, UK

**Style** Pale Ale/Bottled Bitter

**Alcohol content** 3.6 abw (4.5 abv)

**Ideal serving temperature** 55° F (13° C)

***Going for a Burton***
*Burton-style ales are a natural match for the classic steak and fries, shown here with a generous portion of malt vinegar.*

## McMULLEN CASTLE PALE ALE

This pale ale from Hertford, England gains a fruity complexity in a period of warm maturation, during which it is also dry hopped. It starts malty; develops a fresh, pearlike acidity as it warms; and finishes with a cedary, earthy, creamy dryness from the hop.

**Region of origin**
Southern England, UK

**Style** Pale Ale

**Alcohol content** 4.0 abw (5.0 abv)

**Ideal serving temperature** 55° F (13° C)

## BLACK SHEEP ALE

The "black sheep" is Paul Theakston, who fell out with his family over the sale of the famous brewery that bears their name and set up on his own in the same town, Masham in North Yorkshire. His ale has aniseedy, cedary hop aromas and flavors, and a big, dry, smooth, firm maltiness, enhanced by the use of a multistrain yeast and square stone fermenters.

**Region of origin**
Northeast England, UK

**Style** Pale Ale

**Alcohol content** 3.3 abw (4.4 abv)

**Ideal serving temperature** 55° F (13° C)

## WINE AND SHRINE

CLOSE TO SEATTLE'S famous Pike Place food market is a shrine to beer – the Pike brewery. It was created by Charles Finkel, a marketing man in the local wine industry. In the late 1970s he founded the Merchant du Vin company, with the intention of dealing in wine. Then, inspired by the 1977 book *The World Guide to Beer*, he decided instead to import ales, *lambics*, and wheat beers from Europe. His work helped turn Seattle into an American beer capital rivaled only by Portland, Oregon.

### PIKE PALE ALE

The Pike brewery in Seattle embraces a pub (*above, right*), restaurant, and beer museum, as well as a home-brew supply shop called Liberty Malt. The brewery makes some of Seattle's most uncompromising, assertive beers. Its pale ale is very big, with a rich, creamy, sweet malt character; an almost voluptuous body; a hint of peachy fruitiness; with a hit of earthy hop bitterness in the finish.

**Region of origin** Pacific Northwest US

**Style** Pale Ale

**Alcohol content** 3.6 abw (4.5 abv)

**Ideal serving temperature** 50–55° F (10–13° C)

### ST.-AMBROISE PALE ALE

The street where this brewery stands is named after St. Ambroise, a monk believed to be Montreal's first beer-maker. The pale ale is very perfumy, outstandingly hoppy in aroma and flavor, dry, and appetizing. It has a light, soft body but full, long flavors; developing lemony-orangy notes; and an elegant dryness in the finish.

**Region of origin** Province of Quebec, Canada

**Style** Pale Ale

**Alcohol content** 4.0 abw (5.0 abv)

**Ideal serving temperature** 50° F (10° C)

### GEARY'S PALE ALE

American David Geary developed his skills in Britain before setting up this brewery in Portland, Maine, in 1986. This brew has big, assertive flavors. It starts smooth and malty; develops rounded, orangy fruitiness; and finishes with clean, dry, tingly, crisply appetizing hop notes.

**Region of origin** Northeast US

**Style** Pale Ale

**Alcohol content** 3.6 abw (4.5 abv)

**Ideal serving temperature** 50–55° F (10–13° C)

# BEERS WITH PIZZA

To AMERICANS, PIZZA AND BEER (albeit usually a very ordinary kind of lager) is by far the best-known combination of food and brew. It is a transatlantic marriage: the tomatoes, originally from the Americas, may have been introduced by Neapolitan mariners to the oregano, basil, and flat bread of Italy. Beer being "liquid bread," the marriage works. It is happiest if the doughiness of the pizza base and the flavors of the topping are matched by a lager or ale with the spiciness and chewiness of a succulent amber malt.

### MORETTI LA ROSSA

While pizza originates in southern Italy, the country's most characterful beers come from the north. Moretti has its origins in Udine, northeast of Venice. Its La Rossa almost has the aroma of straight-from-the-oven pizza dough; a fresh, sweetish, lively, smooth malt character; finishing in a spicy dryness. The ideal pizza beer, were it not so deceptively strong.

**Region of origin** Northern Italy

**Style** Vienna Lager/*Maibock*

**Alcohol content** 5.8 abw (7.2 abv)

**Ideal serving temperature** 48° F (9° C)

### MOHRENBRÄU SCHLUCK

One of the Three Wise Men was said to have been a Moor, and the Moor's Head is a common name for an inn. Mohrenbräu, in Dornbirn, Austria, makes a soft, smooth, light, balanced, rounded, Vienna-style beer, under the name *Schluck* (implying a quick drink).

**Region of origin** Rhine Valley, Austria

**Style** Vienna Lager

**Alcohol content** 4.2 abw (5.2 abv)

**Ideal serving temperature** 48° F (9° C)

*Beer to go*
*Beer and bread are the most closely related of staples . . . but you need a brew with malty sweetness and spiciness to stand up to pizza toppings.*

### RICKARD'S RED

Signed by E.H. Rickard of the Capilano Brewing Company, of Barrie, Ontario, and Vancouver, British Columbia. The locations of the brewery sites betray the fact that this is a confection of the Canadian national brewer, Molson. Rickard's Red is light in body and flavor, with a pleasantly sweet, caramelly maltiness in the middle. An easily drinkable beer to enjoy with pizza.

**Region of origin**
Province of Ontario, Canada

**Style** Red Beer/Vienna Lager

**Alcohol content** 4.2 abw (5.2 abv)

**Ideal serving temperature** 48° F (9° C)

## FOR THE GOOD OF THE CITIZENS

THE GANG-BUSTER in the 1950s TV series and 1980s movie, *The Untouchables*, Eliot Ness (*right*) was the grandly-titled "Director of Public Safety" in Cleveland, Ohio. The city's Great Lakes brewery, known for the local allusions in the names of several of its beers, honors him with The Eliot Ness (*below*). Great Lakes' Burning River Pale Ale recalls the day the polluted local waterway caught fire. Cleveland has become a smarter and livelier city since then. A great contribution to this revival was made by Great Lakes; its beers are a source of civic pride.

### GREAT LAKES BREWING CO. THE ELIOT NESS

Cleveland's Great Lakes brewery and pub, proud of its bullet holes from the gang-busting days of Eliot Ness, gives his name to their Vienna-style lager. It is rich, creamy, and malty in aroma and palate, with a late balance of whiskeyish oakiness and acidity. A big beer to go with a Chicago-style deep-dish pizza or focaccia bread.

| | |
|---|---|
| **Region of origin** | Midwest US |
| **Style** | Vienna Lager |
| **Alcohol content** | 4.5 abw (5.6 abv) |
| **Ideal serving temperature** | 48° F (9° C) |

### CHELSEA SUNSET RED

This pub and brewery is located in the Chelsea neighbourhood of Manhattan. Specialities include brick-oven pizzas and this reddish, malty, spicy ale. Sunset Red marries a clean, very smooth, chewy, nutty, crystal-malt character with toasty and fruity-ale notes. It is quite dry for the style. Perhaps one for the grilled veggie pizza.

| | |
|---|---|
| **Region of origin** | Northeast US |
| **Style** | Red Ale |
| **Alcohol content** | 4.0 abw (5.0 abv) |
| **Ideal serving temperature** | 50° F (10° C) |

### LAKEFRONT RIVERWEST STEIN BEER

Milwaukee, where several rivers flow into Lake Michigan, was once infamous for watery beers. Today, it has big-tasting beers from little breweries such as Lakefront. Riverwest Stein Beer is a superb lager, with a lovely balance of bigness and drinkability; aniselike malt flavors; and a crisp finish.

| | |
|---|---|
| **Region of origin** | Midwest US |
| **Style** | Vienna Lager |
| **Alcohol content** | 4.7 abw (5.9 abv) |
| **Ideal serving temperature** | 48° F (9° C) |

# BEERS WITH CHEESE

SOME TRAPPIST MONASTERIES in Belgium make both beer and cheese. Abbeys of other orders have these products made for them. The beers are strong ales, some of which develop a portlike character during maturation. Several of the cheeses are typically semisoft and mild (*facing page*), though flavored variations, some with beer added, and cheddar types can also be found. The biggest, fruitiest abbey beers are even better with tasty blue cheeses such as Stilton and Roquefort. Some of the abbeys also make bread.

### LEFFE RADIEUSE

Notre-Dame de Leffe is a Norbertine abbey in Belgium. It has not brewed beer since the French Revolution, but in the 1950s the abbot licensed a local brewer to make Leffe beer. It is now made by Interbrew, at Leuven. Radieuse, meaning halo, is the biggest in flavor. The beer has a cherrylike fruitiness, a portish texture, and a faintly roasty, cinnamon-tinged finish.

**Region of origin**
Province of Namur, Belgium

**Style**  Abbey

**Alcohol content**  6.6 abw (8.2 abv)

**Ideal serving temperature**
59–64° F (15–18° C)

*Hop snack*
*Not only the cheese but also the finest crackers have an affinity with beer: these Bath Oliver biscuits contain hops.*

### WESTVLETEREN 8° (BLUE CAP)

Belgium's smallest Trappist monastery is St. Sixtus, at Westvleteren, near the war graves around Ypres. Its beers have no labels, but are identified on the crown. The blue-capped 8° is the fruitiest, with hints of plum wine or brandy, and an almondy dryness in the finish. Try it with a sweet, soft cheese.

**Region of origin**
Province of West Flanders, Belgium

**Style**  Abbey (Authentic Trappist)

**Alcohol content**  6.4 abw (8.0 abv)

**Ideal serving temperature**
59–64° F (15–18° C)

### LA TRAPPE QUADRUPEL

This beer is made at the Schaapskooi brewery of the Koningshoeven Trappist monastery, near Tilburg, in the Netherlands. The strongest of its beers, Quadrupel, is very long, smooth, oily, syrupy, and fruity; with a dry, warming, corianderlike finish.

**Region of origin**  Province of North Brabant, the Netherlands

**Style**  Abbey (Authentic Trappist)

**Alcohol content**  8.0 abw (10.0 abv)

**Ideal serving temperature**
50–57° F (10–14° C)

## SMOOTH AND SAVORY

CHIMAY IS ONE of several Belgian abbeys that make cheese. Its principal cheese (*right*) is in the classic style known as Trappist. Made from cow's milk, it has a slightly lactic aroma; a velvet-smooth texture, which melts in the mouth; and an appetizingly savory, very mild flavor. The style was first made by Trappists at the monastery of Port-du-Salut, at Entrammes, in Normandy, France, after the Napoleonic period. The monks later sold the brand name Port Salut to a commercial dairy.

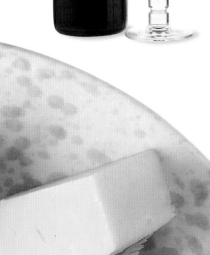

### CHIMAY GRANDE RÉSERVE

The portlike Grande Réserve is made by the Trappist monastery of Notre-Dame, near Chimay, south Belgium. The port flavors develop if the beer is laid down for five years or more. This lively, rich ale has a medium-sweet middle, with suggestions of thyme, pepper, sandalwood, and nutmeg in the finish. It is a complex classic, and a delight with Roquefort cheese.

**Region of origin**
Province of Hainaut, Belgium

**Style** Abbey (Authentic Trappist)

**Alcohol content** 7.2 abw (9.0 abv)

**Ideal serving temperature**
59–64° F (15–18° C)

### BUDELS CAPUCIJN

The Dutch town of Budel once had a Capuchin monastery, but this beer honoring the order was launched by the local brewery in the 1980s. The beer is very lively, and has a fresh, hoppy aroma; a lightly syrupy palate; an apple sweetness; and a rooty, woody dryness in the finish.

**Region of origin** Province of North Brabant, the Netherlands

**Style** Abbey

**Alcohol content** 5.2 abw (6.5 abv)

**Ideal serving temperature** 50° F (10° C)

### ECHIGO LAND BRAUEREI ABBEY-STYLE TRIPEL

Many "abbey-style" beers have been made in the New World in recent years, most of them in the US. This example is from the Japanese Echigo brewery, at Makimachi in the Niigata prefecture. Tripel has an aroma of raspberries; a suggestion of morello cherries in its oily palate; and an intense almondy dryness in the finish.

**Region of origin** Honshu, Japan

**Style** Abbey

**Alcohol content** 7.2 abw (9.0 abv)

**Ideal serving temperature**
50–57° F (10–14° C)

# BEERS WITH FRUITY DESSERTS

THE IDEA OF BEER WITH DESSERTS may surprise, but it can work beautifully. Try a raspberry or cherry beer with a fruit tart, pie, or pudding. While the sharpest, driest fruit beers are best as a party-greeting or aperitif, more rounded ones can highlight the flavors of desserts containing similar ingredients. Apart from the beers suggested here, "white" Belgian wheat beers accompany orangy dishes well; their German counterparts are good with apple desserts; and a *Dunkelweizen* is a delight with banana dishes.

*Two bites . . .*
*The cherry is the most traditional fruit flavoring used in beer. It is also widely used in desserts. These tartlets are half of a marriage made in heaven.*

## RODENBACH ALEXANDER

For years, Belgium's Rodenbach brewery fretted that some consumers, finding its regular beer just too tart, "spoiled" it by adding grenadine syrup. Finally, the brewery realized the value of making a sweetened version. The background of its oak-aged Grand Cru brings a "live yogurt" tartness and an ironlike, passion fruit balance to the clean, sweet, syrupy, cherry character. It is both sharp and sweet.

**Region of origin**
Province of West Flanders, Belgium

**Style** Flemish Red, with fruit essence

**Alcohol content** 4.8 abw (6.0 abv)

**Ideal serving temperature** 53° F (12° C)

## LINDEMANS FRAMBOISE

A raspberry beer based on the *lambic* of this Belgian farmhouse brewery. It has the typically seedlike, stemmy, woody, tobaccoish fragrance of real raspberries. The flavor begins flowery, then becomes very sweet, suggesting a heavy hand with the fruit juice. In the finish, the sherryish acidity and tartness of the *lambic* emerges as a late, surprising balance.

**Region of origin**
Province of Flemish Brabant, Belgium

**Style** *Framboise/Frambozen–lambic*

**Alcohol content** 2.0 abw (2.5 abv)

**Ideal serving temp.** 48–50° F (9–10° C)

## DE TROCH CHAPEAU PÊCHE

The farmhouse brewery De Troch makes crisp *gueuze-lambic* beers in the Belgian village of Wambeek. It also has a sweeter range, Chapeau. This peach beer is very sweet indeed, but has the "fresh apple" flavors of *lambic* beers, and a dry, "fino sherry" finish.

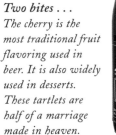

**Region of origin**
Province of Flemish Brabant, Belgium

**Style** Peach *Lambic*

**Alcohol content** 2.4 abw (3.0 abv)

**Ideal serving temperature**
48–50° F (9–10° C)

## NEW WORLD WINNER

DEBORAH AND DAN CAREY (*left*) and their Belgian-style Cherry Beer have twice in succession won the prize for the world's best speciality brew. The awards were made at a contest judged by brewers from all over the world, in Britain's brewing capital, the town of Burton. The Careys typify the enthusiasm and creativity being brought to the world of beer by young American brewers. Other products from their New Glarus brewery, near Madison, Wisconsin, include a *Weissbier*, a Bock, and an *Oktoberfest* lager.

## NEW GLARUS WISCONSIN CHERRY BEER

Cherries grown around Brussels, Wisconsin, are used in this award-winning brew, which also uses wheat, barley malt, and yeasts from Belgium. The beer has almondy, cherry-stone aromas; sweet, fresh-fruit flavors; a textured maltiness; and notes of iron and tart acidity in the finish.

**Region of origin** Midwest US

**Style** Belgian-style Cherry Beer

**Alcohol content** 4.0 abw (5.0 abv)

**Ideal serving temperature**
48–50° F (9–10° C)

## HUYGHE NINKEBERRY

Ninke is not a fruit, but a child's name. The beer, made near Ghent, Belgium, is in the Florisgaarden range of fruit-flavored, "white" wheat brews. It is most obviously flavored with peach, but also apricot and mango. It is syrupy but refreshing, with a spicy, minty balance.

**Region of origin**
Province of East Flanders, Belgium

**Style**
Belgian Wheat Beer, with fruit essences

**Alcohol content** 2.4 abw (3.0 abv)

**Ideal serving temperature**
48–50° F (9–10° C)

*Sweet treat*
*An eclectic beer such as Ninkeberry (left) would suit the treat below: banana fritters with lime-and-caramel syrup.*

## MCAUSLAN RASPBERRY ALE/BIÈRE À LA FRAMBOISE

This fruit beer has a genuine raspberry color and aroma, but a less obviously raspberryish flavor, even though real fruit (purée) is used. There is even a hint of blackberries (which are not used). Because it is based on an ale, it lacks the tartness of *lambic* fruit beers.

**Region of origin**
Province of Quebec, Canada

**Style** Raspberry Ale

**Alcohol content** 4.0 abw (5.0 abv)

**Ideal serving temperature**
48–50° F (9–10° C)

# BEERS WITH CREAMY DESSERTS

THE USE OF ONLY a tiny proportion of oatmeal in the brewing gives beer a delicious creaminess of both texture and flavor. The type of brew in which oatmeal is most often used is stout. Here, the creaminess is married with the typically coffeeish, chocolaty, toasty flavors of the style. A stout clearly labeled as containing oatmeal can be the perfect accompaniment to a creamy dessert. The style has its origins in the fashion for "nutritious" beers in Britain after World War II.

***Move over, Marsala***
*Oatmeal stouts are not only accompaniments but also ingredients of dishes like zabaglione, in place of the more usual Moscato or Marsala wines.*

### SAMUEL SMITH OATMEAL STOUT

The fashion of using oatmeal in stout waned in the 1960s and vanished in the 1970s, but was revived in the 1980s by Samuel Smith's in the brewing village of Tadcaster. This brew has a fresh, flowery, oloroso sherry aroma; a clean, sweet creaminess; and a silky dryness in the finish.

**Region of origin** Northern England, UK

**Style** Oatmeal Stout

**Alcohol content** 4.0 abw (5.0 abv)

**Ideal serving temperature** 55° F (13° C)

### MACLAY OAT MALT STOUT

Oatmeal stouts are usually made with rolled oats, but Maclay uses the malted version to give a fuller, sweeter character. Its stout has a malted-milk aroma, a well-rounded palate, and a light body. It finishes with a buttery, toasty dryness. It is delicious with the Scottish dessert Atholl Brose, which contains cream, honey, and whiskey.

**Region of origin** Central Scotland, UK

**Style** Oat Malt Stout

**Alcohol content** 3.6 abw (4.5 abv)

**Ideal serving temperature** 55° F (13° C)

### MIDDLESEX BREWING CO. OATMEAL STOUT

The Middlesex Brewing Company, established in 1992, is in the former hop-growing town of Wilmington, Massachusetts. Its Oatmeal Stout has a particularly solid ebony color and a dark head. It has the aroma of cinnamon-dusted cappuccino and a firm, smooth, long, coffee-chocolate palate with a good, balancing dryness.

**Region of origin** Northeast US

**Style** Oatmeal Stout

**Alcohol content** 3.4 abw (4.2 abv)

**Ideal serving temperature** 55° F (13° C)

## . . . AND WITH HONEY CAKE

HONEY HAS LONG BEEN USED as an addition to beer. Because honey is very fermentable, much of its obvious flavor quickly vanishes, but some traces always remain. In addition, the interaction of yeast and honey creates new, flowery, creamy flavors. Honey beers are made in several countries, especially Belgium and the US, but the two brews shown on the left are both from England. The notably flowery Enville Ale (3.6 abw, 4.5 abv) is made on the estate of the Earls of Stamford, near Stourbridge. Vaux, of Sunderland, produces the sweeter, more overtly honeyish-tasting Waggle Dance (4.0 abw, 5.0 abv).

### BOSTON BEER WORKS BUCKEYE OATMEAL STOUT

Among the Boston Beer Works' very assertive beers is this full-bodied, rich, oily, oatmeal-tasting, marshmallowlike, sweetish stout. In its rotating range of 30 or 40 products, the Beer Works has brewed a wide selection of porter and stout variations. These have included a creamy, peppery Imperial Stout; and a Cherry Stout with semi-sweet and milk chocolate, for Valentine's Day.

**Region of origin**  Northeast US

**Style**  Oatmeal Stout

**Alcohol content**  4.4 abw (5.5 abv)

**Ideal serving temperature**  55° F (13° C)

### ADLER BRAU OATMEAL STOUT

Adler, of Appleton, Wisconsin, grew out of a German-American lager tradition, but today also makes British styles such as this oatmeal stout. It is medium-sweet, with a rooty, gingery, fruity aroma; a firm, smooth, creamy palate; and a "toasted cookie" finish.

**Region of origin**  Midwest US

**Style**  Oatmeal Stout

**Alcohol content**  3.9 abw (4.9 abv)

**Ideal serving temperature**  55° F (13° C)

*Kiss Kahlúa goodbye?*
*Tiramisu means "pick me up," so it should contain alcohol. It can be infused with stout instead of the more usual Kahlúa.*

### OASIS ZOSER STOUT

With its ancient Egyptian theme, this respected brewery and pub in Boulder, Colorado, names its oatmeal stout after the mythical gatekeeper to heaven. The beer, which has an almost tarlike appearance and a very dense head, has a fragrant, perfumy, bitter-chocolate aroma and palate; a firm body; and a smoky finish reminiscent of a smooth Scotch malt whiskey.

**Region of origin**  Southwest US

**Style**  Oatmeal Stout

**Alcohol content**  4.0 abw (5.0 abv)

**Ideal serving temperature**  55° F (13° C)

# BEERS WITH CHOCOLATE & COFFEE

IT IS HARD TO FIND a dessert wine robust enough to accompany the powerful flavors of chocolate mousses, puddings, or cakes, but many stouts are perfect for the job. The stout chosen must be big, rich, and not too dry. In many stouts, the dark malts used mirror the flavors of chocolate. This alone can create a powerful illusion of chocolate flavors. In recent years, some brewers have begun to add actual chocolate or coffee to speciality stouts – creating the perfect beer for this purpose.

### BROOKLYN BLACK CHOCOLATE STOUT

This outstanding strong stout, from the Brooklyn Brewery, New York, was launched in 1994. It achieves an astonishingly chocolaty taste from malt alone. It is rich, spicy, textured, and fruity. To drink it is like eating the Viennese classic, Sachertorte.

| | |
|---|---|
| **Region of origin** | Northeast US |
| **Style** | Chocolate/Imperial Stout |
| **Alcohol content** | 6.6 abw (8.3 abv) |
| **Ideal serving temperature** | 55° F (13° C) |

*Classic cake*
*Sachertorte, the famous Viennese chocolate cake with apricot preserve, finds an echo in the flavors of some fruity "chocolate" stouts, especially the one from Brooklyn.*

### YOUNG'S DOUBLE CHOCOLATE STOUT

The first stout to be made with added chocolate – both bars and essence – introduced by Young's, of London, in 1997. It is silky smooth and textured, with a lively complexity. The aromas and flavors begin with faint hints of ginger, becoming fudgy and creamy, then balancing this sweetness with a round, bitter-chocolate finish.

| | |
|---|---|
| **Region of origin** | London, England, UK |
| **Style** | Chocolate Stout |
| **Alcohol content** | 4.0 abw (5.0 abv ) |
| **Ideal serving temperature** | 55° F (13° C) |

### MCMULLEN'S CHOCOLATE STOUT

A lighter-bodied example that nonetheless has a very good dark chocolate character, especially when served at room temperature. This beer also has raisiny, sherryish notes: the flavors of a chocolaty trifle or Italian panettone cake. It was introduced by the English country brewery McMullen's, of Hertford, in 1997, initially for the US market.

| | |
|---|---|
| **Region of origin** | Southern England, UK |
| **Style** | Chocolate Stout |
| **Alcohol content** | 4.0 abw (5.0 abv) |
| **Ideal serving temperature** | 55° F (13° C) |

## PERFECTION IN PRALINES

Gouden Carolus ("Golden Charles") is a strong (6.0–6.6 abw, 7.5–8.2 abv), dark ale from Mechelen, Belgium. It is named after Holy Roman Emperor Charles V. The beer's toffeeish, orangy flavors go well with petit fours or chocolates. The sweetmeats shown here are made by Pâtisserie Christian Meyer, of Strasbourg, France. The marzipan "hop flowers" have a curiously authentic perfume (they are aromatized with hop oil). The "mugs" are flavored with beer; the pralines with powdered malt. Beer seems to be an inspiration to Pâtisseur Christian . . . after all, his premises are opposite a famous beer café, The Twelve Apostles.

## CEYLON LION STOUT

Several tropical countries have rich, strong stouts. Perhaps the tastiest is this one, from Ceylon Breweries, of Sri Lanka. Lion Stout is bottle-conditioned, and has big, pruny, mocha aromas and flavors; developing an intense bitter-chocolate finish. In Sri Lanka it is sometimes laced with the local *arrack*, a spirit made from coconuts.

**Region of origin** Sri Lanka

**Style** Strong Tropical Stout

**Alcohol content** 6.0 abw (7.5 abv)

**Ideal serving temperature** 55° F (13° C)

## PYRAMID ESPRESSO STOUT

In espresso-loving Washington State, the Pyramid brewery produces a stout with the local flavor. The espresso character is achieved by the use of dark malts and highly roasted barley. These seem to mimic one of the fruitier varieties of coffee bean. The beer has coffeelike flavors, right through to a long, dry finish.

**Region of origin** Pacific Northwest US

**Style** Coffee Stout

**Alcohol content** 4.5 abw (5.6 abv)

**Ideal serving temperature** 55° F (13° C)

***Mighty mousse***
*This chocolate-decorated coffee mousse cries out for a glass of espresso-tinged stout. The beer can even be used as an ingredient.*

## RED HOOK DOUBLE BLACK STOUT

While Red Hook was popularizing microbrewed beer, another Seattle company, Starbucks, was leading the espresso movement. Both companies were the idea of Seattle entrepreneur Gordon Bowker. His two notions meet in this Red Hook beer flavored with Starbucks coffee. It has a smooth, nutty middle and a rounded espresso bitterness in the finish.

**Region of origin** Pacific Northwest US

**Style** Coffee Stout

**Alc. content** 5.5–5.6 abw (6.9–7.0 abv)

**Ideal serving temperature** 55° F (13° C)

# BEERS FOR AFTER DINNER

THE MORE COMMON DIGESTIF may be a brandy such as Cognac, Armagnac, or Calvados, a fruit eau de vie, single-malt Scotch, or small-batch Bourbon, but the job can also be done by a strong beer. The same fruity flavors develop when yeast has to work hard to ferment a strong beer. The malty richness in a beer (fermented, but not distilled) may exceed that of a fine Scotch. Even the most potent beer has less alcohol than a spirit drink, but may offer a similar soothing warmth to relax the stomach.

### KLOSTER IRSEER ABT'S TRUNK

The abbot may well have got drunk on this very strong lager. The brewery is in a former monastery, at Irsee, in southern Germany. The beer is light-bodied for its strength, with an oily maltiness and vanillalike, oaky, whiskeyish notes. The brewery also has a restaurant, small hotel, crafts gallery, and pottery. The beer is sometimes sold in stoneware flasks.

**Region of origin**
Swabia, Bavaria, Germany

**Style** Extra-strong Lager/Double Bock

**Alcohol content** 9.6 abw (12.0 abv)

**Ideal serving temperature** 48° F (9° C)

### SCHÄFFBRÄU FEUERFEST EDEL BIER

This beer is made at Treuchtlingen, Germany. The seal offers a guarantee of one year's lagering, but maturation can be as long as 18 months. This long sleep makes for a smooth, even lean, beer. The aroma suggests oranges in brandy; the palate is pruny and coffeeish; the finish woody and sappy.

**Region of origin**
Franconia, Bavaria, Germany

**Style** Extra-strong Lager/Double Bock

**Alcohol content** 8.4 abw (10.5 abv)

**Ideal serving temperature** 48° F (9° C)

### UNION CUVÉE DE L'ERMITAGE

Wine terms such as Cuvée are used in Belgium by brewers to imply a very special product. This delicious beer is made at the Union brewery, in Jumet, near Charleroi. It has the flavor of clotted cream; a warming middle; and a smoky, sappy, assertive dryness in the finish. An Armagnac among beers.

**Region of origin**
Province of Hainaut, Belgium

**Style** Strong Dark Ale/Abbey-style

**Alcohol content** 6.8 abw (8.5 abv)

**Ideal serving temperature**
50–57° F (10–14° C)

## THE FINAL, FRAGRANT BREW

FINALLY . . . A BEER to accompany the cigar after dinner. Evenings of fine brews and Havanas have become a fashion since the revival of interest in cigars, especially in the US. With the smokiness of roasted malts and leafiness of the hop, such combinations are more than mere whimsy. Glossy New York magazine *Cigar Aficionado* matched 20 beers with appropriate cigars, in an article by Brooklyn writer-brewer Garrett Oliver (*right*). He nominated his own toasty Brooklyn Brown Ale to pair nothing less than the revered Cohiba Esplendido, of Cuba.

### KASTEEL BIER/ BIÈRE DU CHÂTEAU

The castle, or château, is a moated mansion dating from 1736, at Ingelmunster, West Flanders. The cellars are now used to bottle-age, for 6–12 weeks, Kasteel Bier, which is brewed nearby by Van Honsebrouck. This very powerful beer begins with malty richness, developing to notes of dried fruit and port, drying to a burlaplike finish. There is also a vanillalike golden version.

**Region of origin**
Province of West Flanders, Belgium

**Style** Barley Wine

**Alcohol content** 8.8 abw (11.0 abv)

**Ideal serving temperature**
53–55° F (12–13° C)

### GALES PRIZE OLD ALE

One of the most famous strong, bottle-conditioned ales in Britain. Made by the George Gale brewery of Horndean, near Portsmouth, in Hampshire. Gales Prize Old Ale won the first of its many prizes in the 1920s. It was created by a brewer from Yorkshire, a county once known for a type of strong ale known as stingo. This example starts malty; becomes smoky, winey, and acidic; and finishes with a Calvados-like warmth.

**Region of origin** Southern England

**Style** Strong Old Ale/Barley Wine

**Alcohol content** 7.2 abw (9.0 abv)

**Ideal serving temperature**
53–55° F (12–13° C)

*For the beer nut*
*"From soup to nuts," in the American phrase, there is always a beer to suit . . . right up to an oaky, leafy, earthy, brandyish finale.*

### HAIR OF THE DOG ADAM

This tiny brewery, in Portland, Oregon, specializes in characterful and unusual beers. Adam Bier was a style produced in Dortmund in the days when the city made strong, top-fermenting, dark brews. There is little information on the original Adam Bier, so this is a free interpretation. It is syrupy, with hints of chocolate, roasted peppers, and peat. A beer of astonishing complexity.

**Region of origin** Pacific Northwest US

**Style** Adam Bier

**Alcohol content** 8.0 abw (10.0 abv)

**Ideal serving temperature**
50–57° F (10–14° C)

# COOKING
## WITH
## BEER

BEER WAS FIRST MADE FOR
its nutritional value, and it is
central to the world of food
and drink. Like wine, it also
adds a sensuous element to the
kitchen. Beers that accompany foods
well are often also a useful addition to the
dish itself, whether as a braising liquid or
marinade; an ingredient in a vinaigrette,
soup, or sauce; a yeasty raising agent in a
batter, bread, or cake; or a flavor in a
dessert. The possibilities extend far beyond
the commonly suggested beer batters and
Belgian beef stews. As with wine, there are
no hard-and-fast rules. The recipes that
follow are simply ways of having more fun
with beer and exploring its diversity.

# BEERS FOR VINAIGRETTES

Vinegar originated from sour wine, but is now more often brewed from malt, like a sour beer. Before refrigerators, beer that had gone sour at the brewery was sometimes sold as malt vinegar. Some breweries today deliberately make such a product, or offer beer-flavored condiments. There is, therefore, every logic in using sour styles of beer as an alternative or complement to vinegar.

## CANTILLON KRIEK LAMBIC

Although it is well balanced, this is the tartest-tasting cherry beer, and therefore the most suitable for a fruity vinaigrette. It is based on a very traditional *lambic* (*page 75*), with a distinctly lemony note. There is no lemon added, but this character develops during fermentation. There are also cherry-skin notes; a fresh fruitiness that also hints at raspberry; plenty of intensity; a powerful, oily, zesty aroma; and an attractive cerise color. Cantillon's Rosé de Gambrinus would make a good raspberry vinaigrette.

**Region of origin**
Province of Flemish Brabant, Belgium

**Style** Fruit *Lambic*

**Alcohol content**
4.0 abw (5.0 abv)

**Ideal serving temperature**
55° F (13° C)

## BEERS TO TRY

The classic oil-and-vinegar dressing is given a new twist by the addition of beer. The most obvious beers to use are the *Berliner Weisse* type (*pages 82–83*). Bürgerbräu's example is insufficiently acidic, but examples in this style from Kindl or Schultheiss will do the trick.

In Belgium, the *lambic* family of beers offers many possibilities. Straight, unblended *lambic* is normally available only on draft, though Cantillon has a bottled version, Bruocsella 1900 (*page 140*). The tarter examples of *gueuze* or fruit *lambics* can substitute for raspberry vinegar, as in the recipe below.

The sweet-and-sour "red" ales of Flanders, such as Rodenbach (*page 94*), especially in its Grand Cru version, can also substitute for vinegars. In this instance, distinct acetic characteristics and malty notes emerge.

## ENDIVE SALAD WITH A KRIEK VINAIGRETTE

Both the *kriek* cherry and Belgian endive are especially associated with Schaarbeek, a neighborhood of Brussels. The endive is the whitish-green bud of the chicory root. Its bitter, earthy, yet delicate flavor adds sophistication to a simple salad.

### Ingredients

The vinaigrette:
2 tsp Dijon mustard
1 tsp sugar
½ tsp salt
6 fl. oz (170 ml) olive oil
1 clove garlic, crushed
Juice from ¼ lemon
5 fl. oz (150 ml) kriek lambic

The salad:
Freshly ground pepper, to taste
6 heads endive
6 black olives, stoned
3 radishes, sliced
Chopped chives
1 poached egg
Croutons

1 Pour the *kriek lambic* beer into the oil. Olive oil must be used: a lighter oil, such as sunflower, will not mix with the beer.

**LIQUID COLOR**
*Only a hint of the very attractive cerise color of the* kriek lambic, *but all of the flavors, will be evident in the finished vinaigrette.*

2 Add the Dijon mustard, sugar, salt, lemon juice, and garlic. A German mustard, or any other creamy mustard, can be substituted, but a grainy mustard should be avoided. Blend well with a fork, then strain out the garlic flesh (it is very strong, and will overpower the other flavors). Season with freshly ground pepper (black or white) to taste.

3 Cut the ends off the endive, wash, dry, and then arrange the leaves on a flat plate. Poach an egg. (To make a perfect poached egg, add a teaspoon of vinegar to the water. Swirl the boiling water round with a spoon, then drop in the egg. The water will wrap the white around the yolk.)

4 Scatter the olives, croutons, and sliced radishes on top of the endive, place the poached egg in the center, sprinkle with chives, then dress the salad with the *kriek* vinaigrette.

**SEASONAL SIMILARITY**
*With its poached egg centerpiece, this endive salad is similar to the Flemish dish of hop shoots typically offered in March.*

# BEERS FOR MARINADES

T HE ACIDITY IN BEERS CAN TENDERIZE MEATS and other raw materials in cooking. Acids are created by fermentation, but they are also derived from hops, which also contribute piney elements similar to the flavors in some balsamic vinegars. If a relatively vinegary marinade is required, try the types of beer suggested on page 176. To tenderize red meats, an English ale might be more suitable, but look for one with some acidity.

suggested on page 176

## BEERS TO TRY

Ales such as Adnams' Extra, Bateman's XXXB, Marston's Pedigree, Timothy Taylor's Landlord, and McMullen's Castle Pale Ale, from England, all have enough acidity to work as a marinade. So do St.-Ambroise Pale Ale, from Canada, and US ales such as Oliver's or BridgePort ESB. Very hoppy ales, especially some IPAs, might be just too bitter for long contact with meat. A malty *Helles*, *Oktoberfest*, or *Maibock* will impart both sweetness and

lightly herbal hop flavors to pork, a meat that can easily seem dry. While the beer will tenderize the meat, this action can also be drying – so also use some beer in a sauce. In the recipe below, a beer marinade is used partially to "cook" a salmon, and to impart a smoky flavor. Any smoked beer would make an interesting contribution, but Alaskan Smoked Porter is especially apposite. The malts in this beer are dried over alder in a smokery whose normal function is to prepare Alaskan salmon.

## VINTAGE BREWS

A LASKAN SMOKED PORTER (*page 151*) is one of the few beers to be vintage dated. It is unfiltered and develops with age. Although it is not hugely strong, it has enough residual sugar, and sufficiently complex flavors, to round out. It has at least some living yeast still working in the bottle. When young, it is explosively sooty, with tinges of bitter chocolate and burned fruits. This is not a beer to lay down for long periods, but a bottle of one or two years old might work better in a marinade than a fresh example. With most beers, exactly the opposite would be the case.

*page 151*

## SALMON IN SMOKED PORTER

According to American food historian Waverley Root, the most traditional method of cooking salmon in Alaska was to sandwich the fish between planks of alder and set them over glowing embers.
**Note:** pints referred to in this section are US pints, i.e. 16 fl. oz.

### Ingredients

4–5 lb (1.8–2.3 kg) whole salmon, gutted and cleaned
3 pints (1.4 liters) smoked porter
Few sprigs fresh dill
Few sprigs fresh tarragon
2 lemons, sliced
6 large red onions, sliced
To dress:
2 cucumbers, as thinly sliced as possible
3 lemons, as thinly sliced as possible

1 Line a large baking tray with foil. Allow sufficient overlap on each side of the baking tray to form a rolled-back

**BOTTLE-SMOKED SALMON**
*Marinading salmon in alder-smoked porter imparts flavors associated with the traditional method of cooking salmon in Alaska.*

"pocket," which will prevent the marinade from spilling. Lay the sliced red onions, sliced lemons, and sprigs of fresh tarragon in the baking tray. Place the salmon on top, and cover with the sprigs of fresh dill. Pour the smoked porter over the salmon, and leave to marinate for at least one hour.

2 Preheat the oven to 400° F (200° C). Place another large piece of foil under

the baking tray. Wrap it fairly loosely around, and seal it at the top. Place the baking tray on the top shelf of the oven, and bake for 30 minutes.

3 Remove the baking tray from the oven. Carefully place the salmon on a suitable plate. Peel off the skin, which should come away easily in your fingers. To dress the salmon, cover it in overlapping slices of thinly sliced cucumber, with occasional rows of thinly sliced lemon.

**A BIG FISH**
*"Beer-smoked" salmon makes a wonderful dish for a summer party . . . or perhaps served with bagels and cream cheese for a Sunday brunch. A more European treatment might use crème fraiche and perhaps rye bread.*

# Beers for Soups

The combination of malty sweetness and texture with grassy, herbal hop flavors, and sometimes yeasty tastes, makes beer an excellent base for soups. Malty, sweetish lagers are employed in soups based on barley or other grains, such as corn, or on shellfish such as crab, clams, or oysters. Lactic-tasting beers such as a *Berliner Weisse* or a *lambic* can even be employed in chilled fruit soups.

## Beers to Try

For chilled fruit soups, use a Kindl or Schultheiss Weisse, or a Cantillon or Boon Kriek, or a US brew such as the New Belgium or New Glarus cherry beers. An earthy, yeasty ale such as Orval Trappist makes a wonderful onion soup. Orval's own cookbook proposes a "Brewer's Soup," marrying the beer with beef stock, egg yolks, bread, chicory essence, nutmeg, and parsley. The Shepherd Neame brewery has a soup recipe using its Bishop's Finger strong ale, beef stock, potatoes, and cinnamon-spiced apples. Try a rye brew such as Thurn und Taxis Roggen Bier in a thick bean soup with bacon, pepper, and dill; serve it with rye bread. A French *bière de garde* or an Irish ale would add flavor if plenty of potatoes and salt pork were used in a clam chowder. For a lighter version, try a touch of Samuel Adams' Boston Lager.

## Ridleys ESX Best

The Ridley family brewery has its origins in a grain mill in the 1700s at the hamlet of Hartford End, near the town of Great Dunmow, in the more rural part of Essex, England. The present buildings date from 1842. Ridleys' beers are typically fruity, with suggestions of blackberry and apple emerging from the house yeast. As a change from beers called ESB, Triple X, or Four X, Ridleys plays on the county's name with ESX. This beer has very lively flavors: beginning malty, developing lots of fruit, and finishing long and hoppy.

**Region of origin**
Eastern England, UK

**Style** Bitter/Pale Ale

**Alcohol content**
3.4 abw (4.3 abv)

**Ideal serving temperature**
55° F (13° C)

## Onion and Cheese Soup

Variations on this theme are found in several brewing nations. British styles such as bitter or ESB are often suggested in the US, where beer cheese soup is a classic. In this recipe, the cheese is on croutons in an onion soup. The traditional version involves whisking grated cheddar or Wisconsin Jack into a chicken broth, seasoned with thyme. This calls for great care in the cooking: overheating will damage the flavor, and will also make the cheese become "stringy."

### Ingredients

| | |
|---|---|
| 4 large white onions, thinly sliced | Pinch of sugar |
| 2 red onions, thinly sliced | 4–8 slices French bread, depending on size, thickly cut |
| 4–6 tbsp butter | |
| 1 chicken or beef stock cube | 1 cup (120 g) Gruyère cheese, grated |
| 2 pints (900 ml) pale ale | 1 tbsp chopped parsley |

**SIMMERING, NOT BOILING**
*Overheating or boiling this soup will excessively concentrate the bitterness of the beer, and will spoil the tasty, savory flavors.*

**1** Preheat the oven to 375° F (190° C). Melt 3 tbsp butter in a large, heavy frying pan (ideally, one with a lid). Gently sauté the red and white onions with the sugar until they have collapsed, and are soft and golden brown. Keep stirring to stop them from sticking to the frying pan. Dissolve the chicken or beef stock cube in the beer.

**2** Stir the dissolved beer stock into the onions, cover the frying pan with a lid, and simmer for about 30 minutes.

**3** Generously spread the thick slices of French bread with the remaining butter and bake them in the top of the oven until they are golden brown. Sprinkle the grated Gruyère cheese over the slices of bread, and grill them until the cheese is bubbling. Place the slices of bread in bowls and pour over the soup. Serve with a fine sprinkling of chopped parsley.

**LIQUID LUNCH**
*This thick onion and cheese soup is from the tradition of inexpensive, hearty, filling dishes to go with beer. It makes an excellent snack lunch with ham or tomatoes and French or sourdough bread.*

# BEERS FOR STEWS

**B**EER CAN ADD PIQUANCY TO STEWS. This even works in relatively light dishes such as stewed mussels. A dry, hoppy beer like an IPA, if used with a light touch, also performs well with stews based on oily fish such as eel or salmon. Meat stews need something richer, like an Irish ale, French *bière de garde*, *Märzenbier*, or *Bockbier* for pork or chicken, or a French, English, Scottish, or Belgian ale for lamb or beef.

## BEERS TO TRY

For fish dishes, the American IPAs are often lighter bodied and drier than the British versions. Anchor Liberty is an American beer in broadly this style that can be found in Europe. As fish is cooked only gently, there should not be excessive reduction. To go with meat, the most full-flavored Irish ales are McNally's, from Canada, and McGuire's, from Florida. The latter brewery also makes its own malt vinegar as a culinary ingredient. The ales

actually made in Ireland are less big, but still tasty. Among the widely available *bières de garde*, Jenlain has the fullness of flavour to be very food-friendly. With lamb, consider using a beer in this style with juniper berries or even a splash of gin. The Celebrator Doppelbock from the Ayinger brewery, near Munich, or that city's Paulaner Salvator, also have plenty of flavor to add to a stew. The same is true of Black Sheep Ale, from England, Caledonian's Flying Scotsman, or Belgium's Cuvée De Koninck.

### GRANTED A GIFT

**B**ERT GRANT WAS BORN in Scotland but his family left when he was two. He has spent a lifetime in the hop and brewing businesses in Canada and the US. When he established his own brewery in 1982, his first product was a Scottish ale, but he soon moved on to an extremely hoppy IPA (*page 135*). Grant was the first small brewer in the US to revive the term IPA. The hoppiness is appropriate not only because of Grant's background in the hop industry, but also because his brewery is in Yakima, the hop capital of Washington State.

---

## MUSSELS IN INDIA PALE ALE

Like most shellfish, mussels lend themselves very well to beer. The slightly salty, seaweedy flavors of mussels are a match for a dry, savory, and acidic brew. In northern France or Belgium a *lambic* or *gueuze* is typically used. In Britain an acidic bitter may be considered; in Ireland, a dry stout. American IPAs also have the appropriate qualities, especially in their homelands of Oregon and Washington, northwestern states renowned for shellfish.

**GENTLY DOES IT**
*When pouring the IPA into the pan, gently lift up the mussels with a spoon, allowing the appetizing flavors of the IPA to permeate every shell.*

### Ingredients

| | |
|---|---|
| 4 lb (1.8 kg) mussels, cleaned | 3 tbsp chopped flat-leafed parsley |
| 5 tbsp salted butter | Pinch of salt |
| 1 clove garlic, crushed | Pinch of sugar |
| 2 medium-sized red onions, finely chopped | Freshly ground black pepper |
| 1 ⅓ cups IPA | French bread, to serve |
| 1 tsp fresh thyme | |

about 1 cup IPA, a third of the parsley, and pepper. Simmer for 10 minutes. Strain, then return to the pan. Add the mussels and the rest of the IPA, and cook until the mussels are open. Discard any mussels that are closed or less than one-quarter open. Remove the mussels and keep them warm.

**3** Add the rest of the parsley to the liquid in the pan. Reduce just a little, then pour the liquid over the warm mussels. Serve in individual soup bowls with plenty of French bread to soak up the liquid.

**SCOOP AND SERVE**
*In Belgium, mussels are often eaten straight from the pan in which they are prepared. The shell is used as a spoon, and the cooking liquid is scooped up as a sauce.*

**1** Buy the mussels cleaned, if possible, but if cleaning them yourself, scrub and rinse them thoroughly, and pull off any barnacles and "beardy" attachments. The mussels must be closed – never cook open mussels.

**2** Melt the butter in a pan and fry the onions and garlic until soft. Add the thyme,

# BEERS FOR BRAISING

THE TERM "BRAISE" ORIGINALLY REFERRED to cooking in a pot buried among embers of charcoal. "Carbonade" has the same origin, from *charbon de bois*, French for charcoal. "Flamande" is the French way of saying "Flemish." Often, carbonade flamande is prepared as a braised dish, rather than a stew, in that it is cooked with a relatively small amount of liquid, in a covered pot.

## BEERS TO TRY

The first people to use braising probably had no other means available, but it does provide a distinct result, somewhere between a roast and a stew. A "pot roast" is much the same thing. Because the steam cooks and tenderizes the meat very thoroughly, the beef emerges dryish but crumbly, and the liquid can be poured over it as a naturally dense, intensely flavored sauce. The ideal beer for braising meat is an acidic Belgian "old brown" such as

Liefman's Goudenband or the redder Petrus Oud Bruin. Failing that, a Belgian-style *saison* might do the trick. The great French chef Escoffier suggested either a Belgian old *lambic* or a stout for braising. Either of these works, but the *lambic* is arguably too thin-bodied and a modern stout not always sufficiently acidic to tenderize the meat.

## LIEFMANS GOUDENBAND

The wineyness and slight sourness of "Gold Riband" place it as the classic brown ale in the style of its original home, Oudenaarde, in East Flanders. It is brewed in Dentergem, just across the West Flanders border, but is still fermented and matured in Oudenaarde. Its distinctive, irony, salty, and toasty flavors derive from sodium bicarbonate water treatment; a multi-strain yeast; between four months and one year's maturation; a blending of young and old beers; and bottle-aging.

**Region of origin** Province of East Flanders, Belgium

**Style** Oudenaarde Brown

**Alcohol content** 6.4–6.8 abw (8.0–8.5 abv)

**Ideal serving temperature** 55° F (13° C)

## GAME BIRDS IN FLEMISH BROWN ALE

A beer such as Liefmans Goudenband from the "Flemish Ardennes" performs well in the braising of pigeon, quail, partridge, or pheasant, especially older birds, moistened with a larding of smoked bacon. After being browned, these birds can be braised with root vegetables, cabbage, or peas.

### Ingredients

| | |
|---|---|
| 2 game birds | 1 tbsp fresh thyme or |
| 12 slices bacon | mixed herbs |
| 1 lb (455 g) shallots | 3 tbsp sunflower oil |
| 1½ lb (680 g) carrots, | 2 cloves garlic |
| sliced in rounds | 2 pints (1 liter) |
| 1½ lb (680 g) parsnips, | Flemish brown ale |
| sliced lengthways | 1 chicken stock cube |
| 1 large onion, chopped | Pinch of sugar |

1 Peel the shallots and fry them until they are golden brown. Place the

**PERFECT PARTNERS**
*For a gravy, a full-bodied beer, with plenty of flavor, but without too much bitterness, is an ideal complement to the caramelly sweetness of onions.*

prepared parsnips and carrots into a roasting pan and coat them with a little oil. Add the shallots to the roasting pan.

2 Put a garlic clove in the cavity of each bird. Place the birds on the vegetables in the pan, sprinkle them with half of the thyme, and the sugar, then cover them with the bacon.

Pour three-quarters of the beer over the game birds. Place them in a preheated oven, 425° F (220° C), and cook for 45–60 minutes, basting every 15 minutes.

3 For the gravy, fry the onion with the remaining thyme. Add the stock cube, dissolved in a little hot water. Pour in the rest of the beer. Bring to the boil and reduce by 50 percent. Put the cooked birds on a serving platter with the vegetables. Add the gravy to the roasting pan and mix well. Pour the gravy into a gravy boat, and serve.

**INTERESTING VARIATIONS**
*Try using apple, Belgian endive, or asparagus in place of the root vegetables. Or serve slices of the meat on lettuce, with a beer vinaigrette.*

# BEERS FOR BASTING

**B**ASTING MOISTENS, TENDERIZES, and adds flavor to meat. If a dark, rich, and malty beer is used in the basting liquid, the malt sugars will caramelize, leaving a hint of toffeeish crustiness and sweet flavors. Perhaps because pork and ham are often served with sweet or fruity accompaniments, these meats lend themselves especially well to being basted with a sweetish beer.

## BEERS TO TRY

A dark lager in the German *Dunkel* or *Schwarzbier* style, or a wheat beer in the same vein, can be used in the basting of almost any meat. *Schwarzbier* will provide a more chocolaty character that suits chicken or lamb. A *Dunkelweizen* will be fruitier. A Belgian honey beer or Dutch "old brown" will add sweetness, and a German Bock or Double Bock, or one of the sweeter, darker barley wines, richness. Smoked beers will give a roast an appetizingly toasted taste.

A more elaborate basting sauce can be made by adding to the beer about a quarter of a cup of a malty Scotch whiskey, and perhaps fruits such as pitted and diced apricots or prunes. A spicier basting sauce might include honey, ginger, chili paste, or garlic. Try these variations as an overnight marinade, then keep the liquid for basting.

## CHRISTOFFEL ROBERTUS

As well as its renowned dry, Pilsner-style Blond (*page 126*), this Dutch producer of unfiltered, unpasteurized lager makes the ruby colored Robertus: something between a Vienna, a Munich-style dark, and a Bock. This is styled a "Double Malt," though this claim has no specific meaning. The brew has a fresh, grainy aroma; a firm, smooth body; complex, nutty, malty, fruity flavors; and a dryish finish.

**Region of origin**
Province of Limburg, the Netherlands

**Style** Dark Lager

**Alcohol content**
4.8 abw (6.0 abv)

**Ideal serving temperature**
50° F (10° C)

## HAM BASTED WITH DARK LAGER

The German, and especially Bavarian, passion for smoked pork and ham seems to know no bounds. Bavarian hams are often basted with dark brews. A knuckle may be served, or a whole ham sliced at the table, often with a second serving coming along behind. As a student at brewing school in Weihenstephan, near Munich, St. Christoffel's Dutch founder Leo Brand no doubt enjoyed several variations of the theme. A caramelized onion "chutney" or orange marmalade will enhance the savory/sweet interplay: so will sweet Bavarian mustard.

### Ingredients

| | |
|---|---|
| Approx. 6–8 lb (2.7–3.5 kg) cured ham | 1 ¾ cups sweet, dark lager |
| 1 ½ cups (360 g) soft, dark brown sugar | 24 cloves |

**A GOOD BASTING**
*When pouring the dark lager over the ham, thoroughly moisten the skin, and the ends of the joint, to impart the maximum flavor of the beer.*

**1** Soak the ham in cold water for 2–3 hours. Remove the ham and place it in a very large pan. Cover it with fresh water, and add 1 ½ cups beer, and 1 cup sugar.

**2** Bring the ham to the boil, cover, and simmer for 3–4 hours. Turn off the heat, and leave the ham in the liquid until cool.

**3** Preheat the oven to 450° F (230° C). Lift out the ham, wipe and dry it thoroughly with a clean, absorbent cloth, and trim off the skin. Run a sharp knife over the skin, forming 1 in (2.5 cm)-wide squares. Insert a clove in the center of each square, then cover the ham with the remaining brown sugar.

**4** Bake the ham for 30 minutes or until it is golden brown. Baste the ham with the remaining dark lager at least twice during the cooking period. Allow the ham to rest, and cool, before carving.

**HAM FEASTED**
*With new potatoes, this is a simple and appetizing dish. It could also be served with potato dumplings or noodles such as Spätzle (made with egg). Rocket will add texture and color.*

# BEERS FOR BATTERS & BAKING

ONE OF THE BEST-ESTABLISHED uses of beer is in batters, bread, and cakes. In the US, beer batters are commonly used on vegetables served as finger food or in the style of tempura, or on oysters or cod. The carbonation and, in sedimented beers, the yeastiness, will make batters crisper (it is especially effective in Yorkshire puddings) and help breads to rise. Richer, darker beers will give moisture to puddings and cakes.

## BEERS TO TRY

For a batter on vegetables, try a *Hefeweizen*, a style that has lots of carbonation and some fruity flavors to complement, for example, broccoli florets, zucchini, or slices of eggplant. The Japanese have very strong conventions about the presentation of their favorite dishes, but a more informal oriental flavor can be added by using a little ginger or soy sauce in the batter. For oysters, perhaps a dry stout (*pages 142–143*). For Yorkshire pudding, a pale ale, added to the batter just as it goes into a hot oven. Beer bread can be made by adding a dark lager or Bock to the dough, and perhaps using some barley. Brewpubs often offer breads made with grain recovered from the mash tun. This is hard to find unless you live near a very small brewery. It adds graininess and a touch of sourdough flavor. In dark, fruity cakes, a Guinness is often recommended, but it can be too bitter for this purpose.

### FORBIDDEN FRUIT

AFTER THE HOEGAARDEN brewery, in Belgium, achieved popularity with its "white" wheat beer, its subsequent products included this darker ale. It is labelled Verboden Vrucht, in Flemish, and Le Fruit Défendu, in French. This follows in the Belgian tradition of beer names implying sudden death or diabolic encounters. It is made with barley malt, not with wheat, but has the typical spicing of Curaçao orange peels and coriander.

At 7.2 abw (9.0 abv), Forbidden Fruit is earthy, vanilla-like, and chocolaty, with hints of apricots, coffee, and almonds. It is a luxurious, voluptuous, and seductive brew.

## FRUIT CAKE WITH SPICED BEER

A Guinness, perhaps with a touch of rum, could be used in a fruit cake that is intended to be moist in texture but dry in flavor, but usually a sweet or imperial stout is preferable. A sweet stout adds creaminess; an imperial style enhances the "burned fruit." A spiced dark brew like Forbidden Fruit or Liefmans Glühkriek (*page 108*) will be even more effective.

### Ingredients

| | |
|---|---|
| 1 ½ cups (360 g) butter | 2 ⅓ cups (360 g) sultanas |
| 1 ½ cups (360 g) soft, dark brown sugar | 1 ⅓ cups (225 g) seedless raisins |
| 6 medium eggs, beaten | 1 cup (225 g) chopped prunes |
| 1 lb (480 g) flour, sifted with 1 tsp mixed spice or mace | ½ cup (125 g) glacé cherries, quartered |
| 2 tbsp golden syrup | ½ cup (125 g) almonds, sliced and blanched |
| ½ pint (300 ml) spiced beer | Grated zest of 2 oranges |
| 2 ⅓ cups (360 g) currants | 5 tbsp dark rum |

**CHERRY NICE INDEED**
*The additional flavorings in spiced beer make it perfect for a fruit cake. If a spiced cherry beer is used, the cake should ideally contain cherries.*

1 Grease a 23 cm (9 in) round pan; line it with greaseproof paper; grease the paper. Preheat oven to 300° F (150° C).

2 Cream together the butter and sugar until pale and fluffy. Gradually beat in the eggs and add half the sifted flour, a little at a time. Fold in the rest with a large metal spoon. Add the beer to the fruit, nuts, orange zest, and golden syrup, then mix this into the butter, sugar, eggs, and flour. Spoon the mixture into the pan and level the top with the back of a spoon, making a slight hollow in the cake's center. Bake in the middle of the oven for 4–4½ hours. Cool for 1 hour in the pan then skewer the center; gently pour in the rum.

3 Let the cake rest, then turn it out onto a wire rack, and allow it to cool completely. Wrap the cake in greaseproof paper and cover it with foil.

**SPICED SLICE**
*If the spiced fruit cake is served as a dessert, add a cherry sauce, using a* kriek *beer. To provide a color contrast, a second, orange-cream sauce could be made with a Belgian white beer.*

# BEERS FOR DESSERTS

CERTAIN BEERS MAKE SURPRISINGLY GOOD accompaniments to desserts, as well as being ingredients in them. The fortified wines that are used as marinades for fruits can be substituted by rich, sherryish, or portlike beers. Strawberries or oranges can be steeped in wheat beers, with a dash of brown sugar. Honey beers or oatmeal stouts can add creaminess to desserts; imperial or chocolate stouts can add moisture.

## BEERS TO TRY

Berliner Weisse from Kindl or Schultheiss is ideal in raspberry sorbets. Other North German wheat beers, like those from Berliner Bürgerbräu or Pinkus Müller, are less fruitily tart, but can be used nonetheless. A mild example of a South German *Weisse* or *Weizenbier* can be tried in banana dishes, perhaps with ice cream; a clovier one or a Belgian *wit* with oranges, plums, or in apple pie, sticky toffee, or bread pudding; a *kriek* with cherries; or a *pêche* with peaches. In a "beer sorbet," use a malty lager or a *bière de garde*. Consider adding a dash of gin or (very sparingly) pastis. An oatmeal stout will add character to the classic Scottish dessert Atholl Brose with the grain itself, cream, honey, and whiskey. England has its well-known example from Samuel Smith, while Scotland's interpretations from Broughton and Maclay have a special affinity with such dishes. Young's, McMullen's, and Brooklyn all have excellent chocolate stouts, to moisten truffles, mousses, or brownies.

### TRAVELLING PORTER

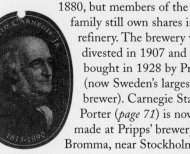

DAVID CARNEGIE WAS BORN in Scotland in 1813. His uncle ran a trading company in Gothenburg, Sweden, and in 1836 the young Carnegie bought a combined sugar refinery and porter brewery there. The business became one of Gothenburg's most important enterprises, reaching a peak of porter production in 1875 (924,000 gallons/ 42,000 hectoliters). Carnegie died in 1880, but members of the family still own shares in the refinery. The brewery was divested in 1907 and bought in 1928 by Pripps (now Sweden's largest brewer). Carnegie Stark Porter (*page 71*) is now made at Pripps' brewery in Bromma, near Stockholm.

## CHOCOLATE TRUFFLES WITH PORTER

The Swiss have a reputation for good chocolate, the Germans and French have some fine chocolate products that are insufficiently known, but the Belgian interpretation is surely the one to marry with beer. The Belgians use African chocolate beans, which are stronger in flavor than those grown in South America. Belgium has countless beers that go well with chocolate, not least the stronger versions of malty ales from the Trappist abbeys like Rochefort and Westvleteren. Dutch dark wheat Bocks and Baltic porters are other possibilities.

### Ingredients

| | |
|---|---|
| 8 oz (225 g) semisweet chocolate | ¾ cup unsalted butter |
| 6 tbsp porter | 1 cup (125 g) ground almonds |
| 1 cup (125 g) powdered sugar | 2 ½ tbsp chopped raisins |
| | Cocoa powder for coating |

**HOT CHOCOLATE**
*Keep the chocolate constantly moving over the heat when adding the porter and the other ingredients. Do not allow it to boil – overcooked chocolate coagulates, and cannot be worked with at all.*

1 Gently melt the chocolate with the butter, in a bowl over a pan of hot water. Make sure that the bowl does not make contact with the hot water, and do not allow the mixture to boil. Whisk or stir in the porter. Beat in the powdered sugar, ground almonds, and chopped raisins. Allow the mixure to cool at room temperature, then chill it in a refrigerator until the mixture has set.

2 Roll the mixture into small balls in your hands, then chill. Gently roll the truffles in cocoa powder using your fingertips, then place the truffles in paper sweetcases, and chill again. Serve the truffles straight from the refrigerator. This chocolate truffle recipe could also be adapted to make delicious treats such as brownies, mud pies, or death-by-chocolate, all incorporating a strong porter or stout.

**SNUFFLE A TRUFFLE**
*A small dessert, or an extra indulgence with the coffee? These truffles can be given a toasty coating if they are rolled in chocolate malt, available from homebrew stores.*

# POURING BEER

DEBATE RAGES OVER THE WAY in which beer should be poured, but there is considerably less disagreement about the end result. Whether the head should be modest, creamy, blossomy, or towering depends partly upon local custom, but also upon the aroma and flavor desired from the beer.

## POURING AN ALE

*A gentle, steady pour down the side of the tilted glass will stop the beer from foaming excessively.*

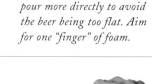

*Steepen the angle and pour more directly to avoid the beer being too flat. Aim for one "finger" of foam.*

*Too much creaminess will rob the beer of its appetizingly bitter character. The hop oils will migrate from the beer itself and hide in the head.*

## POURING A STOUT

*Pour stout slowly, to allow the head to develop. If it grows too quickly, stop for a moment.*

*A two-stage pour will make for a denser, creamier, more solid head, which will suit the coffeeish flavors of the stout.*

*A bottled stout will have a rockier, less rich head and a more natural flavor than the "draft" versions containing a "widget" (nitrogen capsule).*

## POURING A PILSNER

*Bottles may take less than the seven minutes prescribed for a draft, but a real Pilsner must have a blossoming head.*

*A soft, sustained carbonation further enlivens the golden color with a consistent rise of small bubbles (known as the "bead").*

*The head should rise, almost like a soft ice cream, above the rim of the glass. This brings forward the hop aroma and holds back bitterness to the finish.*

## POURING A WHEAT BEER

*Beers containing yeast have a high carbonation, so an especially gentle pour is required. The Belgians wet the glass to control the head.*

*In Bavaria, wheat beer is typically served with a huge head, especially if it is a bottle-conditioned example. Some yeast is included in the pour.*

*If the beer is deemed insufficiently cloudy, the last few drops may be rolled in the bottle to loosen the remaining yeast sediment. This is then added to the glass.*

# GLOSSARY

**Abbey (Abbaye, Abdij) beer** Belgian family of strong, fruity-tasting ales. Some Benedictine and Norbertine abbeys license commercial brewers to produce these beers for them. Such products are inspired by those of the authentic Trappist monastery brewers.

**abw** Alcohol by weight, as a percentage. The simplest and most widely used measure. Alcohol by volume (**abv**) is generally used in Europe.

**Ale** English-language term for a beer made by warm fermentation, traditionally with a "top" yeast. For example, mild, bitter, pale, brown ales.

*Altbier* German style of beer similar to British bitter or pale ale. Especially associated with Düsseldorf.

**Amber** Tends to indicate an amber-red ale in broadly the Irish style, but sometimes a Vienna lager.

**Barley wine** English-language term for extra-strong ale.

**Bavaria** Former kingdom and republic, now the biggest state in Germany (and the one with the most breweries by far). Bavaria's capital is Munich.

**Beer** A fermented drink made from grain, most often malted barley, and usually flavored with hops. Includes ales, lagers, wheat beers, and all styles reviewed in this book.

*Bière de garde* Strong, ale-like style, originally brewed to be kept in storage. Typical in the northwest of France.

**Bitter** Implies a well-hopped ale.

**Bo(c)k** Germanic term for an extra-strong beer. Often, but not always, dark. Usually a lager, but can also be a strong wheat beer. Usually 4.8 abw (6.0 abv) or more.

**Bohemia** With Moravia, comprises the Czech Republic. Bohemia's capital is Prague. Other main cities include Pilsen and Budweis.

**Bottle-conditioned** With living yeast in the bottle.

**Brabant** Former duchy, centered on the city of Brussels. Now three provinces: Walloon and Flemish Brabant (including the brewing city of Leuven), both in Belgium; and North Brabant, across the border in the Netherlands.

**Brewpub** Pub or restaurant making its own beer, sometimes also for sale elsewhere.

**Doppelbock** "Double" Bock. Usually around 6.0 abw (7.5 abv) or more.

**Dortmunder Export** Golden lager with a mineralish dryness and slightly above-average strength. (*See* Export.)

*Dunkel/Dunkle/Dunkles* German words for dark.

**ESB** Extra Special Bitter. In Britain, a specific beer from the Fuller's brewery. Has inspired many similar beers in North America.

**Export** In the German tradition, a beer of slightly above-average strength, typically 4.2–4.4 abw/5.25–5.5 abv, most often in the Dortmunder style.

**Flanders** One of two regions (the other being French-speaking Wallonia) that form the Kingdom of Belgium. Provinces include East and West Flanders, Flemish Brabant, Antwerp, and Belgian Limburg. The Flemish language is a version of Dutch.

*Framboise/Frambozen* French and Flemish words used in Belgium to indicate raspberry beers.

**Franconia** Regional name for the three northernmost counties of Bavaria, including the cities of Nuremberg and Bamberg.

*Gueuze/Gueze* Young and old *lambics*, blended to achieve a sparkling, champagnelike beer.

*Hefeweizen* An unfiltered wheat beer.

*Hell/Helles* German for "pale." Indicates a golden beer, often a malt-accented lager. Typical in Bavaria.

**Imperial stout** Extra-strong stout, originally popular in Imperial Russia.

**IPA** India Pale Ale. Type of ale originally made for Britain's Indian Empire. Should be above average in both hop bitterness and strength.

**Irish ale** Typically has a reddish color and a malt accent, sometimes with a suggestion of butterscotch.

*Kellerbier* "Cellar beer" in German. Usually an unfiltered lager, high in hop and low in carbonation.

*Kloster* German term for a beer that is, or once was, made in a monastery. May be any style.

*Kölsch* Means "from Cologne" in German. Applied to the style of top-fermenting golden ale made in and around that city.

*Kriek* Flemish term for a type of cherry that is grown in Belgium and used in making some fruit beers.

**Lager** Beer fermented and matured at low temperatures. Can be any color or strength.

*Lambic* Belgian term for beer fermented with wild yeasts.

**Limburg** Brewing province in the Netherlands, centered on the city of Maastricht. The name Limburg is shared with an adjoining province of Belgium and a city in Germany.

*Maibock* Bock released in late spring (March, April, or May). Often relatively pale, hoppy, and spritzy.

*Märzenbier* Traditionally, a beer brewed in March and matured until September or October. In Germany and the US, implies a reddish-bronze, aromatically malty, medium-strong (4.4 abw/5.5 abv or more) lager.

**Microbrewery** One of the new generation of small breweries that have sprung up since the mid- to late-1970s.

**Mild** Ale that is only lightly hopped, and thus mild-tasting. Usually modest in alcohol. Sometimes dark. The word mild also exists in Germany, and appears on some (relatively) gently hopped Pilsners.

**Münchner, Munchener, Munich-style** Typically a malt-accented lager of conventional strength, whether pale (*Helles*) or dark (*Dunkel*).

*Oktoberfest* Traditionally a *Märzenbier*, but today often paler.

**Old ale** Usually dark and classically medium-strong (around 4.8 abw/6.0 abv). Some are much stronger.

*Oud Bruin* In the Netherlands, a very sweet dark lager. In Belgium, a sourish brown ale in the Oudenaarde style, but at a conventional strength.

**Pale ale** Originally a British style. Classically ranges from bronze to a full copper color. "Pale" as opposed to a brown ale or porter.

**Pils/Pilsner/Pilsener** Widely misused term. A Pilsner is more than just a standard golden lager of around 3.4–4.2 abw/4.25–5.25 abv. It should be an all-malt brew, with a flowery hop aroma and dryness, typically using the Saaz variety. The original is Pilsner Urquell.

**Pint** Pints referred to in recipes in this book are US pints. 1 US pint = 16 fl. oz. (1 imperial pint = 20 fl. oz.)

**Porter** Dark brown or black. Made with highly kilned malts, with a good hop balance, and traditionally top-fermenting. Associated with London.

*Rauchbier* German term for beer (usually lager) made with smoked malts. Especially associated with Bamberg, Franconia.

**Red ale** See Irish ale.

*Saison* Style of dry, sometimes slightly sour, refreshing, but strongish (4.0–6.4 abw/5.0–8.0 abv) summer ale, often bottle-conditioned. Typical in the province of Hainaut, Belgium.

*Schwarzbier* "Black" beer. Usually a very dark lager with a bitter-chocolate character. Especially associated with Thuringia and the former East Germany.

**Scotch ale** Smooth, malty style classically made in Scotland. Often dark, sometimes strong.

**Stout** Dark brown to black. Made with highly-roasted grains and traditionally top-fermenting. Sweet stouts historically associated with London, hoppier dry examples with Dublin and Cork.

**Trappist** Strict order of monks making strong ales of great character in several monasteries in Belgium and the Netherlands. Labels include a logo saying "Authentic Trappist."

*Tripel/Triple* Usually an extra-strong, golden, aromatic, hoppy golden ale, modelled on Westmalle Tripel.

**Vienna-style lager** Bronze-to-red lager with a sweetish malt aroma and flavor. No longer readily available in its city of origin, but increasingly made in the US. The *Märzen-Oktoberfest* type is a stronger version.

*Weisse/Weissbier* "White" beer. German term for a wheat beer. Implies a pale head and often a cloudy brew.

*Weizen* "Wheat." Also used to describe the above.

**White/Wit** English-language and Flemish terms for Belgian-style spiced wheat beer.

# USEFUL ADDRESSES

**The Beer Hunter®**
News and articles from Michael Jackson, with beer reviews.
www.beerhunter.com

**The Real Beer Page**
The principal worldwide web publication for beer lovers. Links to many other sites.
www.realbeer.com

**Beer Paradise**
In English, French, and Flemish. Consumer-friendly information from the Belgian Confederation of Brewers.
www.beerparadise.be

**Association of Brewers**
For information on US brewers, especially micros and brewpubs, and the Great American Beer Festival.
736 Pearl St., PO Box 1679, Boulder, CO 80306-1679
tel: 303-447-0816
fax: 303-447-2825
Internet: www.beertown.org

**All About Beer**
National magazine for beer lovers.
tel: 919-490-0589
fax: 919-490-0865
e-mail: AllAbtBeer@ad.com

**Malt Advocate**
National magazine for lovers of beer and malt whiskey.
tel: 610-967-1083
fax: 610-965-2995
e-mail: maltman999@aol.com
Internet: www.whiskeypages.com

## Importers

ALL SAINTS BRANDS
tel: 612-378-7820
fax: 612-378-7823
e-mail: saintale@wavetech.net

B. UNITED INTERNATIONAL
tel: 914-345-8900
fax: 914-354-9019
e-mail: BUNITEDINT@mcimail.com

MERCHANT DU VIN
tel: 206-322-5022
e-mail: info@mdv-beer.com
Internet: www.mdv-beer.com

PAULANER – NORTH AMERICA
tel: 303-792-3242
fax: 303-792-3430

PHOENIX IMPORTS
tel: 800-700-4253
fax: 410-465-1197
e-mail: mythbird@aol.com
Internet: www.mythbirdbeer.com

Will Shelton
tel: 305-859-8877
fax: 800-809-7725
e-mail: Shelton@tiac.net

WETTEN IMPORTERS
tel: 703-503-2083
fax: 703-503-9732

## Northeast

ALE STREET NEWS
Newspaper published for beer lovers throughout the region. Based in New York/New Jersey area.
tel: 800-351-ALES

fax: 201-368-9100
e-mail: tony@alestreetnews.com
Internet: www.alestreetnews.com

YANKEE BREW NEWS
Newspaper for beer lovers in New England.
tel. 800-423-3712
e-mail: Brett@ynakee brew.com
Internet: realbeer.com:80/ybn/

**Massachusetts**
Kappy's
175-177 Andover Street
Peabody, MA 01960
tel: 508-532-2330

**New Jersey**
Grand Opening Liquors
1068 Belmont Ave.
N. Haledon, NJ 0750815
tel: 973-427-4477

**New York City**
B & E Quality Beverage
511 West 23rd St.
New York, NY 10011
tel: 212-243-6812

**New York (Long Island)**
Big Z Beverage
1675 E. Jericho Turnpike
Huntington, NY 11743
tel: 516-499-3479

**Pennsylvania**
Shangy's
601 State Avenue
Emmaus, PA 18049
tel: 610-967-1701

## Mid-Atlantic

BARLEY CORN
Newspaper based in Washington DC.
tel: 301-831-3759
fax: 301-831-6376

**District of Columbia**
Chevy Chase Wine & Spirits
5544 Connecticut Ave. NW
DC 20015
tel: 202-363-4000
fax: 202-537-6067

**Maryland**
Bun Penny
1364 Columbia Mall
Columbia, MD 21044
tel: 410-730-4100
fax: 410-730-1703

**Delaware**
State Line Liquors
1610 Elkton Road
Elkton, MD 21921
tel: 1-800-446-9463 / 410-398-3838
fax: 410-398-1303
e-mail: stateline@dpnet.net

**Virginia**
Corks & Kegs
7110 Patterson Avenue, Suite A
Richmond, VA 23229
tel: 804-288-0816
fax: 804-648-3914

## Southeast

SOUTHERN DRAFT
Based in Atlanta.
tel: 770-345-1512
fax: 770-345-2852
e-mail: brewnews@Southerndraft.com
Internet: southerndraft.com/sodraft/

**Florida**
World of Beer
2809 Gulf to Bay Blvd
Clearwater, FL 34619
tel: 813-797-6905

**Georgia**
Mac's Beer & Wine
925 Spring Street
Altanta, GA 30309
tel: 404-872-4897

## Midwest

GREAT LAKES BREWING NEWS
Based in upstate New York, but excellent coverage of region to west.
tel: 716-689-5841
fax: 716-689-5789
e-mail: glbrewing@aol.com

MIDWEST BEER NOTES
Based in Minnesota/Wisconsin region.
tel: 715-837-1120
e-mail: beernote@realbeer.com

**Illinois**
Sam's Wines & Spirits
1720 N. Marcey St.
Chicago, IL 60614
tel: 312-664-4394 / 800-777-9137
fax: 312-664-7037

Total Beverage
1163 East Ogden Avenue
Naperville (Chicago), IL 60563
tel: 630-428-1122

**Minnesota**
Surdyk's Liquors
303 E. Hennepin Avenue
Minneapolis, MN 55414
tel: 612-379-3232

**Ohio**
Warehouse Beverage
4364 Mayfield Road
South Euclid
Cleveland, OH 44121
tel: 216-382-2400

## Southwest

ROCKY MOUNTAIN BEER NOTES
Based in Colorado.
tel: 715-837-1120
e-mail: beernote@realbeer.com

SOUTHWEST BREWING NEWS
Based in Texas.
tel: 1-800-474-7291 / 512-443-3607
fax: 512-443-3607
e-mail: swbrewing@aol.com

**Colorado**
Liquor Mart Inc.
1750 15th Street
Boulder, CO 80302-6338
tel: 303-449-3374
fax: 303-938-9463

**Austin**
Whip-In
1950 So. IH-35
Austin, TX 78704
tel: 512-442-5337
fax: 512-442-1443
Internet: whipin@swbell.com

**Dallas**
Mr G's
1453 Coit & 15th
Plano, TX 75075
tel: 972-867-2821
fax: 972-867-2821, ext. 8

**Houston**
Spec's
2410 Smith Street

Houston, TX 77006
tel: 713-526-8787
fax: 713-526-6129
Internet: www.specsonline.com

Central Market
4821 Broadway
San Antonio, TX 78209
tel: 210-368-8600
fax: 210-826-3253

## California

CELEBRATOR
Based in the San Francisco Bay area. Covers the whole of the west, also with national news.
tel: 510-670-0121
fax: 510-670-06 39
e-mail: tdalldorf@celebrator.com
Internet: www.celebrator.com

**Northern California**
Beverages & more!
201 Bay Shore Blvd,
San Francisco, CA
tel: 1-888-77 BEVMO

**Southern California**
Beverages & more!
2775 Pacific Coast Hwy,
Torrance, CA
tel: 1-888-77 BEVMO

## Hawaii

GUSTO MAGAZINE
tel: 808-259-6884
fax: 808-259-6755
e-mail: editor@getgus.to
Internet: getgus.to

**Oahu**
The Liquor Collection
Ward Warehouse
Honolulu, HI 96814
tel: 808-524-8808

**Maui**
Kihei Wine & Spirit
Maui, HI 96744
tel: 808-879-0555

## Northwest

NORTHWEST BEER NOTES
tel: 715-837-1120
e-mail: beernote@realbeer.com

**Oregon**
Belmont Station
4520 SE Belmont
Portland, OR 97215
tel: 503-232-2202
fax: 503-232-1315

Burlingame Grocery
8502 SW Terwilliger
Portland, OR 97219
tel: 503-232-8538

**Washington**
Larry's Market
Totem Lake – Store # 6
12321 – 120th Pl. NE
Kirkland, WA 98034
tel: 425-820-2300
fax: 425-820-8176

## Canada

BIÈRE MAG
tel: 514-658-8133
fax: 514-447-0426
Internet: www.biermag.ca

**Alberta**
Beerland at Cecil Hotel
415 - 4 th Avenue S.E.
Calgary, Alberta T2G 0C8

tel: 403-266-3344
fax: 403-234-9756

Château Louis
11727 Kingsway Avenue
Edmonton, Alberta T5G 3A1
tel: 403-452-7770
fax: 403-454-3436

**British Columbia**
Cambie Street Liquor
5555 Cambie Street
Vancouver, B.C. V5Z 3A3
tel: 604-266-1321
fax: 604 -264-9071

Fort Street Liquor
1960 Foul Bay Road
Victoria, B.C. V8R 5A7
tel: 250-952-4220
fax: 250-595-0768

**Manitoba**
Grant Park Shopping Centre Store #45
1120 Grant Avenue
Winnipeg, Manitoba R3M 2A6
tel: 204-284-4204
fax: 204-475-8172
Internet: www.mlcc.mb.ca

**Quebec**
l'Epicier du Marché
128 Atwater
Atwater Market
Montreal, Quebec H4C 2G3
tel: 514-846-3224
fax: 514-932-7753

Epicier des Halles
145 St. Joseph
St. Jean, Quebec J3B 1W5
tel: 450-348-6100
fax: 450-348-0936

**Saskatchewan**
8th Street Liquor Store #505
3120 8th Street East
Saskatoon, SK S7H 0W2
tel: 306-933-5318

Albert South #557
2626 28th Avenue
Regina, SK S4S 6P3
tel: 306-787-4251

# INDEX

## A

Aass Bock 105
Abbaye des Rocs see L'Abbaye des Rocs
Abbey Affligem Nöel Christmas Ale 41
abbey beers, dry 128-9
Abita Springs Andygator 31
ABT's Trunk 172
acidity in flavor, explanation of 23
Adam 173
additional flavors used in brewing 16-17
Adelshoffen
  Adelscott 116
  Adelscott Noir 116
Adler Bräu
  Dopple Bock 31
  Oatmeal Stout 169
Adnams Suffolk Strong Ale 59
  hops used in 15
Aecht Schlenkerla Rauchbier 150
after dinner, beers for 172
Alaskan Amber 55
Alaskan Brewing Co. Smoked Porter 151
  as a marinade 177
Alba Scots Pine Ale 38
  and pine tips in brewing 16
Ale of Atholl 65
ales
  pouring of 184
  and top fermentation 19
Alexander 166
Alfa
  Lente Bok 30
  Oud Bruin 99
Alken-Maes
  Judas 131
  Zulte 95
Altbier 52-5
amber malt 13
Amberley 116
Ambre des Flandres 158
Ambrée 159
Amstel Herfstbock 106
Anchor
  Liberty Ale 136
  in fish stews 179
  hops used in 15
  Old Foghorn 122
  Our Special Holiday Ale 42
Anderson Valley, High Rollers Wheat Beer 93
Andygator 31
aperitifs
  dry abbey beers 128-9
  extra-hoppy ales 136-7
  India pale ales 132-5
  Pilsner lagers 124-7
  strong golden ales 130-31
appetizers, beers to accompany 140-41
apple flavor, explanation of 23
appreciation of beer 22-3
Arabier 35
Arcen
  Hertog Jan Grand Prestige 122
  Het Elfde Gebod 131
aroma, appreciation of 22-3
aromas produced by hops 15
aromatic malt 13
Auer Pils 152
August Schell
  Doppel Bock 105
  Schmaltz's Alt 55
Australia, beers of
  Burragorang Bock Beer 104
  Coopers Best Extra Stout 143
  Coopers Sparkling Ale 35
  Tooheys Old Black Ale 110
Austria, beers of
  Mac Queen's Nessie 116
  Mohrenbräu Schluck 162

Nussdorf Sir Henry's Dry Stout 73
Nussdorfer Old Whisky Bier 116
Nussdorfer St. Thomas Bräu 54
Schloss Eggenberg Urbock 23° 146
Autumn Ale 39
autumn, beers for 36-9
Autumn Frenzy 39
Autumn Gold 39
Aventinus 106
Ayinger
  Celebrator 29
  in stews 179
  Oktober Fest-Märzen 37

## B

Bacchus 95
Bachelor Bitter 68
Back Bay India Pale Ale 134
baking, beer as an ingredient in 182
Baltic porters and stouts 118-19
Baltika Porter 119
banana flavor, explanation of 23
Banks's 101
barley, malting, growing regions for 10
Barley Wine, Smithwick's 123
barley wines 120-23
barley-growing regions 10
Barock-Dunkel 148
Bass
  No 1 121
  Younger of Alloa Sweetheart Stout 123
basting, beer as an ingredient for 181
Batemans XXXB 59
  as a marinade 177
batters, beer as an ingredient for 182
Beamish Irish Stout 142
Beantown Nut Brown Ale 145
beef, beers to accompany 160-61
beer
  appreciation of 22-23
  baking ingredient 182
  basting ingredient 181
  batters ingredient 182
  braising ingredient 180
  complexity of flavors in 22
  desserts ingredient 183
  early history of 11
  judging of 22
  marinades ingredient 177
  pouring of 184
  selection of 26-7
  serving of 184
  serving temperature for 22
  soup ingredient 178
  stews ingredient 179
  tasting of 22-3
  time to drink 26
  vinaigrettes ingredient 176
beer drinkers' calendar 43
beers to accompany
  appetizers 140-41
  beef 160-61
  cheese 164-5
  chicken 154-5
  chocolate 170-71
  cigars 173
  coffee 170-71
  desserts 166-9
  fish 152-3
  lamb 158-9
  pâtés 146-7
  pickles 146-7
  pizza 162-3
  pork 156-7
  salads 144-5

sausages 148-9
shellfish 142-3
smoked foods 150-51
soups 140-41
starters 144-5
Belgian ales 56-7
Belgian-style wheat beers 78-81
**Belgium,** beers of
  Abbey Affligem Nöel Christmas Ale 41
  Alken-Maes Judas 131
  Alken-Maes Zulte 95
  Belle-Vue Kriek 75
  Belle-Vue Kriek Primeur 75
  Bière du Château 173
  Bosteels Tripel Karmeliet 129
  Bush 7% 137
  Bush Clovis see Bush 7
  Bush de Noël 41
  Cantillon Grand Cru Bruocsella 1900 140
  Cantillon Kriek Lambic 176
  in chilled fruit soups 178
  Chimay Cinq Cents 129
  Chimay Grande Réserve 165
  Con Domus 127
  Cristal Alken 152
  Cuvée De Koninck 56
  in stews 179
  De Dolle Brouwers Arabier 35
  De Koninck 56
  De Troch Chapeau Pêche 166
  Domus Leuvendige Witte 79
  Echte Kriek 76
  Framboise Boon 74
  Geuze Boon 140
  and fermentation 19
  Ginder Ale 57
  Gouden Carolus 171
  Gueuze Vigneronne Cantillon 75
  Haecht Witbier 79
  Hoegaarden DAS 78
  Hoegaarden Grand Cru 144
  Hoegaarden Special 78
  Horse Ale 57
  Huyghe Ninkeberry 167
  Julius 131
  Kasteel Bier 173
  Kriek Mort Subite 75
  L'Abbaye des Rocs Blanche des Honnelles 79
  Le Fruit Défendu 182
  Lefèbvre Saison 1900 34
  Leffe Radieuse 164
  Liefmans Glühkriek 108
  Liefmans Goudenband 76
  and braising 180
  Liefmans Kriekbier 76
  Lindemans Cuvée René 141
  Lindemans Framboise 166
  Louwaege Hapkin 131
  Martens Sezoens 35
  Mater Wit Bier 79
  Moortgat Duvel 130
  hops used in 15
  Mort Subite Fond Gueuze 75
  Op-Ale 57
  Orval 128
  in onion soup 178
  Palm Speciale 57
  Petrus Oud Bruin 95
  for braising 180
  Petrus Speciale 57
  Poperings Hommel Bier 137
  Riva Dentergems Wit 81
  Rodenbach 94
  Rodenbach Alexander 166
  Rodenbach Grand Cru 147
  as a vinegar 176
  Roman Sloeber 144
  Rosé de Gambrinus 75
  flavorings in 26
  Saison de Pipaix 34
  Saison Dupont 34

Saison Silly 35
  Steendonk Brabants Witbier 81
  use of spices in 17
  Timmermans Caveau 75
  Timmermans Kriek 75
  Timmermans Lambic Wit 81
  Union Cuvée de l'Ermitage 172
  Van Eecke Watou's Wit 81
  Van Eecke Winter Wit 81
  Van Honsebrouck Bacchus 95
  Van Steenberge Bios 95
  Verboden Vrucht 182
  Verhaeghe Vichtenaar 95
  Vieux Temps 57
  Villers Trippel 129
  Westmalle Trappist 129
  Westvleteren 8° (Blue Cap) 164
Belhaven
  80/- Export Ale 63
  90/- 117
  Wee Heavy 117
Belle-Vue
  Kriek 75
  Kriek Primeur 75
Bell's Porter 73
Belzebuth 131
Bergische Löwen
  Gilden Kölsch 49
  Sester Kölsch 50
  Sion Kölsch 49
Bering, Ceres 47
Berlin-style wheat beers 82-3
Berliner Bürgerbräu
  Bernauer Schwarzbier 97
  Maibock 31
  Weissbier 82
  in sorbets 183
Berliner Kindl
  Märkischer Landmann Schwarzbier 97
  Weisse 83
  in chilled fruit soups 178
  for raspberry sorbets 183
Berliner Weisse
  and Himbeer (raspberry) 83
  and Waldmeister (woodruff) 83
Bernauer Schwarzbier 97
Bert Grant and IPA 179
Bert Grant's
  India Pale Ale 135
  Perfect Porter 72
  Scottish Ale 64
Best Extra Stout, Coopers 143
Bhagwan's Best India Pale Ale 133
Bière à la Framboise 167
Bière des Sans Culottes 159
Bière du Château 173
Big Horn Bitter 68
Big Rock McNally's Extra Ale 157
  in stews 179
Big Time
  Bhagwan's Best India Pale Ale 133
  Old Wooly 122
Bigfoot Ale 123
Bilé 89
Binding, Schöfferhofer Kristallweizen 85
Bios 95
biscuit malt 13
Bishop's Finger, in soup 178
Bisucuit Weizen 80
Bitburger Premium Pils 152
bitterness, explanation of 23
Black Beer 96
black beers 96-7
Black Chocolate Stout 170
  in desserts 183
Black Douglas 63
black malt 13
Black Sheep Ale 160
  in stews 179
Blackstone St. Charles Porter 72
Blanche de Chambly 80

Blanche des Honnelles 79
Blind Faith IPA 135
Blue Cap 164
Blue Moon Belgian White 81
Blue Star 116
Bock beers 104-7
body in flavor, explanation of 23
Bohemian Pilsner 127
Bolten Ur-Alt 54
Bombardier 61
Boon
  Framboise Boon 74
  Geuze Boon 140
  and fermentation 19
Borve Ale 115
Boscos Flaming Stone 150
Bosteels Tripel Karmeliet 129
Boston Beer Works
  Back Bay India Pale Ale 134
  Beantown Nut Brown Ale 145
  Buckeye Oatmeal Stout 169
  Cock Ale 17
Boston Lager 178
bottom fermentation (lager) 19
Boulder Creek
  Dizzy Lizzy 123
  Highlands Amber 65
Brabandere see De Brabandere
Brains IPA 134
braising, beer as an ingredient for 180
Brakspear Special 59
Brand
  Doublebock 29
  Oud Bruin 99
Brassin Robespierre 159
Breckenridge Autumn Ale 39
brewing
  additional flavorings in 16-17
  colours produced by grain and malts 13
  early history of 11
  and fermentation 21
  flavors produced by grain and malts 13
  fruit as an additional flavoring in 16-17
  hop addition in 21
  hops, processing of 14
  hops, varieties of 14-15
  lactose and its use in stout 12
  mashing 20
  maturation 21
  process of 21
  sugars 12
  temperatures 20
  timing 20
  water, the use of 18
  yeast 19
Brick Bock 105
BridgePort
  ESB 67
  as a marinade 177
  India Pale Ale 135
  Old Knucklehead 123
Brooklyn
  Black Chocolate Stout 170
  in desserts 183
  Brown Ale, and cigars 173
  East India Pale Ale 133
Broughton
  Black Douglas 63
  Greenmantle 63
  Old Jock 115
Bruocsella 1900 140
bubblegum flavor, explanation of 23
Buckeye Oatmeal Stout 169
Budels
  Alt 55
  Capucijn 165
  Mei Bock 31
  Oud Bruin 99
  Parel Kölsch 51
Budweiser Budvar 153
  and water 18
Bürgerbräu see Berliner Bürgerbräu
burned flavor, explanation of 23
Burragorang Bock Beer 104

Burton Bridge
  Empire Pale Ale 133
  Porter 70
Bush
  7% 137
  Clovis see Bush 7%
  de Noël 41
butterscotch flavor, explanation of 23

## C

Cains Formidable Ale 57
Caledonian
  Edinburgh Strong Ale 62
  Flying Scotsman 62
  in stews 179
  Merman 62
calendar for beer drinkers 43
Calvinator 107
camomile as a flavoring in brewing 17
**Canada,** beers of
  Big Rock McNally's Extra Ale 157
  in stews 179
  Brick Bock 105
  Creemore Springs Premium Lager 153
  Denison's Bock 107
  Denison's Dunkler Weizenbock 107
  Granite Brewery Peculiar 111
  McAuslan Raspberry Ale / Bière à la Framboise 167
  Molson Dave's Scotch Ale 65
  Molson Signature Cream Ale 68
  Rickard's Red 162
  St. Ambroise Pale Ale 161
  as a marinade 177
  and Ringwood brewery yeast 19
  Unibroue Blanche de Chambly 80
  Unibroue Maudite 144
  Unibroue Quelque Chose 109
  Unibroue Raftman 117
Cantillon
  Cantillon Kriek Lambic 176
  in chilled fruit soups 178
  Cantillon Gueuze Vigneronne 75
  Grand Cru Bruocsella 1900 140
  Rosé de Gambrinus 75
  flavorings in 26
Capstone ESB 67
Captivator 107
Capucijn, Budels 165
caramel flavor, explanation of 23
Carl Dinkelacker, Dinkel Acker Volksfest Bier 37
Carnegie, David and porter 183
Carnegie Stark Porter 77
Cascade (hop variety) 15
Castelain Ch'ti 158
Castle Pale Ale 160
Catamount
  Octoberfest 154
  Porter 72
  10 IPA 134
Caveau 75
cedary flavor, explanation of 23
Celebration Ale 42
Celebrator 29
  in stews 179
Celis
  Grand Cru 144
  White 80
Ceres
  Bering 47
  Dansk Dortmunder 47
  Stowt 47
  Ceylon Lion Stout 171
Challenger (hop variety) 15
Chapeau Pêche 166
Charles Wells
  Bombardier 61
  Wells Fargo 61

cheese, beers to accompany 164-5
Chelsea
　Old Titanic 122
　Sunset Red 163
cherry, as a flavoring in
　brewing 17
chicken, beers to accompany
　154-5
chili, as a flavoring in brewing 17
Chiltern John Hampden's Ale 61
Chimay
　Cinq Cents 129
　Grande Réserve 165
　Trappist (cheese) 165
Chinook (hop variety) 15
Chiswick Bitter 58
chocolate
　beers to accompany 170-71
　as a flavoring in brewing 17
chocolate malt 13
Chocolate Stout 170
　in desserts 183
chocolate truffles with porter
　(recipe) 183
chocolaty flavor, explanation
　of 23
Chojugura Blond 35
choosing beer 26
Choulette see La Choulette
Christian Merz Spezial
　Rauchbier 150
Christmas, beers for 40-42
Christoffel
　Blond 126
　Robertus 181
Ch'ti 158
cinnamon, as a flavoring in
　brewing 17
Cinq Cents 129
Classic Yorkshire Ale 101
Climax ESB 67
clover, as a flavoring in
　brewing 17
cloves flavor, explanation of 23
Clovis see Bush 7
Cobbold IPA 133
Cock Ale 17
Cocker Hoop 60
coffee
　beers with 170-71
　as a flavoring in brewing 17
coffeeish flavor, explanation of
　23
colors, produced by grains and
　malts 13
complexity of flavors in beer 22
Con Domus 127
cookielike flavor, explanation
　of 23
cooking with beer 175-83 see
　also recipes
Coopers
　Best Extra Stout 143
　Sparkling Ale 35
Coors Blue Moon Belgian
　White 81
Coors Brewery, and hop study 15
coriander, as a flavoring in
　brewing 17
Cottage Norman's Conquest 121
Cougan's Bock 107
Courage Imperial Russian
　Stout 118
Creemore Springs Premium
　Lager 153
Cristal Alken 152
Cristal Preta Dark 149
crystal malt 13
Csarda Sweet Stout 103
Curaçao orange zest, as a
　flavoring in brewing 16
Cuvée De Koninck 56
　in stews 179
Cuvée de l'Ermitage 172
Cuvée René 141
**Czech Republic**, beers of
　Budweiser Budvar 153
　Gambrinus Bílé 89
　Pilsner Urquell 124
　Staropramen Dark 148

**D**
DAB see Dortmunder Actien-
　Brauerei
Damson Beer 77
damson, as a flavoring in
　brewing 17
Dansk Dortmunder 47
Dark Island 65
dark lager, ham basted with
　(recipe) 181
dark malts and beer strength 13
Dark Ruby 112
DAS 78
Das Feine Hofmark Würzig
　Herb 126
Dave's Scotch Ale 65
De Brabandere
　Petrus Oud Bruin 95
　　for braising 180
　Petrus Speciale 57
De Dolle Brouwers Arabier 35
De Koninck
　Cuvée De Koninck 56
　　in stews 179
　De Koninck 56
De Leeuw
　Valkenburgs Wit 81
　Winter Wit 81
De Ridder Wieckse Witte 80
De Smedt, Op-Ale 57
De Troch Chapeau Pêche 166
Dead Horse India Pale Ale 133
decoction in brewing 20
Denison's
　Bock 107
　Dunkler Weizenbock 107
**Denmark**, beers of
　Ceres Bering 47
　Ceres Dansk Dortmunder 47
　Ceres Stowt 47
Dentergems Wit 81
Deschutes Bachelor Bitter 68
desserts
　beer as an ingredient in 183
　beers to accompany 166-9
Diebels Alt 53
Dinkel Acker Volksfest Bier 37
Dizzy Lizzy 123
Dock Street
　Bohemian Pilsner 127
　Grand Cru 147
　Illuminator 107
Dolle see De Dolle
Dom Kölsch 49
Domus
　Con Domus 127
　Leuvendige Witte 79
Dort, Gulpener 47
Dortmunder Actien-Brauerei 46
　Hansa 46
Dortmunder Export 46-7
Dortmunder Gold 47
Dortmunder Union Export 46
Dos Equis 42
Double Black Stout 171
Double Chocolate Stout 170
　and chocolate 17
　in desserts 183
Double Maxim 145
Douglas Xmas 41
Dragon Stout 102
dry abbey beers 128-9
dry stouts 70-73
DUB see Dortmunder Union
Dubuisson see Bush
Dunkler Weizenbock 107
Dupont, Saison Dupont 34
Duvel 130
　hops used in 15
Duyck Jenlain 158
　in stews 179

**E**
early history of beer 11
earthy flavor, explanation of 23
Echigo Land Brauerei Abbey-
　style Tripel 165
Echte Kriek 76

Edinburgh Strong Ale 62
Ed's Best Bitter 69
Eggenberg
　Mac Queen's Nessie 116
　Schloss Eggenberg Urbock
　　23° 146
1812 India Pale Ale 132
1859 Porter 71
Einbecker Maibock 31
EKU 28 146
Elblag Porter 119
Eldridge Pope Thomas Hardy's
　Ale 120
Elgood's Flag Porter 143
Elysian The Wise ESB 69
Emerson's
　1812 India Pale Ale 132
　London Porter 73
Empire Pale Ale 133
endive salad with kriek
　vinaigrette (recipe) 176
**England**, beers of
　Adnams Suffolk Strong Ale 59
　　hops used in 15
　Banks's 101
　Bass No 1 121
　Batemans XXXB 59
　　as a marinade 177
　Black Sheep Ale 160
　　in stews 179
　Brakspear Special 59
　Burton Bridge Empire Pale
　　Ale 133
　Burton Bridge Porter 70
　Cains Formidable Ale 57
　Charles Wells Bombardier 61
　Chiltern John Hampden's
　　Ale 61
　Cobbold IPA 133
　Cottage Norman's Conquest
　　121
　Courage Imperial Russian
　　Stout 118
　Eldridge Pope Thomas
　　Hardy's Ale 120
　Elgood's Flag Porter 143
　Enville Ale 169
　Everards' Tiger 61
　Freedom Pilsener 153
　Fuller's Chiswick Bitter 58
　Fuller's Extra Special Bitter 58
　Fuller's London Pride 58
　Fuller's Summer Ale 35
　Gales Prize Old Ale 173
　Golden Hill Exmoor Gold 33
　Greene King Strong Suffolk
　　147
　Guernsey Milk Stout 103
　Harveys 1859 Porter 71
　Highgate & Walsall Old Ale
　　112
　Hopback Summer Lightning
　　32
　Hopback Thunderstorm 93
　Hull Mild 101
　Jennings Cocker Hoop 60
　King & Barnes Rye Beer 149
　King & Barnes Wheat Mash
　　92
　King and Barnes Old Porter 73
　Mackeson Stout 103
　McMullen Castle Pale Ale 160
　　as a marinade 177
　McMullen Haytime Summer
　　Ale 33
　McMullen's Chocolate Stout
　　170
　　in desserts 183
　Manns Original Brown Ale
　　101
　Marston's India Export 134
　Marston's Owd Rodger 111
　Marston's Oyster Stout 143
　Marston's Pedigree 160
　Marston's Summer Wheat
　　Beer 33
　Mash and Air Scotch Ale 117
　Mordue's Workie Ticket 61
　Morland "Old Speckled
　　Hen" 61

Newcastle Brown Ale 145
Pitfield Dark Star 113
Ridleys ESX Best 178
Ringwood Old Thumper 61
Robinson's Old Tom 112
St. Peter's Spiced Ale 109
Samuel Smith Imperial Stout
　118
Samuel Smith Oatmeal Stout
　168
　in desserts 183
Sarah Hughes Dark Ruby 112
Shepherd Neame Bishop's
　Finger 178
Shepherd Neame Original
　Porter 71
Shepherd Neame Spitfire 60
Strawberry Bank Damson
　Beer 77
Tetley Mild 100
Theakston Old Peculier 111
Timothy Taylor's Landlord 60
　as a marinade 177
Umbel Ale 17
Ushers Autumn Frenzy 39
Ushers Summer Madness 35
Vaux Double Maxim 145
Vaux How's Your Father
　Summer Ale 33
Vaux St. Nicholas's
　Christmas Ale 42
Wadworth 6X 61
Wadworth Farmer's Glory 112
Wadworth Old Timer 112
Waggle Dance 169
Ward's Classic Yorkshire Ale
　101
Wells Fargo 61
Whitbread Gold Label 121
Woodforde Headcracker 123
Woodforde's Norfolk
　Wherry 61
Young's Double Chocolate
　Stout 170
　and chocolate 17
　in desserts 183
Young's Old Nick 121
Young's Special 60
Young's Special London Ale
　137
Young's Winter Warmer 111
English bitter 58-61
Enville Ale 169
ESB 67
　as a marinade 177
Espresso Stout 171
**Estonia**, beers of
　Saku Hele 45
　Sillamäe München 149
ESX Best 178
Evening Star, Pitfield Dark
　Star 113
Everards' Tiger 61
Exmoor Gold 33
Extra Special Bitter, Fuller's 58
Extra Stout, Guinness 142
extra-hoppy ales 136-7

**F**
Farmer's Glory 112
Farsons Lacto Traditional Stout
　102
Feldschlösschen
　Schwarzer Steiger 97
　Warteck Alt 54
fermentation
　controlled 19
　and maturation 21
Feuerfest Edel Bier 172
**Finland**, beers of
　Koff Jouluolut 41
　Palvasalmi Real Ale Brewery
　　"Valte" 113
　sahti 32
　Sinebrychoff Porter 119
Firehouse Kölsch Lager 51
First Gold (hop variety) 15
First United Brewery, EKU 28
　146

Fischerstube Ueli Reverenz 45
fish, beers to accompany 152-3
Fish Poseidon Old Scotch Ale
　117
Fish Tale Mud Shark Porter 72
Flag Porter 143
Flaming Stone 150
Flatlander's Eighty Shilling Ale
　64
flavorings, additional, used in
　brewing 16-17
flavors
　appreciation of 22
　explanation of 23
　produced by grains and malts
　　13
　produced by hops 15
Flemish brown ale, game birds
　in (recipe) 180
Flemish sweet and sour red ales
　94-5
Flying Dog Scottish Ale 65
Flying Scotsman 62
　in stews 179
Fond Gueuze 75
food
　beer as an ingredient in
　　175-83 see also recipes
　beers to accompany 139-72
Fordham Calvinator 107
Formidable Ale 57
**France**, beers of
　Adelscott 116
　Adelscott Noir 116
　Brassin Robespierre 159
　Castelain Ch'ti 158
　Duyck Jenlain 158
　　in stews 179
　Heineken Kylian 156
　Jeanne d'Arc Ambre des
　　Flandres 158
　Jeanne d'Arc Belzebuth 131
　La Choulette Ambrée 159
　La Choulette Bière des Sans
　　Culottes 159
　La Choulette Framboise 77
　Pelforth Amberley 116
　Pelforth George Killian's 156
　Saint Sylvestre 3 Monts 159
Frankenheim Alt 53
Franklinfest 155
Franziskaner Dunkel
　Hefe-Weissbier 91
Franziskaner Kristallklar
　Weissbier 85
Fraoch Heather Ale 38
Freedom Pilsener 153
fresh bread flavor, explanation
　of 23
Früh Kölsch 48
fruit beers 76-8
fruit cake with spiced beer
　(recipe) 182
Fruit Défendu see Le Fruit
　Défendu
fruit, as a flavoring in brewing
　16-17
fruit lambics 74-5
Fuggle (hop variety) 15
Full Sail Wassail Winter Ale 113
Fuller's
　Chiswick Bitter 58
　Extra Special Bitter 58
　London Pride 58
　Summer Ale 35

**G**
Gales Prize Old Ale 173
Gambrinus Bílé 89
game birds in Flemish brown
　ale (recipe) 180
Garde Kölsch 49
Gatzweiler Alt 53
Geary's Pale Ale 161
George Killian's 156
German dark wheat beers 90-91

German-style Hefeweizen 86-9
**Germany**, beers of
　Aecht Schlenkerla Rauchbier
　　150
　Ayinger Celebrator 29
　　in stews 179
　Ayinger Oktober Fest-
　　Märzen 37
　Berliner Bürgerbräu
　　Bernauer Schwarzbier 97
　Berliner Bürgerbräu
　　Weissbier 82
　　in sorbets 183
　Berliner Kindl Weisse 83
　　in chilled fruit soups 178
　　for raspberry sorbets 183
　Berliner Weisse and Himbeer
　　83
　Berliner Weisse and
　　Waldmeister 83
　Bitburger Premium Pils 152
　Bolten Ur-Alt 54
　Brand Doublebock 29
　Christian Merz Spezial
　　Rauchbier 150
　Das Feine Hofmark Würzig
　　Herb 126
　Diebels Alt 53
　Dinkel Acker Volksfest Bier 37
　Dom Kölsch 49
　Dortmunder Union Export 46
　Einbecker Maibock 31
　EKU 28 146
　Frankheim Alt 53
　Franziskaner Dunkel Hefe-
　　Weissbier 91
　Franziskaner Kristallklar
　　Weissbier 85
　Früh Kölsch 48
　Garde Kölsch 49
　Gatzweiler Alt 53
　Gilden Kölsch 49
　Gose Ohne Bedenken 141
　Hacker-Pschorr Alt Munich
　　Dark 148
　Hallertau Auer Pils 152
　HB Mai-Bock 30
　HB Oktoberfestbier 37
　HB Schwarze Weisse 91
　Hellers Wiess 51
　Herrenhäuser Weizen Bier 88
　Herrnbräu Hefe-Weissbier
　　Dunkel 91
　Hoepfner Blue Star 116
　Hoepfner Pilsner 126
　Hoepfner Porter 73
　Holsten Maibock 31
　Hopf Dunkle Weisse 91
　Im Füchschen Alt 53
　Jever Pilsner 125
　Kaltenberg Ritterbock 29
　Kloster Irseer ABT's Trunk 172
　Kneitinger Bock 105
　Köstritzer Schwarzbier 97
　Küppers Kölsch 49
　Lammsbräu Kristall Weizen 85
　Maisel's Weisse Kristallklar 85
　Märkischer Landmann
　　Schwarzbier 97
　Mönchshof Kapuziner
　　Schwarze Hefeweizen 90
　Moravia Pils 125
　Mühlen Kölsch 50
　Oberdorfer Weissbier 87
　Päffgen Kölsch 50
　Paulaner Salvator 28
　　in stews 179
　Pinkus Müller Alt 54
　Pinkus Müller Hefe Weizen 88
　　in sorbets 183
　Radeberger Pilsner 125
　Rauchenfelser Steinbier 151
　Reissdorf Kölsch 50
　Rhenania Alt 53
　Richmodis Kölsch 50
　Roggen Bier 149
　　in soup 178
　St Georgen Keller Bier 126
　Schäffbräu Feuerfest Edel
　　Bier 172

Scheidmantel Hefe Weisse 87
Schlösser Alt 53
Schneider Aventinus 106
Schneider Weisse 86
  fermentation of 19
Schöfferhofer Kristallweizen 85
Schultheiss Berliner Weisse 83
  in chilled fruit soups 178
  in sorbet 183
Schumacher Alt 53
Schwaben Bräu Märzenbier 37
Schwarzer Steiger 97
Sester Kölsch 50
Sion Kölsch 49
Spaten Oktoberfestbier 37
  fermentation 19
Steiner Märzen 36
Sticke Bier 52
Sünner Hefeweizen 88
Sünner Kölsch 51
Tucher Helles Hefe Weizen 87
Uerige Alt 52
Ueriges Weizen 88
Unertl Weissbier 87
Unions Bräu Hell 45
Victory St. Victorious 29
Weihenstephaner Kristall
  Weissbier 84
Weltenburger Kloster
  Barock-Dunkel 148
Wernesgrüner Pils Legende
  125
Würzburger Hofbräu
  Sympator 107
Geuze Boon 140
  and fermentation 19
Gilden Kölsch 49
Ginder Ale 57
Girardin, Gueuze 140
Glühkriek 108
Gold Label 121
golden ales, strong 130-31
Golden Hill Exmoor Gold 33
golden lagers 44-5
Golding (hop variety) 15
Goose Island Honker's Ale 69
Gordon Biersch
  Blonde Bock 107
  Märzen 155
Gordon Highland Scotch
  Ale 115
Gordon Xmas 41
Gose Ohne Bedenken 141
Gouden Carolus 171
Goudenband 76
  and braising 180
grain
  colors produced by 13
  and the effect of drying 12
  flavors produced by 13
grains of paradise, as a
  flavoring in brewing 17
Grand-Place Blanche 81
Grande Réserve, Chimay 165
Granite Brewery Peculiar 111
Grant's
  Bert Grant's Perfect Porter 72
  Bert Grant's Scottish Ale 64
  India Pale Ale 135
grapefruit flavor, explanation
  of 23
grass flavor, explanation of 23
Great Divide Saint Brigid's
  Porter 73
Great Lakes Brewing Co.
  Dortmunder Gold 47
  The Eliot Ness 163
  Wits' End, and camomile 17
Greene King Strong Suffolk 147
Greenmantle 63
Gritty McDuff's Best Bitter 69
Grolsch
  Herfstbok 107
  Lentebok 31
  Wintervorst 109
  and clover 17
Grozet Gooseberry & Wheat
  Ale 38
Guernsey Milk Stout 103
Gueuze Boon see Geuze Boon

Gueuze Girardin 140
Gueuze Vigneronne Cantillon 75
Guinness
  for batters and baking 182
  Extra Stout 142
  Kilkenny Irish Beer 157
  Macardles Traditional Ale 156
  Smithwick's Ale 157
  Smithwick's Barley Wine 123
  and water usage 18
Gulpener
  Dort 47
  Korenwolf 81

**H**

Hacker-Pschorr Alt Munich
  Dark 148
Haecht Witbier 79
Hair of the Dog Adam 173
Hale's
  Harvest Ale 39
  Special Bitter 68
Hallertau Auer Pils 152
Hallertau Mittelfrüh (hop
  variety) 15
ham basted with dark lager
  (recipe) 181
hand-pumps 58
Hansa Urbock 30
Hapkin 131
Harvest Ale 39
Harveys 1859 Porter 71
Harvey's brewery, using hops in
  14
Harviestoun Montrose Ale 65
hay aroma, explanation of 23
Haytime Summer Ale 33
HB
  Mai-Bock 30
  Oktoberfestbier 37
  Schwarze Weisse 91
H.C. Berger Maibock 31
Headcracker 123
Heather Ale, Fraoch 38
heather ale in Orkney 16
Heineken
  Amstel Herfstbock 106
  De Ridder Wieckse Witte 80
  Kylian 156
  Oud Bruin 98
  Ridder Donker 99
  Tarwebok 106
Hellers Wiess 51
hemp, as a flavoring in
  brewing 17
herbal flavor, explanation of
  23
herbs, as a flavoring in
  brewing 16-17
Herfstbok 107
Herrenhäuser Weizen Bier 88
Herrnbräu Hefe-Weissbier
  Dunkel 91
Hertog Jan Grand Prestige 122
Het Elfde Gebod 131
High Rollers Wheat Beer 93
Highgate & Walsall Old Ale
  112
Highlands Amber 65
Himbeer and Berliner Weisse 83
Hoegaarden
  DAS 78
  Grand Cru 144
  Le Fruit Défendu 182
  Special 78
  Verboden Vrucht 182
Hoepfner
  Blue Star 116
  Pilsner 126
  Porter 73
Hofbräuhaus see HB
Hofbräuhaus Freising 84
Holland see Netherlands, the
Holsten
  Maibock 31
  Moravia Pils 125
honey, as a flavoring in
  brewing 12
honey malt 13

Honker's Ale 69
hop-growing regions 11
Hopback
  Summer Lightning 32
  Thunderstorm 93
Hopf Dunkle Weisse 91
hopping (addition of hops) 21
hoppy ales, extra 136-7
hoppy flavor, explanation of 23
hops
  flavors and aromas
    produced by 15
  and Harvey's brewery 14
  processing of 14
  varieties of 15
Horse Ale 57
Hoster's Captivator 107
How's Your Father Summer
  Ale 33
Hübsch Sudwerk Helles 45
Hull Mild 101
Hürlimann, Samichlaus Bier 40
Hurricane Premium Pure Malt
  Beer 113
Huyghe Ninkeberry 167

**I**

Illuminator 107
Im Füchschen Alt 53
Imperial Stout 118
Independence Franklinfest 155
India Export 134
India pale ale, mussels in
  (recipe) 179
India pale ales 132-5
Inselkammer, Tucher Helles
  Hefe Weizen 87
Interbrew
  Ginder Ale 57
  Hoegaarden DAS 78
  Hoegaarden Grand Cru 78
  Hoegaarden Special 78
  Horse Ale 57
  Julius 131
  Leffe Radieuse 164
  Vieux Temps 57
Ireland, beers of
  Beamish Irish Stout 142
  Guinness Extra Stout 142
  Kilkenny Irish Beer 157
  Macardles Traditional Ale 156
  Murphy's Irish Stout 142
  Porterhouse Plain Porter 73
  Smithwick's Ale 157
  Smithwick's Barley Wine 123
Italy, beer of, Moretti La Rossa
  162

**J**

Jacobite Ale 38
Jamaica, beer of, Dragon Stout
  102
Japan, beers of
  Chojugura Blond 35
  Csarda Sweet Stout 103
  Echigo Land Brauerei
    Abbey-style Tripel 165
  Grand-Place Blanche 81
  Moku Moku Bisucuit
    Weizen 80
  Moku Moku Smoked Ale 151
  Okhotsk Mild Stout 71
  Otaru Helles 44
  Sapporo Black Beer 96
Jeanne d'Arc
  Ambre des Flandres 158
  Belzebuth 131
Jenlain 158
  in stews 179
Jennings Cocker Hoop 60
Jever Pilsner 125
John Hampden's Ale 61
Jopen Bok Bier 106
Judas 131
judging of beer 22
Julius 131
juniper berries, as a flavoring
  in brewing 17

**K**

Kalamazoo Brewing
  Bell's Porter 73
  Third Coast Old Ale 113
Kaltenberg Ritterbock 29
Kasteel Bier/Bière du Château
  173
Keller Bier 126
Kilkenny Irish Beer 157
Kindl see Berliner Kindl
King & Barnes
  Old Porter 73
  Rye Beer 149
  Wheat Mash 92
King Lear Old Ale 113
Kloster Irseer ABT's Trunk 172
Kneitinger Bock 105
Koff see Sinebrychoff
Koff Jouluolut 41
Kölschbier 48-51
Koninck see De Koninck
Korenwolf 81
Köstritzer Schwarzbier 97
Kriek Lambic, Cantillon 176
  in chilled fruit soups 178
Kriek Mort Subite 75
kriek vinaigrette, endive salad
  with (recipe) 176
Kulmbach, Mönchshof
  Kapuziner Schwarze
  Hefewizen 90
Küppers Kölsch 49
Kylian 156

**L**

La Choulette
  Ambrée 159
  Bière des Sans Culottes 159
  Brassin Robespierre 159
  Framboise 77
La Rossa 162
La Trappe Quadrupel 164
L'Abbaye des Rocs Blanche des
  Honnelles 79
Lacto Traditional Stout 102
lactose, its use in stout brewing 12
lager
  and bottom fermentation 19
  decoction-mashed 20
Lakefront Riverwest Stein Beer
  163
lamb, beers to accompany 158-9
lambic and wild fermentation 19
Lammsbräu Kristall Weizen 85
Landlord 60
  as a marinade 177
Lang Creek Trimotor Amber 69
Larson, Alaskan Amber 55
Le Fruit Défendu 182
Leeuw see De Leeuw
Lefèbvre Saison 1900 34
Leffe Radieuse 164
Leinenkugel's Autumn Gold 39
Lente Bok, Alfa 30
Leuven, Domus Leuvendige
  Witte 79
Liberty Ale 136
  in fish stews 179
  hops used in 15
licorice flavor, explanation of 23
licorice, as a flavoring in
  brewing 16
Liefmans
  Glühkriek 108
  Goudenband 76
  and braising 180
  Kriekbier 76
Lindemans
  Cuvée René 141
  Framboise 166
Lion Nathan, Tooheys Old
  Black Ale 110
Lion Stout 171
London Porter, Emerson's 73
London Pride 58
Louwaege Hapkin 131
Lublin (hop variety) 15

**M**

Mac Queen's Nessie 116
Macardles Traditional Ale 156
McAuslan Raspberry Ale /
  Bière à La Framboise 167
McEwan's 80/- 63
McGuire's Old Style Irish Ale
  157
  in stews 179
Mackeson Stout 103
Maclay
  Eighty Shilling Export Ale 63
  Oat Malt Stout 168
  in desserts 183
  Scotch Ale 63
McMullen
  Castle Pale Ale 160
  as a marinade 177
  Chocolate Stout 170
  in desserts 183
  Haytime Summer Ale 33
McNally's Extra Ale 157
  in stews 179
McNeill's Dead Horse India
  Pale Ale 133
MacTarnahan's Gold Medal 64
Madeira flavor, explanation of 23
Magic Hat Blind Faith IPA 135
Maibock, Berliner Bürgerbräu 31
Maisel's Weisse Kristallklar 85
**Malta**, beer of, Farsons Lacto
  Traditional Stout 102
malting 12
malting barley regions 10
malts, colors and flavors
  produced by 13
malty flavor, explanation of 23
Malzmühle, Mühlen Kölsch 50
Manns Original Brown Ale 101
maple syrup, as a flavoring in
  brewing 12
Marin "Old Dipsea" 123
marinades, beer as an
  ingredient in 177
Märkischer Landmann
  Schwarzbier 97
Marston's
  India Export 134
  Owd Rodger 111
  Oyster Stout 143
  Pedigree 160
  Summer Wheat Beer 33
  and water usage 18
Mârten Trotzig's Öl 109
Martens Sezoens 35
Märzenbier 37
Mash and Air Scotch Ale 117
mashing 20
Mater
  Roman Sloeber 144
  Wit Bier 79
maturation 21
Maudite 144
meat, as a flavoring in
  brewing 17
Mechelen, Gouden Carolus 171
Merman 143
**Mexico**, beers of
  Moctezuma Dos Equis 42
  Moctezuma Noche Buena 42
  Michelob HefeWeizen 89
Middlesex Brewing Co.
  Oatmeal Stout 168
Mike's Mild Ale 100
mild ales 100-101
Milk Stout, Guernsey 103
minty flavor, explanation of 23
Mitchell's
  Old 90/- Ale 114
  Raven Stout 73
Moctezuma
  Dos Equis 42
  Noche Buena 42
Mohrenbräu Schluck 162
Moku Moku
  Bisucuit Weizen 80
  Smoked Ale 151
Molson
  Molson Dave's Scotch Ale 65

Rickard's Red 162
  Signature Cream Ale 68
Mönchshof Kapuziner
  Schwarze Hefeweizen 90
Montrose Ale 65
Moortgat Duvel 130
  hops used in 15
Moravia Pils 125
Mordue's Workie Ticket 61
Moretti La Rossa 162
Morland "Old Speckled Hen" 61
Mort Subite
  Fond Gueuze 75
  Kriek Mort Subite 75
Moulin Ale of Atholl 65
Mount Hood (hop variety) 15
Mount Hood Pittock Wee
  Heavy 117
Mud Shark Porter 72
Mühlen Kölsch 50
München 149
Munich 149
Munich malt 13
Munich Oktoberfest 36
Murphy's Irish Stout 142
mussels in India pale ale 179

**N**

**Namibia**, beer of, Hansa
  Urbock 30
Nessie 116
Nethergate, Umbel Ale 17
**Netherlands, the**, beers of
  Alfa Lente Bok 30
  Alfa Oud Bruin 99
  Amstel Herfstbock 106
  Arcen Het Elfde Gebod 131
  Berliner Bürgerbräu Maibock
    31
  Brand Oud Bruin 99
  Budels Alt 55
  Budels Capucijn 165
  Budels Mei Bock 31
  Budels Oud Bruin 99
  Budels Parel Kölsch 51
  Christoffel Blond 126
  Christoffel Robertus 181
  De Leeuw Valkenburgs Wit 81
  De Leeuw Winter Wit 81
  De Ridder Wieckse Witte 80
  Grolsch Herfstbok 107
  Grolsch Lentebok 31
  Grolsch Wintervorst 109
  and clover 17
  Gulpener Dort 47
  Gulpener Korenwolf 81
  Heineken Kylian 156
  Heineken Oud Bruin 98
  Heineken Tarwebok 106
  Hertog Jan Grand Prestige 122
  Jopen Bok Bier 106
  La Trappe Quadrupel 164
  Ridder Donker 99
  Speculator 107
  Winter Vorst 17
New Belgium
  Old Cherry Ale 77
  in chilled fruit soups 178
  Porch Swing Ale 35
New Glarus Wisconsin Cherry
  Beer 177
  and cherries 17
  in chilled fruit soups 178
**New Zealand**, beers of
  Emerson's 1812 India Pale
    Ale 132
  Emerson's London Porter 73
  Mike's Mild Ale 100
  Petone Owd Jim 113
  Renwick Hurricane Premium
    Pure Malt Beer 113
  Shakespeare King Lear Old
    Ale 113
Newcastle Brown Ale 145
nightcap beers, barley wines
  120-23
Ninkeberry 167
Noche Buena 42
Noël, Bush de 41

Nöel Christmas Ale 41
Norfolk Wherry 61
Norman's Conquest 121
North American ales 66-9
North Coast Old Rasputin
   Russian Imperial Stout 119
North Holland Foundation of
   Alternative Brewers,
   Speculator 107
Norway, beer of, Aass Bock 105
Nugget (hop variety) 15
Nussdorfer
   Nussdorf Sir Henry's Dry
   Stout 73
   Old Whisky Bier 116
   St. Thomas Bräu 54
nut flavor, explanation of 23

**O**
Oasis
   Capstone ESB 67
   Zoser Stout 169
Oat Malt Stout 168
   in desserts 183
oats in brewing 13
Oberdorfer Weissbier 87
occasions, special and the right
   beer 26-7
Odell's 90 Shilling 64
Okhotsk Mild Stout 71
Okocim Porter 119
Oktober Fest-Märzen, Ayinger 37
old ales 110-13
Old Bawdy 123
old brown lagers 98-9
Old Cherry Ale 77
   in chilled fruit soups 178
Old Dipsea 123
Old Dominion
   Spring Brew 31
   Octoberfest 154
   Tupper's Hop Pocket Ale 137
Old Foghorn 122
Old Jock 115
Old Knucklehead 123
Old Nick 121
Old 90/- Ale 114
Old Porter, King & Barnes 73
Old Rasputin Russian Imperial
   Stout 119
Old Speckled Hen 61
Old Thumper 61
Old Timer 112
Old Titanic 122
Old Tom 112
Old Whisky Bier 116
Old Wooly 122
Oliver ESB 66
   as a marinade 177
onion and cheese soup (recipe)
   178
Op-Ale 57
orange peel (Curaçao), as a
   flavoring in brewing 16
orangy flavor, explanation of 23
Original Porter 71
Orkney
   Dark Island 65
   Skullsplitter 117
Orval 128
   in onion soup 178
Otaru Helles 44
Otto Brothers' Teton Ale 69
Our Special Holiday Ale 42
Owd Jim 113
Owd Rodger 111
Oxford Brewing, Oxford Class
   Ale 69
Oyster Stout 143

**P & Q**
Päffgen Kölsch 50
Palm
   Speciale 57
   Steendonk Brabants Witbier 81
   Steendonk, use of spices in 17
Palvasalmi Real Ale Brewery
   "Valte" 113

paradise, grains of, as a
   flavoring in brewing 17
Parel Kölsch 51
Park Slope India Pale Ale 135
party beers
   fruit beers 76-8
   fruit lambics 74-5
pâtés, beers to accompany 146-7
Paulaner Salvator 28
   in stews 179
peach, as a flavoring in
   brewing 17
pear flavor, explanation of 23
Peconic County Reserve Ale 77
Peculiar 111
Pedigree 160
Pelforth
   Amberley 116
   George Killian's 156
Penn Oktoberfest 154
pepper flavor, explanation of 23
Perfect Porter, Bert Grant's 72
Pete's Summer Brew 35
Petone Owd Jim 113
Petrus Oud Bruin 95
   for braising 180
Petrus Speciale 57
pickles, beers to accompany 146-7
Pike
   Old Bawdy 123
   Pale Ale 161
Pils Legende 125
Pilsner lagers 124-7
   pouring of 184
Pilsner malt 13
Pilsner Urquell 124
pine tips, as a flavoring in
   brewing 16
piney flavor, explanation of 23
Pinkus Müller
   Alt 54
   Hefe Weizen 88
   in sorbets 183
Pipaix, Saison de Pipaix 34
Pitfield Dark Star 113
Pittock Wee Heavy 117
pizza, beers to accompany 162-3
plain porters 70-73
plum flavor, explanation of 23
Poe's Tell Tale Ale 123
Poland, beers of
   Elblag Porter 119
   Okocim Porter 119
   Zywiec Porter 119
Poperings Hommel Bier 137
Porch Swing Ale 35
pork, beers to accompany 156-7
porter, chocolate truffles with
   (recipe) 183
porter and David Carnegie 183
Porterhouse Plain Porter 73
porters and top fermentation 19
Portland Brewing MacTarnahan's
   Gold Medal 64
Portugal, beers of
   Cristal Preta Dark 149
   Sagres Dark 149
Poseidon Old Scotch Ale 117
pouring of beer 184
Prima Pils 127
Pripps, Carnegie Stark Porter 71
Prize Old Ale 173
process of brewing 21
Progress (hop variety) 15
Pullman Pale Ale 69
Pyramid
   Espresso Stout 171
   Scotch Ale 117
   Wheaten Ale 93
Quelque Chose 109

**R**
Radeberger Pilsner 125
Raftman 117
raisiny flavor, explanation of 23
Raspberry Ale / Bière à La
   Framboise 167
Rauchenfelser Steinbier 151
Raven Stout 73

recipes
   chocolate truffles with porter
      183
   endive salad with kriek
      vinaigrette 176
   fruit cake with spiced beer 182
   game birds in Flemish
      brown ale 180
   ham basted with dark lager 181
   mussels in India pale ale 179
   onion and cheese soup 178
   salmon in smoked porter 177
Red Hook
   Double Black Stout 171
   ESB 67
Reissdorf Kölsch 50
Renwick Hurricane Premium
   Pure Malt Beer 113
resiny flavor, explanation of 23
restoratives
   black beers 96-7
   mild ales 100-101
   old brown lagers 98-9
   sweet stouts 102-3
Rhenania Alt 53
Richbrau Poe's Tell Tale Ale 123
Richmodis Kölsch 50
Rickard's Red 162
Ridder see De Ridder
Ridder Donker 99
Ridleys ESX Best 178
Ringwood brewery yeast 19
Ringwood Old Thumper 61
Ritterbock 29
Riva Dentergems Wit 81
Riverside Pullman Pale Ale 69
Riverwest Stein Beer 163
Road Dog see Flying Dog
   Scottish Ale
Robertus 181
Robinson's Old Tom 112
Rodenbach
   Alexander 166
   Grand Cru 147
   as a vinegar 176
   Rodenbach 94
Roggen Bier 149
   in soup 178
Rogue
   Maierbock Ale 30
   Rogue-N-Berry 76
Roman Sloeber 144
Rosé de Gambrinus 75
   flavorings in 26
rose flavor, explanation of 23
Russia, beers of
   Baltika Porter 119
   Stepan Razin Porter 119
   Vienna Porter 119
Rye Beer 149
   rye in brewing 13

**S**
Saaz (hop variety) 15
sagebrush, as a flavoring in
   brewing 17
Sagres Dark 149
sahti 32
St. Ambroise Pale Ale 161
   as a marinade 177
   and Ringwood brewery yeast
      19
Saint Arnold Kristall Weizen 93
Saint Brigid's Porter 73
St. Charles Porter 72
St. Galler Klosterbräu
   Schützengarten Naturtrüb 47
St. Georgen Keller Bier 126
St. Nicholas's Christmas Ale 42
St. Peter's brewery and
   Jerusalem Tavern 108
St. Peter's Spiced Ale 109
Saint Sylvestre 3 Monts 159
St. Thomas Bräu 54
St. Victorious 29
Saison 1900 34
Saison de Pipaix 34
Saison Dupont 34
Saison Silly 35

Saku Hele 45
salads, beers to accompany 144-5
salmon in smoked porter
   (recipe) 177
Salvator 28
   in stews 179
Sam Adams
   Boston Lager 178
   Triple Bock 146
Samichlaus Bier 40
Samuel Smith
   Imperial Stout 118
   Oatmeal Stout 168
   in desserts 183
Sapporo Black Beer 96
Sarah Hughes Dark Ruby 112
sausages, beers to accompany
   148-9
sausages (Weisswurst), beers to
   accompany 86
Schaapskooi
   Jopen Bok Bier 106
   La Trappe Quadrupel 164
Schäffbräu Feuerfest Edel Bier
   172
Scheidmantel Hefe Weisse 87
Schlenkerla 151
Schloss Eggenberg Urbock 23°
   146
Schlösser Alt 53
Schluck 162
Schmaltz's Alt 55
Schneider
   Aventinus 106
   Weisse 86
   fermentation of 19
Schöfferhofer Kristallweizen 85
Schultheiss Berliner Weisse 83
   in chilled fruit soups 178
   in sorbet 183
Schumacher Alt 53
Schützengarten, St. Galler
   Klosterbräu Schützengarten
   Naturtrüb 47
Schwaben Bräu Märzenbier 37
Schwarzbier, Köstritzer 97
Schwarzer Steiger 97
Scotland, beers of
   Alba Scots Pine Ale 38
   and pine tips in brewing 16
   Belhaven 80/- Export Ale 63
   Belhaven 90/- 117
   Belhaven Wee Heavy 117
   Borve Ale 115
   Broughton Black Douglas 63
   Broughton Greenmantle 63
   Broughton Old Jock 115
   Caledonian Flying Scotsman
      62
   in stews 179
   Caledonian Merman 62
   Douglas Xmas 41
   Fraoch Heather Ale 38
   Gordon Highland Scotch
      Ale 115
   Gordon Xmas 41
   Grozet Gooseberry & Wheat
      Ale 38
   Harviestoun Montrose Ale 65
   McEwan's 80/- 63
   Maclay Eighty Shilling
      Export Ale 63
   Maclay Oat Malt Stout 168
   in desserts 183
   Maclay Scotch Ale 63
   Moulin Ale of Atholl 65
   Orkney Dark Island 65
   Orkney Skullsplitter 117
   Tomintoul Wild Cat 65
   Traquair House Ale 115
   Traquair Jacobite Ale 38
   Younger of Alloa Sweetheart
      Stout 103
   Scots Pine Ale 38
   and pine tips in brewing 16
Scottish ales 62-5
Scottish ales and shilling
   symbol 62
Scottish ales, strong 114-17
Scottish Courage

Douglas Xmas 41
Gordon Highland Scotch
   Ale 115
Gordon Xmas 41
McEwan's 80/- 63
Newcastle Brown Ale 145
Theakston Old Peculier 111
seasonal beers
   for autumn 36-9
   for Christmas 40-42
   for spring 28-31
   for summer 32-5
Secret 55
selecting beers 26-7
serving temperature of beer 22
Sester Kölsch 50
Sezoens 35
Shakespeare King Lear Old
   Ale 113
shellfish, beers to accompany
   142-3
Shepherd Neame
   Bishop's Finger, in soup 178
   Original Porter 71
   Spitfire 60
Sherlock's Home Piper's Pride 65
sherry flavor, explanation of 23
shilling symbol, and Scottish
   ales 62
Shirayuki, Grand-Place
   Blanche 81
6X 61
Sierra Nevada
   Bigfoot Ale 123
   Celebration Ale 42
Signature Cream Ale 68
Sillamäe München 149
Silly, Saison 35
Sinebrychoff
   Koff Jouluolut 41
   Porter 119
Sion Kölsch 49
Sir Henry's Dry Stout 73
Sissons Wise Guy Weissbier 89
Skullsplitter 117
Sloeber 144
Smedt see De Smedt
Smithwick's
   Ale 157
   Barley Wine 123
Smoked Ale 151
smoked foods, beers to
   accompany 150-51
smoked malt 13
Smoked Porter 151
   as a marinade 177
smoked porter, salmon in
   (recipe) 177
smoky flavor, explanation of 23
sociable beers
   Altbier 52-5
   Belgian ales 56-7
   Dortmunder export 46-7
   dry stouts 70-73
   English bitter 58-61
   golden lagers 44-5
   Kölschbier 48-51
   North American ales 66-9
   plain porters 70-73
   Scottish ales 62-5
Sofiero, Mårten Trotzig's Öl 109
soups
   beer as an ingredient in 178
   beers to accompany 140-41
sour flavor, explanation of 23
South Africa, beers of
   Mitchell's Old 90/- Ale 114
   Mitchell's Raven Stout 73
South German wheat beers 84-5
Southampton Publick House
   Peconic County Reserve Ale 77
   Southampton Saison 34
   and grains of paradise 17
   Southampton Secret 55
Sparkling Ale, Coopers 35
Spaten
   Franziskaner Dunkel Hefe-
      Weissbier 91
   Oktoberfestbier 37
   fermentation of 19

Special London Ale 137
special occasions, selection of
   beer for 26-7
Speculator 107
Spezial Rauchbier, Christian
   Merz 150
Spiced Ale 109
spiced beer, fruit cake with
   (recipe) 182
spiced beers 108-9
spices, as a flavoring in
   brewing 16-17
Spitfire 60
spring, beers for 28-31
Sri Lanka, beer of, Ceylon
   Lion Stout 171
Stark Porter 71
Staropramen Dark 148
starters, beers to accompany 144-5
Steendonk Brabants Witbier 81
Steendonk, use of spices in 17
Stein, Steiner Märzen 36
Stepan Razin Porter 119
stews, beers as an ingredient in
   179
Sticke Bier 52
Stoudt's Pils 127
stouts
   and lactose 12
   pouring of 184
   and top fermentation 19
Stowt, Ceres 47
Strawberry Bank Damson Beer 77
strawberry flavor, explanation
   of 23
strong golden ales 130-31
strong Scottish ales 114-17
Strong Suffolk, Greene King 147
Styrians (hop variety) 15
Sudwerk, Hübsch Sudwerk
   Helles 45
Suffolk Strong Ale, Adnams 59
   hops used in 15
sugars in brewing 12
Summer Ale, Fuller's 35
summer, beers for 32-5
Summer Lightning 32
Summer Madness 35
Summer Wheat Beer 33
Summit Winter Ale 113
Sünner
   Hefeweizen 88
   Kölsch 51
Sunset Red 163
Sweden, beers of
   Carnegie Stark Porter 71
   Mårten Trotzig's Öl 109
Sweet Stout, Csarda 103
sweet stouts 102-3
Sweetheart Stout 103
sweets see desserts
Switzerland, beers of
   Fischerstube Ueli Reverenz 45
   St. Galler Klosterbräu
      Schützengarten Naturtrüb
      47
   Samichlaus Bier 40
   Warteck Alt 54
Sympator 107

**T**
Tabernash
   Munich 149
   Weisse 89
Target (hop variety) 15
Tarwebok 106
tasting beer 22-3
tea flavor, explanation of 23
temperature, serving 22
temperatures in brewing 20
Tetley Mild 100
Teton Ale 69
The Eliot Ness 163
The Wise ESB 69
Theakston Old Peculier 111
Theakston, and use of wooden
   casks 110
Third Coast Old Ale 113
thirst quenchers

Belgian-style wheat beers 78-81
Berlin-style wheat beers 82-3
Flemish sweet and sour red ales 94-5
German dark wheat beers 90-91
German-style Hefeweizen 86-9
South German wheat beers 84-5
wheat ales 92-3
Thomas Hardy's Ale 120
Thomas Kemper Oktoberfest 155
3 Monts 159
Thunderstorm 93
Thurn und Taxis, Roggen Bier 149
in soup 178
Tiger 61
timing in brewing 20
Timmermans
Caveau 75
Kriek 75
Lambic Wit 81
Timothy Taylor's Landlord 60
as a marinade 177
toast flavor, explanation of 23
tobacco flavor, explanation of 23
toffee flavor, explanation of 23
Tomintoul Wild Cat 65
Tooheys Old Black Ale 110
top-fermentation (ales, porters, stouts) 19
top-fermentation (wheat beers) 19
Trappe see La Trappe
Trappist 129
Traquair
House Ale 115
Jacobite Ale 38
Trimotor Amber 69
Tripel Karmeliet, Bosteels 129
Troch see De Troch
Tucher Helles Hefe Weizen 87
Tupper's Hop Pocket Ale 137

**U**
Ueli, Fischerstube Ueli Reverenz 45
Uerige Alt 52
Ueriges Weizen 88
Umbel Ale 17
Unertl Weissbier 87
Unibroue
Blanche de Chambly 80
Maudite 144
Quelque Chose 109
Raftman 117
Union Cuvée de l'Ermitage 172
Unions Bräu Hell 45
Ur-Alt, Bolten 54
Urbock 23° 146
Urbock, Hansa 30
USA, beers of
Abita Springs Andygator 31
Adler Bräu Dopple Bock 31
Adler Bräu Oatmeal Stout 169
Alaskan Amber 55

Alaskan Brewing Co.
Smoked Porter 151
as a marinade 177
American root beer 16
Anchor Liberty Ale 136
in fish stews 179
hops used in 15
Anchor Old Foghorn 122
Anchor "Our Special Holiday Ale" 42
Anderson Valley High Rollers Wheat Beer 93
August Schell Doppel Bock 105
Bert Grant's Perfect Porter 72
Bert Grant's Scottish Ale 64
Big Time Bhagwan's Best India Pale Ale 133
Big Time Old Wooly 122
Blackstone St. Charles Porter 72
Boscos Flaming Stone 150
Boston Beer Works Back Bay India Pale Ale 134
Boston Beer Works Beantown Nut Brown Ale 145
Boston Beer Works Buckeye Oatmeal Stout 169
Boston Beer Works Cock Ale 17
Boulder Creek Dizzy Lizzy 123
Boulder Creek Highlands Amber 65
Breckenridge Autumn Ale 39
BridgePort ESB 67
as a marinade 177
BridgePort India Pale Ale 135
BridgePort Old Knucklehead 123
Brooklyn Black Chocolate Stout 170
in desserts 183
Brooklyn Brown Ale, and cigars 173
Brooklyn East India Pale Ale 133
Catamount 10 IPA 134
Catamount Octoberfest 154
Catamount Porter 72
Celis Grand Cru 144
Celis White 80
Chelsea Old Titanic 122
Chelsea Sunset Red 163
Climax ESB 67
Cock Ale 17
Coors Blue Moon Belgian White 81
Cougan's Bock 107
Deschutes Bachelor Bitter 68
Dock Street Bohemian Pilsner 127
Dock Street Grand Cru 147
Dock Street Illuminator 107
Elysian The Wise ESB 69
Firehouse Kölsch Lager 51
Fish Poseidon Old Scotch Ale 117

Fish Tale Mud Shark Porter 72
Flatlander's Eighty Shilling Ale 64
Flying Dog Scottish Ale 65
Fordham Calvinator 107
Full Sail Wassail Winter Ale 113
Geary's Pale Ale 161
Goose Island Honker's Ale 69
Gordon Biersch Blonde Bock 107
Gordon Biersch Märzen 155
Grant's India Pale Ale 135
Great Divide Saint Brigid's Porter 73
Great Lakes Brewing Co. The Eliot Ness 163
Great Lakes Brewing Co. Dortmunder Gold 47
Gritty McDuff's Best Bitter 69
H. C. Berger Maibock 31
Hair of the Dog Adam 173
Hale's Harvest Ale 39
Hale's Special Bitter 68
Hoster's Captivator 107
Hübsch Sudwerk Helles 45
Independence Franklinfest 155
Kalamazoo Brewing Bell's Porter 73
Kalamazoo Brewing Third Coast Old Ale 113
Lakefront Riverwest Stein Beer 163
Lang Creek Trimotor Amber 69
Leinenkugel's Autumn Gold 39
McGuire's Old Style Irish Ale 157
in stews 179
McNeill's Dead Horse India Pale Ale 133
Magic Hat Blind Faith IPA 135
Marin "Old Dipsea" 123
Michelob HefeWeizen 89
Middlesex Brewing Co. Oatmeal Stout 168
Mount Hood Pittock Wee Heavy 117
New Belgium Old Cherry Ale 77
in chilled fruit soups 178
New Belgium Porch Swing Ale 35
New Glarus Wisconsin Cherry Beer 167
and cherries 17
in chilled fruit soups 178
North Coast Old Rasputin Russian Imperial Stout 119
Oasis Capstone ESB 67
Oasis Zoser Stout 169
Odell's 90 Shilling 64
Old Dominion Brewing Co. Spring Brew 31
Octoberfest 154

Oliver ESB 66
as a marinade 177
Otto Brothers' Teton Ale 69
Oxford Class Ale 69
Park Slope India Pale Ale 135
Peconic County Reserve Ale 77
Penn Oktoberfest 154
Pete's Summer Brew 35
Pike Old Bawdy 123
Pike Pale Ale 161
Portland Brewing MacTarnahan's Gold Medal 64
Pyramid Espresso Stout 171
Pyramid Scotch Ale 117
Pyramid Wheaten Ale 93
Red Hook Double Black Stout 171
Redhook ESB 67
Richbrau Poe's Tell Tale Ale 123
Riverside Pullman Pale Ale 69
Rogue Maierbock Ale 30
Rogue-N-Berry 76
Saint Arnold Kristall Weizen 93
Sam Adams Boston Lager 178
Sam Adams Triple Bock 146
Schmaltz's Alt 55
Sherlock's Home Piper's Pride 65
Sierra Nevada Bigfoot Ale 123
Sierra Nevada Celebration Ale 42
Sissons Wise Guy Weissbier 89
Southampton Saison 34
and grains of paradise 17
Southampton Secret 55
Stoudt's Pils 127
Summit Winter Ale 113
Tabernash Munich 149
Tabernash Weisse 89
Thomas Kemper Oktoberfest 155
Tupper's Hop Pocket Ale 137
Vermont Pub and Brewery Wee Heavy 117
Victory Prima Pils 127
Walnut Big Horn Bitter 68
Waterloo Brewing Ed's Best Bitter 69
Watou's Wit 81
Weeping Radish 90
Wits' End 17
Yellow Rose Vigilante Porter 73
Ushers
Autumn Frenzy 39
Manns Original Brown Ale 101
Summer Madness 35

**V**
Valkenburgs Wit 81
Valte 113
Van Eecke
Poperings Hommel Bier 137
Watou's Wit 81

Winter Wit 81
Van Honsebrouck
Bacchus 95
Bière du Château 173
Kasteel Bier 173
Van Steenberge Bios 95
Vaux
Double Maxim 145
How's Your Father Summer Ale 33
St. Nicholas's Christmas Ale 42
Waggle Dance 169
Verboden Vrucht 182
Verhaeghe
Duchesse de Bourgogne 95
Echte Kriek 76
Vichtenaar 95
Vermont Pub and Brewery Wee Heavy 117
Vichtenaar 95
Victory
Prima Pils 127
St. Victorious 29
Vienna malt 13
Vienna Porter 119
Vieux Temps 57
Vigilante Porter 73
Villers Trippel 129
vinaigrettes, beer as an ingredient in 176
vinegary flavor, explanation of 23

**W**
Wadworth
Farmer's Glory 112
Old Timer 112
6X 61
Waggle Dance 169
Waldmeister and Berliner Weisse 83
Wales, beer of, Brains IPA 134
Walnut Big Horn Bitter 68
Ward's Classic Yorkshire Ale 101
Warteck Alt 54
Wassail Winter Ale 113
water in brewing 18
Waterloo Brewing Ed's Best Bitter 69
Waterloo Brewing Ed's Best Bitter 69
Watou's Wit 81
Weeping Radish 90
Weihenstephaner Kristall Weissbier 84
Weissbier, Berliner Bürgerbräu 82
Weisswurst (sausage) 86
Wells Fargo 61
Weltenburger Kloster Barock-Dunkel 148
Wernesgrüner Pils Legende 125
Westmalle Trappist 129
Westvleteren 8° (Blue Cap) 164
wheat ales 92-3
wheat beers
pouring of 184
and top-fermentation 19

wheat in brewing 13
Wheat Mash 92
Wheaten Ale 93
whiskey-malt beers 114-17
Whitbread
Gold Label 121
Mackeson Stout 103
White Cliffs, Mike's Mild Ale 100
Wicked Ale, Pete's Summer Brew 35
Wild Cat 65
wild fermentation (lambic) 19
Williams
Alba Scots Pine Ale 38
Fraoch Heather Ale 38
Grozet Gooseberry & Wheat Ale 38
winey flavor, explanation of 23
Winter Ale 113
Wintervorst 17
Winter Warmer, Young's 111
winter warmers
Baltic porters and stouts 118-19
Bock beers 104-7
old ales 110-13
spiced beers 108-9
strong Scottish ales 114-17
whiskey-malt beers 114-17
Winter Wit 81
Wintervorst 109
and clover 17
Wisconsin Cherry Beer 167
and cherries 17
in chilled fruit soups 178
Wise Guy Weissbier 89
Wits' End, and camomile 17
Woodforde Headcracker 123
Woodforde's Norfolk Wherry 61
Workie Ticket 61
Würzburger Hofbräu Sympator 107
Würzig Herb 126

**X, Y & Z**
XXXB, Batemans 59
as a marinade 177
yeast in brewing 18-19
yeast flavor, explanation of 23
Yellow Rose Vigilante Porter 73
Younger of Alloa Sweetheart Stout 103
Young's
Double Chocolate Stout 170
and chocolate 17
in desserts 183
Special 60
Special London Ale 137
Winter Warmer 111
Zoser Stout 169
Zulte 95
Zum Uerige
Sticke Bier 52
Uerige Alt 52
Ueriges Weizen 88
Zywiec Porter 119

# ACKNOWLEDGMENTS

**Author's Acknowledgments**
All the beers in this book were chosen by the author on the basis of past tastings. The brewers were then requested to supply current bottles for retasting and photography. The author and publishers would like heartily to thank all of the brewers who supplied beer, especially those whose products for one reason or another did not make the final selection. In the longer term, we hope to produce further editions, in which some of these beers will feature. Many of the glasses were supplied by the brewers but a large number were provided directly by the Rastal company, of Höhr-Grenzhausen, Germany; special thanks to them. For this book and over the years, the following have all offered great help:

Larry Baush, Stephen Beaumont, Eugene Bohensky, Kathleen Boyen, Ian Burgess, Vince Cottone, Tom Dalldorf, Stephen D'Arcy, Erich Dederichs, René Descheirder, Alan Dikty, Sarah and Phil Doersam, Jim Dorsch, Pierre-André Dubois, Drew Ferguson, David Furer, Gary and Libby Gillman, Geoff Griggs, Thomas Halpin, Ainsley Harriot, Erik Hartman, Dr. Alfred Haunold of Oregon State University, Bob Henham, Hans J. Henschien, Graham Howard, Miles Jenner, Eric Källgren, Nirbhao Khalsa, Alan Knight, Konishi Brewing, Jim Krecjie, Michiko Kurita, Graham Lees, Lars Lundsten, Rob Maerz, Franz Mather, Peter McAuslan, Ed McNally, Bill Metzger, Steve Middlemiss, Mikko Montonen, Multilines, Father Ronald Murphy of Georgetown University, Professor Doctor Ludwig Narziss of Weihenstephan, Hans Nordlov, Ryouji Oda, Barrie Pepper, Chris Pietruski, Portugalia Wines (UK), Bernard Rotman, John Rowling, Rüdiger Ruoss, Silvano Rusmini, Margarita Sahm, the late Dr. Hans Schultze-Berndt, Frau Schultze-Engels, Professor Paul Schwarz of North Dakota State University, Todd Selbert, Conrad Seidl, Willie Simpson, Simpson's Malt, Ritchie Stolarz, Peter Terhune, Unto Tikkanen, Anastasy and Jo Tynan, Mike Urseth, Derek Walsh, De Wolff Cosijns Malt, Sabina Weyerman, Przemyslaw Wisniewski, Kari Ylane . . .

. . . and everyone else who has helped me or shared a beer on the road.

Michael Jackson's necktie by Cynthia Soboti.

**Bibliography**
BOOKS CONSULTED
*Additives in Beer* Jeffrey Patton (self-published)
*On Food and Cooking* Harold McGee (Scribners)

FURTHER READING
*Michael Jackson's Beer Companion* (Running Press)
*Simon & Schuster Pocket Guide to Beer* (Simon & Schuster)
*Michael Jackson's Great Beers of Belgium* Michael Jackson (Running Press)
*Everybody Eats Well in Belgium* Ruth Van Waerebeek (Workman)
*American Brasserie* Gale Gand, Julia Moskin, Rick Tramonto, and Tim Turner (Macmillan)
*Cooking with Beer* Lucy Saunders (Time-Life)
*Designing Great Beers* Ray Daniels (Brewers Publications)

**Publisher's Acknowledgments**
*Photography:* Steve Gorton, Ian O'Leary, Sarah Ashun
*Additional photography:* Philip Dowell, Neil Fletcher, Dave King, David Murray, Martin Norris, Roger Phillips, Jules Selmes, Matthew Ward.
Thanks to Harveys brewery at Lewes, East Sussex, for kind permission to take photographs.
*Home economist:* Ricky Turner
*Artwork:* Ruth Hall 9, 15; Janos Marffy 11
*Design assistance:* Simon Oon, Fay Singer
*Index:* Margaret McCormack

**Picture Credits**
The publisher would like to thank the following for their kind permission to reproduce their photographs:

a=above; c=center; b=bottom; l=left; r=right; t=top

**AKG London:** 52 br, 96 br, 118 br; **Bass PLC:** 18 tc, 18 c; **Bières de Chimay S.A.:** 165 tr; **Boston Beer Company:** 16bl; **Brasserie Friart S.A.:** 20 bl; **Brasserie d'Orval S.A.:** 128br; **Brouwerij Palm:** 56tr; **Brouwerij Rodenbach:** 94tr, 147 tl; **Brouwerij Verhaege:** 76tr; **Budweiser Budvar:** 153 tr; **Pierre Celis:** 78 tr; **Christie's Images:** 98 br; **Colorphoto Hans Hinz:** © Jasper Johns/VAGA, NY and DACS, London 1998, 66 br; **Corbis UK Ltd:** 162 tr; **Antoine Denooze:** 130 tr; **E.T. Archive:** 70 br; **Teri Fahrendorf:** 132 tr; **Charles Finkel:** 28 br; **Guinness:** 18 cr; **Robert Harding Picture Library:** Adam Woolfitt 58 tr; R. Richardson 32 tr; **Heather Ale Ltd:** 16 br; **Hans Hennebach:** 141 tr; **Ian Howes:** 21br; **Illustrated London News Picture Library:** 40 tr; **Images Colour Library:** 70 tr; **Michael Jackson:** 14 bl, 18 bl, 19 bl, 20 bc, 66tr, 74 tr, 90 tr, 92 tr, 94 br, 114tr, 114br, 136 tr, 150tr, 151 tr; **Klosterbrauerei Weltenburg GmbH:** 148 tl; **Hank Koshollek:** 167 tl; **Franz Mather:** 48 br; **National Maritime Museum Picture Library:** 132 br; **Pilsner Urquell:** 124 br; © **Retrograph Archive Ltd:** 46 tr; **Royal Horticultural Society, Lindley Library:** 78 br; **St. Peter's Brewery:** 108 br; **Schlossbrauerei Kaltenberg:** 28 tr; **Frau Schulze-Engels:** 46br; **Claus Schunk:** 86 br; **Staatliches Hofbräuhaus München:** 44 tr; **Still Moving Picture Company:** Doug Corrance 62 tr; **Tony Stone Images:** John Lawrence 145 tr; Stephen Studd 36 tr; **T & R Theakston:** 110 br; **United Distillers & Vintners:** 10; **University of Pennsylvania Museum:** (negs #B16688 & #B17694) 11 bl; **Bethany Versoy:** 173tr; **Yakima Brewing & Malting Co.:** 179tr.